Captain

OF THE Ash

CAPTAINS
OF THE ASH

Brendan Fullam

WOLFHOUND PRESS

Published in 2002 by
Wolfhound Press
An imprint of Merlin Publishing
16 Upper Pembroke Street
Dublin 2
Ireland
Tel: + 353 1 6764373
Fax: + 353 1 6764368
publishing@merlin.ie
www.merlin-publishing.com

Text © 2002 Brendan Fullam
Design and Layout © 2002 Merlin Publishing
Cover photographs:
Top – All-Ireland Final 1996, Wexford v Limerick.
(Courtesy of Ibar Carty, Enniscorthy)
Bottom left – September 15th, 2002 Joanne O'Callaghan, Cork,
against Clare Grogan, Tipperary, Cork v Tipperary All-Ireland Camogie Final.
(© Ray McManus/SPORTSFILE)
Bottom right – September 8th, 2002, Andy Comerford, Kilkenny, against
David Hoey, Clare, Kilkenny v Clare, All-Ireland Hurling Final.
(© Damien Eagers/SPORTSFILE)
Internal photographs © of individuals
and agencies indicated.

British Library Cataloguing in Publication Data
A catalogue record for this book is available from the British Library.

ISBN 0–86327–900–7

The publishers have made every reasonable effort to contact the copyright
holders of photographs reproduced in this book. If any involuntary
infringement of copyright has occurred, sincere apologies are offered and
the owner of such copyright is requested to contact the publisher.

Typeset by Carrigboy Typesetting Services
Cover design by Pierce Design, Dublin
Printed by ColourBooks Ltd., Dublin

Dedication

I am dedicating *Captains of the Ash* to the following – all now deceased – whose GAA writings have given me immense pleasure:

Thomas F. O'Sullivan, a native of Tralee, Co. Kerry, author of *The Story of the GAA*, published in 1916 and covering the period 1884 to 1908.

Paddy D. Mehigan (Carbery) player, journalist and author of many works including *Carbery's Annual* – a native of Co. Cork.

Phil O'Neill (Sliabh Ruadh) author of *History of the GAA 1910-1930*, born in Co. Cork and spent much of his life in Kilkenny as a journalist.

Pádraig Puirséal, author of *The GAA in its Time*, a native of Mooncoin, Co. Kilkenny.

Tom Ryall, a native of Co. Kilkenny, author of *Kilkenny – The GAA Story 1884-1984*.

Raymond Smith, a native of Thurles, Co. Tipperary, author of many hurling books including *Decades of Glory*.

Val Dorgan, a native of Cork, journalist and author of the book *Christy Ring*.

> 'When I am dead
> Of me may it be said,
> His sins were scarlet
> But his books were read.'
>   (Belloc)

Contents

Réamhrá

Is mór liom an chaoi fáilte is fiche a chur roimh an fhoilseachán breá, suimiúil seo, agus i dteannta san, tréaslú leis an údar díograiseach as an sárobair atá déanta aige, an foilseachán seo a chur ar fáil comh maith leis na cinn eile roimhe, chun scéal na h-iomána, mar a déarfá, a choimeád beo agus a chur in a luí ar ár muintir chomh tábhachtach is atá an iomáint i saol agus i gcultúr ar dtíre agus ár muintire sa bhaile agus i gcéin.

In welcoming this excellent publication, the author Brendan Fullam is to be sincerely thanked and highly complimented on his dedication, commitment and thorough research in making available this very fine and extremely interesting publication to add to his other works of equal merit on hurling and hurlers.

The author being an ardent lover and keen student all his life of our unique and most distinctive national game, his work springs from the heart which makes it all the more acceptable as a worthy and deserved tribute to all the great players included. This publication now also includes a very worthwhile and thoughtful section on some of our great camogie players who have figured with distinction in making a valued contribution to the entertainment and social life of our people. This is a timely step at a time when both organisations are moving closer together with the promotion of our national games.

All of this is in keeping with the author's lifelong ambition, expressed in his own words, to personalise the great game of hurling — to keep memories, anecdotes and names alive, to leave a folklore for future generations, to capture the atmosphere, economic and political, through which our great game has travelled for over a century; nor has he forgotten here to, of course, record the prominence, the skill, the performances, the personalities and devotion of great players down the generations who may have missed the accolades and the limelight in comparison with others, but are nonetheless among the greats. This is a well-deserved focus. We thank them all for the many stirring games and top class individual performances which were experienced in every generation. However, in the recall of those great players and the debt we owe them and as we absorb the narratives we are attracted to thinking about hurling and its welfare into the future for which I am grateful to the author. For instance, on reflection we are indirectly reminded of the major contribution of that great band of voluntary workers at all levels, particularly at club and schools levels who have put so many players on the road to participation in games, success and eventual greatness in the mastery of the art of hurling. This is invaluable work. This combination of players and voluntary workers supported by evolving prudent techniques in coaching and organisation imbued with a pride in our national game and by the individual players in their performances, have made players and the Gaelic Athletic Association great. It is worth remembering as we enjoy the chronicle of the great players that this combination of players and voluntary workers is more vital to the future than it ever was in the past, no matter how we look at things in an era of ever changing values and growing materialism.

Publications such as this also serve to remind us of our responsibility to the game of hurling itself. We can be proud that hurling is regarded as one of the fastest, if not the fastest, field game in the world. It has the greatest range of skills which when coupled with instinctive, controlled sporting abandon by players make it a most attractive spectacle for everybody and even a source of astonishment to first time viewers, now further enhanced by television. The mastery of the art, using the full range of skills, is a very fulfilling experience for players and a major contributor to the magic and image of the game. It must be the aim of all involved, particularly those very dedicated people involved with the youth and indeed some referees and players, to keep this attractive format intact. The range of fundamental skills must be neither diluted, lost nor replaced. Example: the hand-pass is now becoming very prevalent even in our major games, which could be regarded as a lack of skill on the part of the players or a tactic by mentors. This is just a case in point; there are others. Some will say that there is a new game of hurling evolving. Do we really want to replace traditional hurling? I don't believe we do. Let us cultivate the fundamental and basic skills with enthusiasm and positive expertise. While game plans are essential in a broad sense, the programming of hurling games should not have any place in such plans. Programming limits or dilutes the use of spontaneous natural skills, introduces what can be described as predictable hurling into games, curtails the freedom of accomplished skilful players – indeed all players – to blossom to their full potential, affects the overall team performance and the game as a spectacle.

On perusing the list of players profiled we cannot but also sadly observe how hurling has declined over the years where it was once strong and produced great players. While it is a priority today to maintain hurling strong where it is strong or reasonably strong, we have a serious obligation to do everything possible to restore hurling to its rightful place in all areas. It is a major challenge and will require a massive investment of manpower and finance over and above the present level of work and support. There are positive signs that progress can be made. There are very devoted people on the ground, always living in the hope that the existing gap in standards will be bridged and in certain instances that a new beginning on the road back will be made. Hopefully some day players from such areas will again figure among the greats.

Personally I feel very privileged to have been invited to submit this *Réamhrá* and to be associated with the publication which I am certain will be an item treasured by many and a permanent tribute, not alone to the players profiled but, to the author whose writings have always sought to enhance the game of hurling.

Guidhim rath Dé ar an obair. Molaim an foilseachán do chách agus gabhaim buíochas ó chroí leis an údar.

Conchúr Ó Murchú
Uachtarán CLCG 1976–1978

Preface

Captains of the Ash joins its predecessors *Giants of the Ash, Hurling Giants* and *Legends of the Ash* in paying tribute to more of hurling's great exponents.

The vast bulk of those who feature in this book had the honour of captaining an All-Ireland winning team. A few, while playing at the highest level, had to settle for the captaincy honour in other competitions. All, however, brought glory to the game and the men they led.

Those who feature in *Captains of the Ash* span every decade of the GAA from its inception to date – magic names from distant times to the present moment, among them Mikey Maher, Jim Kelliher, Sim Walton, Bob McConkey, Dinny Barry Murphy, Timmy Ryan, Frankie Walsh, Billy Rackard, Joe Connolly, Anthony Daly and Willie O'Connor – names that conjure up hurling epics, deeds of valour and tales of 'battles long ago'.

Some of the hurlers in this book were profiled in earlier publications. But these articles give a new insight, a deeper profile into their hurling life.

Nor have I forgotten the ladies who demonstrated their superb skills on the camogie field – Kathleen Mills, Una O'Connor, Brigid Doyle, Angela Downey, Elsie Cody and Jovita Delaney.

The hurling careers of in excess of 270 players have been covered in my four publications – men who played our ancient game, the game our forefathers played, the game that is part of the legend of Cúchulainn, the game whose origin is lost in the mists of time and found in the twilight of fable.

Ar aghaidh leis an iomáint.

All-Ireland Winning Hurling Captains

YEAR	NAME	COUNTY	YEAR	NAME	COUNTY7
1887	Jim Stapleton	Tipperary	1935	Lory Meagher	Kilkenny
1888	No final	(U.S. Invasion)	1936	Mick Mackey	Limerick
1889	Nicholas O'Shea	Dublin	1937	Jimmy Lanigan	Tipperary
1890	Dan Lane	Cork	1938	Mick Daniels	Dublin
1891	John Mahony	Kerry	1939	Jimmy Walsh	Kilkenny
1892	W. O'Callaghan	Cork	1940	Mick Mackey	Limerick
1893	John Murphy	Cork	1941	Connie Buckley	Cork
1894	Steven Hayes	Cork	1942	Jack Lynch	Cork
1895	Mikey Maher	Tipperary	1943	Mick Kenefick	Cork
1896	Mikey Maher	Tipperary	1944	Sean Condon	Cork
1897	Denis Grimes	Limerick	1945	John Maher	Tipperary
1898	Mikey Maher	Tipperary	1946	Christy Ring	Cork
1899	T. Condon	Tipperary	1947	Dan Kennedy	Kilkenny
1900	Ned Hayes	Tipperary	1948	Jim Ware	Waterford
1901	Jack Coughlan	London	1949	Pat Stakelum	Tipperary
1902	Jim Kelliher	Cork	1950	Sean Kenny	Tipperary
1903	Steva Riordan	Cork	1951	Jimmy Finn	Tipperary
1904	Jer Doheny	Kilkenny	1952	Paddy Barry	Cork
1905	D.J. Stapleton	Kilkenny	1953	Christy Ring	Cork
1906	Tom Semple	Tipperary	1954	Christy Ring	Cork
1907	Dick 'Drug' Walsh	Kilkenny	1955	Nick O'Donnell	Wexford
1908	Tom Semple	Tipperary	1956	Jim English	Wexford
1909	Dick 'Drug' Walsh	Kilkenny	1957	Mick Kelly	Kilkenny
1910	Dick Doyle	Wexford	1958	Tony Wall	Tipperary
1911	Kilkenny walk-over from Limerick		1959	Frankie Walsh	Waterford
1912	Sim Walton	Kilkenny	1960	Nick O'Donnell	Wexford
1913	Dick 'Drug' Walsh	Kilkenny	1961	Matt Hassett	Tipperary
1914	Amby Power	Clare	1962	Jimmy Doyle	Tipperary
1915	Jack Finlay	Laois	1963	Seamus Cleere	Kilkenny
1916	Johnny Leahy	Tipperary	1964	Mick Murphy	Tipperary
1917	John Ryan	Dublin	1965	Jimmy Doyle	Tipperary
1918	Willie Hough	Limerick	1966	Gerald McCarthy	Cork
1919	J. Kennedy	Cork	1967	Jim Treacy	Kilkenny
1920	Bob Mockler	Dublin	1968	Dan Quigley	Wexford
1921	Bob McConkey	Limerick	1969	Eddie Keher	Kilkenny
1922	Wattie Dunphy	Kilkenny	1970	Paddy Barry	Cork
1923	Mick Kenny	Galway	1971	Tadhg O'Connor	Tipperary
1924	Frank Wall (non-playing)	Dublin	1972	Noel Skehan	Kilkenny
			1973	Eamon Grimes	Limerick
1925	Johnny Leahy	Tipperary	1974	Nicky Orr	Kilkenny
1926	Sean Óg Muprhy	Cork	1975	Billy Fitzpatrick	Kilkenny
1927	Mick Gill	Dublin	1976	Ray Cummins	Cork
1928	Sean Óg Murphy	Cork	1977	Martin Doherty	Cork
1929	Dinny Barry Murphy	Cork	1978	Charlie McCarthy	Cork
			1979	Ger Fennelly	Kilkenny
1930	John Joe Callinan	Tipperary	1980	Joe Connolly	Galway
1931	Eudi Coughlan	Cork	1981	Padraig Horan	Offaly
1932	Jimmy Walsh	Kilkenny	1982	Brian Cody	Kilkenny
1933	Ned Doyle	Kilkenny	1983	Liam Fennelly	Kilkenny
1934	Timmy Ryan	Limerick	1984	John Fenton	Cork

YEAR	NAME	COUNTY	YEAR	NAME	COUNTY
1985	Pat Fleury	Offaly	1994	Martin Hanamy	Offaly
1986	Tom Cashman	Cork	1995	Anthony Daly	Clare
1987	Conor Hayes	Galway	1996	Martin Storey	Wexford
1988	Conor Hayes	Galway	1997	Anthony Daly	Clare
1989	Bobby Ryan	Tipperary	1998	Hubert Rigney	Offaly
1990	Tomas Mulcahy	Cork	1999	Mark Landers	Cork
1991	Declan Carr	Tipperary	2000	Willie O'Connor	Kilkenny
1992	Liam Fennelly	Kilkenny	2001	Tommy Dunne	Tipperary
1993	Eddie O'Connor	Kilkenny	2002	Andy Comerford	Kilkenny

All-Ireland Winning Camogie Captains

YEAR	NAME	COUNTY	YEAR	NAME	COUNTY
1932	Maura Gill	Dublin	1967	Sue Cashman	Antrim
1933	Maura Gill	Dublin	1968	Mary Walsh	Wexford
1934	Kate Delea	Cork	1969	Brigid Doyle	Wexford
1935	Josie McGrath	Cork	1970	Ann Comerford	Cork
1936	Kitty Cotter	Cork	1971	Betty Sugrue	Cork
1937	Mary Walsh	Dublin	1972	Hannah Dineen	Cork
1938	Emmy Delaney	Dublin	1973	Marie Costine	Cork
1939	Renee Fitzgerald	Cork	1974	Teresa O'Neill	Kilkenny
1940	Lil Kirby	Cork**	1975	Gretta Kehoe	Wexford
1941	Kitty Buckley	Cork	1976	Mary Fennelly	Kilkenny**
1942	Peggy Griffin	Dublin	1977	Angela Downey	Kilkenny
1943	Peggy Griffin	Dublin	1978	Nancy O'Driscoll	Cork
1944	Doreen Rogers	Dublin	1979	Mairead McAtamney	Antrim
1945	Marie O'Gorman	Antrim	1980	Mary Geany	Cork
1946	Marjorie Griffin	Antrim	1981	Liz Neary	Kilkenny
1947	Celia Quinn	Antrim	1982	Pat Lenihan	Cork
1948	Sophie Brack	Dublin	1983	Catherine Landers	Cork
1949	Doreen Rogers	Dublin	1984	Anne Colgan	Dublin
1950	Pat Raftery	Dublin	1985	Bridie McGarry	Kilkenny
1951	Sophie Brack	Dublin	1986	Liz Neary	Kilkenny
1952	Sophie Brack	Dublin	1987	Bridie McGarry	Kilkenny
1953	Sophie Brack	Dublin	1988	Angela Downey	Kilkenny
1954	Sophie Brack	Dublin	1989	Anne Downey	Kilkenny
1955	Sophie Brack	Dublin	1990	Breda Holmes	Kilkenny
1956	Madge Rainey	Antrim	1991	Angela Downey	Kilkenny
1957	Eileen Duffy	Dublin	1992	Sandy Fitzgibbon	Cork
1958	Kathleen Mills	Dublin	1993	Linda Mellerick	Cork
1959	Brid Reid	Dublin	1994	Anne Downey	Kilkenny
1960	Doreen.Brennan	Dublin	1995	Denise Cronin	Cork
1961	Gerry Hughes	Dublin	1996	Imelda Hobbins	Galway
1962	Gerry Hughes	Dublin	1997	Linda Mellerick	Cork
1963	Una O'Connor	Dublin	1998	Eithne Duggan	Cork
1964	Una O'Connor	Dublin	1999	Meadhbh Stokes	Tipperary
1965	Kay Ryder	Dublin	2000	Jovita Delaney	Tipperary
1966	Kay Ryder	Dublin	2001	Emily Hayden	Tipperary
			2002	Una O'Donoghue	Cork

Both with ** later became Presidents of the Camogie Association.
My thanks to Sheila Wallace for her kind assistance with many of the above names.
Sheila captained Dublin in the 1976 final when they lost to Kilkenny on the score 0:6 to 1:2
She was marking the great Angela Downey.

All-Ireland Winning
Hurling Captains
2002 – 1887

Andy Comerford
KILKENNY
2002

My father manufacturing a hurl for me from a flooring board was my intro to hurling but after all these years I'm delighted he did. From there to the school in St. John's I served my hurling apprenticeship under Dan Kennedy, Padraig O'Neill, Felix Nolan and John Cooney. Although unsuccessful it was a good education – hurling education, that is.

From there to St. Kieran's College where success was bred into players. Father Fergus Farrell (Johnstown), Tom Lanigan, Seamus Knox, Nicholas Cashin and Denis Philpott. A great period but the education suffered – unfortunately, mother. I met players there whom I would have the honour of winning All-Irelands in later years with. Graduation to Kilkenny Seniors was easy after a hurling upbringing like that.

My biggest thrill in hurling has to have been winning the senior county final with my brothers Martin and Jimmy and my friends who hurled with me throughout the lean periods with O'Loughlin's and St. John's.

Hail to the chief who in triumph advances!

It was around 5 p.m. on the afternoon of Sunday 8 September 2002. Referee Aodhán Mac Suibhne of Dublin blew the final whistle in Croke Park to bring to an end an absorbing All-Ireland hurling final between Clare and Kilkenny.

The scoreboard was a source of joy and elation to every Kilkenny supporter in the official attendance of 76,254.

Andy Comerford, Kilkenny's 22nd successful captain had guided the Noresiders to their 27th All-Ireland crown. Earlier in the year he had led them to a tenth National League success.

The chart to MacCarthy Cup glory in 2002 read as follows:

v Offaly (2:20 to 1:14)
v Wexford (0:19 to 0:17)

v Tipperary (1:20 to 1:16)
v Clare (2:20 to 0:19)

There was a glow of modest triumph and satisfaction in Andy Comerford's face as he held aloft the MacCarthy Cup to exultant Kilkenny followers. Later in the dressing room he exhorted his colleagues to celebrate victory with pride and dignity. 'Don't spoil this great victory by doing rash things now or some weeks or months down the line. We have gained the respect of the entire hurling world so let's not blow it.'

This big, rangy man of 6'2" and turning the scales fit at 13.5 stone was born in London in 1972 where he spent the first seven years of his life and 'never caught a hurley'.

Back in Ireland he developed his hurling skills at under-age level with his club, O'Loughlin-Gaels, in Kilkenny city.

At St. Kieran's College his hurling talents won him a place on the college senior team and he won successive All-Ireland titles in 1989 and 1990.

Further honours came his way in 1990 when after a replay Kilkenny defeated Cork in the All-Ireland minor final by 3:16 to 0:11 (drawn game, 3:14 each). Andy played at right half forward. At third level he won a Fitzgibbon Cup in 1992 with Waterford RTC.

Under-21 success eluded him. The final of 1993 was lost to Galway in a replay 2:9 to 3:3 following a drawn result of 2:14 to 3:11 for Kilkenny.

Sometime after that Andy emigrated to England. Hurling remained a major part of his recreation. He played his hurling with Brother Pearse's Club and practised at Ruislip and on occasions at Ealing soccer pitch. 'In London the hurling was tough.'

Andy won an All-Ireland senior B medal with London – place of his birth – in 1995 following victories over New York and Wicklow. That qualified London for a quarter-final place in the All-Ireland senior championship against Down at Ruislip but they lost by 16 points to 9.

Back in Ireland Andy won his place on the Kilkenny senior team. He made his début against Dublin in the championship of 1997, lost the All-Ireland finals of '98 and '99 to Offaly and Cork respectively, but won the All-Ireland contest of 2000 when Kilkenny gave a display of precision and power-packed hurling to record a fine victory over Offaly.

4

Andy is a player in the mould of a Frank Cummins rather than that of a John Fenton. When he moves well at midfield — his favourite position — Kilkenny's performance is enhanced. He excelled in this year's All-Ireland semi-final against Tipperary, having shaken off an injury that had plagued him for some time and curtailed his mobility.

As captain Andy has that essential gift of being a great leader and inspirational captain both prior to a game and on the field of play. He is also a wonderful motivator and brings a spirit of total commitment to the task on hand.

He operates at midfield like a hungry forager. His style is determined, tenacious and speedy of delivery. It is exceedingly difficult to outshine Andy because of his capacity to disrupt play. He has a great engine and his high energy levels enable him to instinctively fall back towards defence or advance forward as the tide of battle demands. You find him at the main action with remarkable regularity. And he can pick off that vital score, too — we saw a few classic examples in the games against Tipperary and Clare.

His brother, Martin, who had a great game in the All-Ireland final on Clare's Brian Lohan, is the current Kilkenny full forward, while a third brother Jimmy completes a trio on the O'Loughlin-Gaels senior team.

In the All-Ireland final Andy led a Kilkenny hurling outfit fine tuned and trained to the ounce by their manager Brian Cody, that were majestic and awesome in almost everything they did.

Andy will always look back on 2002 with great pride and the honour and privilege of being captain will gather added value and nostalgic glory as the years speed on.

Diarmuid O'Flynn writing in the *Irish Examiner* summed matters up well in his Monday morning report on the game.

> The thunder and lightning All-Ireland final of 1939, Kilkenny and Cork, has gone into the annals of GAA history.
>
> The Cats won that one too, but yesterday, in the new magnificence that is Croke Park, they blew up a storm all on their own. Thunder at the back, lightning up front, the cyclonic force that is Captain Comerford with Lyng alongside at midfield, an immense Kilkenny team took what has been probably the most physical force ever in hurling and blitzed them off the park . . .
>
> The thunder, the lightning, but on this year, it all came up from the pitch. Split the heavens above, tore the Banner apart.
>
> Privilege to have been there.

Tommy Dunne
TIPPERARY
2001

'Hurrah for Toomevara
May your banners never fall.
You beat Galway and Queen's County
And you levelled Cork's stone wall.
I never will forget the day
Kilkenny's pride went down
Before the skill of Wedger's men
In sweet Dungarvan town.'

The name Toomevara – the parish Tommy Dunne hails from – is legendary in the hurling world and synonymous with the great game in Co. Tipperary. The fame of Toomevara goes back to the early years of the twentieth century when Patrick 'Wedger' Meagher – later to emigrate to America – captained Tipperary with a Toomevara selection in the All-Ireland campaign of 1913. Fleet of foot and trained to the ounce they were dubbed the Toomevara Greyhounds. They won their way to the final against Kilkenny, represented by a Mooncoin selection. They failed at the last hurdle by 2:4 to 1:2. Their performance wasn't helped by a dispute between the Tipperary County Board and the Central Council over the allocation of funds collected from the Croke Memorial tournament. There was domestic pressure on Toomevara not to travel for the game. At first they agreed but later changed their minds. The affair, no doubt, had a negative impact on the team.

Garrett Howard, who hurled with Limerick, Tipperary and Dublin, regarded the Tipperary county final of 1930 between Toomevara and Boherlahan as the most memorable club game he played in. Victory went to Toomevara after a replay. A year later they repeated the success.

So when Tommy Dunne set forth, for the third year in a row in 2001, to lead Tipperary in the All-Ireland championship he had, historically speaking, much to look back on – much from which to draw inspiration.

Tipperary's path to the final, which brought them face to face with a Galway team that had given a devastating performance in dethroning reigning All-Ireland champions Kilkenny in the semi-final, had been a testing one.

The results were as follows:

v Clare (0:15 to 0:14)
v Limerick (2:16 to 1:17)
v Wexford (1:16 to 3:10)
v Wexford (3:12 to 0:10 (replay))

All were cliffhangers. In the first three games the result was in doubt up to the final whistle. In the Munster final against Limerick, Bobby Ryan and Donie O'Connell, Tipperary heroes of yesteryear, sat beside each other. With less than five minutes to go and the teams level and Limerick dominating possession-wise, the tension became unbearable. Donie, who had been off the fags for years, turned to Bobby and said 'Give me a fag' – anything to ease the pressure. The first round clash with Clare was a teak tough encounter. It was a test of courage and spirit. Both prevailed. Wexford had a chance to steal the drawn game in the dying moments but the effort sailed wide of the posts.

Came final day against Galway – Sunday 9 September 2001. Tommy Dunne, age 26, was now in his eighth year in county senior ranks, having made his début in the senior championship against Clare in 1994. A year later, at the age of 21, he wore the captain's jersey in the Munster semi-final, only to see his native county go under to Limerick. He had lots of honours under his belt – county titles, Railway Cups, National League, All-Star, a Munster title, an under-21 All-Ireland success in 1995 following which he was nominated RTÉ Man of the Match. But the ultimate dream, an All-Ireland medal, had so far proved elusive.

It was a great day for Tommy Dunne, Toomevara and Tipperary when referee Pat O'Connor sounded the final whistle and the scoreboard read Tipperary 2:18 Galway 2:15 in a game that had been gripping, thrilling, pulsating and brimful of excitement. As Tommy proudly took possession of the coveted and fabled Liam MacCarthy Cup he could reflect with deep satisfaction on a superb personal performance. On a day when Tipperary functioned as a cohesive unit, Tommy captained by example. He was an inspiration – his endless energy producing a high work rate, his accurate passing and excellent distribution of the sliotar being invaluable. And it was all done with style and élan and sportsmanship. He richly deserved his Man of the Match award.

Martin Breheny, writing in the *Irish Independent* the following day had this to say, 'Dunne hit the hectic pace of the game very quickly, firing over the opening point after three minutes. It was the launch pad for a superb performance which mixed energy, effort and touch with a smartness which took him to the point of action sooner than others. He decorated it with consistent accuracy, shooting five points (three from 65s).'

Victory brought Tipperary their 25th All-Ireland crown and their first since 1991. The success in 2001 placed them third in the All-Ireland senior hurling honours list – three behind Cork and one behind Kilkenny.

If there is one word that describes Tipperary's success in the campaign of 2001, it is, I believe, composure. Ally to that the superb management of Nicky English who placed huge emphasis on hurling skills, an indomitable spirit founded on conviction and you had a team that was always going to be very hard to beat.

Tom Humphries writing in *The Irish Times* the following Monday summed it well up for team and captain. 'They have hurled hardest, they have hurled the most often and they have hurled best . . . There were moments of genius amid granite shoulder challenges . . . Tommy Dunne scored some sublime points . . . He is inhaling the moment, the implications of it, the symmetry of it . . . He led his men and dealt with victory with a humility which runs in proportion to his greatness.'

It all came good for Tommy Dunne in 2001. The jigsaw pieces of his hurling world fell beautifully into place after a campaign, occasionally fraught, oft times arduous, but always nail-bitingly exciting, that had tested to the limits of human endurance, physical stamina and grit of the spirit. Hurrah for Toomevara. Hurrah for Tommy Dunne.

Willie O'Connor
KILKENNY
2000

'Hurling survives and is indestructible because of its stern naked grandeur.'

(Carbery)

The sun set on a glorious and colourful county career in 2001, when Willie decided at the age of 34 to call it a day.

He had much on which to reflect and much to savour. Honours came his way aplenty – Leinster titles; Railway Cup honours – he captained Leinster to victory in 1998; All-Star trophies; National League victories and what every hurler dreams of, an All-Ireland medal. Three times the dream came true for Willie, in 1992, 1993 and 2000. At club level with Glenmore, county, provincial and All-Ireland success came his way. His athletic prowess wasn't confined to just hurling. He was no mean footballer either and to prove it he won two county titles with his native parish.

Willie, at 5'7" and turning the scales at over 12 stone, was one of the great cornerbacks of hurling. He played with fiery defiance. He always attacked the sliotar with assurance and confidence. His covering and reading of the game were superb. He advanced and cleared in no nonsense fashion and his clearances were rarely misplaced. He was a first-touch master and extremely difficult to outwit. It was this combination of qualities that inspired and aroused those around him.

Enda McEvoy, sports journalist with the *Sunday Tribune*, rated Willie tops among modern day players on the art of tackling. 'Experienced defenders have a variety of tricks for one-on-one situations. Standing one's ground, hooking an opponent, shouldering him, insinuating one's body in his way when the ball is loose, flicking the sliotar away just as he's about to connect with it. Willie O'Connor deploys such tricks better than most.' Enda listed Brian Lohan of Clare and Stephen McDonagh of Limerick as contenders.

Babs Keating of Tipperary had this to say about Willie. 'His reading of the game is unreal. When he is under pressure he has the cunning to force a free and lift the siege. I think he must have been born in Croke Park.' And on the pressure felt by players on All-Ireland final day, Babs had this to say. 'It won't matter a damn to Willie O'Connor. He plays the same everyday regardless of pressure.'

When Willie was selected as Kilkenny captain for the year 2000 he had family pride and county pride to spur him on.

First of all was family pride. Kilkenny's last title was won in 1993 at the expense of Galway – a late goal finally clinching the issue. On that occasion his brother Eddie, playing at right fullback, captained the Noresiders. Willie played at left halfback that day. Now seven years later Willie would hope to emulate his brother Eddie and return in triumph to the Marble City, bearing the MacCarthy Cup. Victory would be special to the O'Connor family. It would be the second time only in the history of the senior hurling championship that brothers would have led their county to All-Ireland honours. On the first occasion the glory also fell to a Kilkenny family. Ger Fennelly led a victorious Kilkenny team in 1979 when Galway had to be satisfied with second best. His brother Liam had his moments of triumph in 1983 and 1992 with a win over Cork on each occasion.

Now to county pride. Kilkenny were appearing in their third-in-a-row All-Ireland final when Willie led his team around Croke Park on a sunny autumn afternoon on Sunday 10 September. Fixed in all Kilkenny minds was the fact that they had lost the two previous finals – in 1998 to Offaly, in 1999 to Cork. To lose three in a row would be humiliating to the team and devastating to Kilkenny's passionate supporters. Only once before were they faced with such a prospect. That was away back in the forties. Tipperary beat them in 1945 (5:6 to 3:6). They fell to Cork (7:5 to 3:8) in 1946. The following year it was Lee versus Nore again. Kilkenny pride was restored. Terry Leahy, with a point on the call of time, gave Kilkenny a famous victory.

The year 2000 brought a different kind of victory to that of 1947. This time it was far more decisive. Right from the throw-in Kilkenny tore into the game. They fired on all cyclinders. Offaly errors – so untypical of them – were punished mercilessly by the rampant Noresiders. By the tenth minute the Kilkenny men were cruising and led by 2:3 to 1 point. Their forwards were operating like a pack of marauding wolves. Everything Kilkenny did was classy and clinical, yet laced with grim resolve. They were on a mission and by half time had surged into an intimidating and daunting ten-point lead. By full time a masterly team display was reflected on the scoreboard – Kilkenny 5:15 Offaly 1:14.

The indefatigable Willie O'Connor, giving his usual rock-like defensive display had captained a team of wonderful hurlers – chief among them, on the day, was that prince of the modern game, D.J. Carey, who gave a capital performance. For his hurling was 'all sunshine and dazzling splendour'.

The supporters celebrated in rare style. Over and over again they sang the Rose of Mooncoin. It was sung with gusto and abandon, with elation and relief. The occasion called to mind these lines from Wordsworth's 'Tintern Abbey'.

'Sensations sweet
Felt in the blood, and felt along the heart'

Seven years of waiting had ended.

Willie's post-game thoughts were edifying and tender. In the glow of victory he remembered in a special way his mother, Bridie. 'It was the saddest year of my life. My mother died but I know she was looking down on us today. It would have been great if my mother could have been here for it too. She was in my thoughts today. Mammy is never far from my thoughts.

From a family point of view, I am so, so proud. To repeat what Eddie did was brilliant.'

The victorious team of 2000 had just three survivors from the previous winning team of 1993 – Willie O'Connor, the lion-hearted John Power and D.J. Carey – and lined out as follows:

James McGarry

Michael Kavanagh   Noel Hickey   Willie O'Connor

Phil Larkin   Eamon Kennedy   Peter Barry

Andy Comerford   Brian McEvoy

Denis Byrne   John Power   John Hoyne

Charlie Carter   D.J. Carey   Henry Sheflin

Canice Brennan replaced Brian McEvoy after 28 minutes.
Eddie Brennan replaced Canice Brennan after 67 minutes.

Hubert Rigney
OFFALY
1998

'O Captain! my Captain, our fearful trip is done,
The ship has weathered every rack, the prize we sought is won.'

I was brought up, I suppose, in the thick of hurling tradition in the townland of Coolfin, Banagher, Co. Offaly. I grew up in the famed club, St. Rynagh's, who by the time I was born had made a name for themselves all around the country. I first played a competitive hurling match for St. Rynagh's when I was eleven. My first hurling medal arrived when I was thirteen in a competition in Galway. We beat Portumna in that match. I would have been encouraged to keep hurling by my father and older brother Kieran who, when I was under 14, was a selector. I have a lot to thank Kieran for. Other influences in my early career would have been 'Chirsty Hough', Ger Fogarty and Kieran Pat Kelly. I have been fortunate to have grown up in an era when Offaly were making great progress on the hurling field. This would have had a huge influence.

At school level Pat McNamara would have been the main influence. Looking back I have had many ups and downs but thankfully I was always encouraged to keep training and listening. I have been fortunate to have been selected to play for my county at minor, under-21, and senior level. I have many great memories of those years and games which are history now but will never be forgotten.

The highlight of my career would have to be All-Ireland day 1998 and the feeling when you have just won an All-Ireland title. I have been fortunate to have been part of a great bunch of players and the fact that I was captain made it all the more special in 1998.

Finally, I think nobody will ever know it all about hurling and this is probably the beauty of this one of our native sports. To me there is always something to learn.

I want to thank Brendan for asking me to write something but to be signing my name beside other more illustrious players and famous players is hard to believe.

Hubert Rigney was born in 1971 – son of Hubert and Philomena (née Gothery), a Galway lady from the parish of Tynagh.

He was ten years old in 1981 as he watched on T.V. the men of the Faithful County defeat Galway and take their first ever All-Ireland crown. Damien Martin, Padraig Horan and Aidan Fogarty became his heroes.

Hubert won an All-Ireland minor title in 1989 when Offaly defeated Clare in the final. A year later, in the winter of 1990, he made his début in the green, white and gold senior jersey of Offaly. 'It was a league game against Derry on a rural pitch in Derry – a wet windy day. We beat them – not by much – and went on to win the league title – our first and only one to date.'

From then on Hubert became a key figure in the Offaly defence. He has always played with a quiet authority – a style that is a reflection of his personality. Attention and adherence to the basics of the game and the execution of same with a simple and phlegmatic approach stand out as his forte. In the 1998 Leinster final against Kilkenny he was absent through injury – and he was missed.

He has played in many epic contests with Offaly. Among them must surely rank the Leinster final of 1995. It was, without doubt, the best game of the year and one of the great ones in the history of the game. Thunder and lightning and torrential rain presaged the drama that the game would unfold. This was hurling of rare splendour – fast, furious and first time; the stuff traditionalists love. Hubert was at the centre of the defence where he controlled the stout-hearted and energetic John Power – a defence that was phalanx-like in the face of every Kilkenny assault. A defence in which he joined with his colleagues in blocking, hooking, parrying, harassing, covering, batting and chasing with a spirit of no surrender. We witnessed a game for the gods.

1998 dawned and the hurling championship began. It was a brave pundit that would have attempted a forecast. There was a strong field. As always the 'Big Three' were there – Tipp. Kilkenny and Cork. But you also had Waterford and Galway, both knocking at the door; Limerick who had contested and lost the finals of 1994 and 1996; Clare who had won the titles of 1995 and 1997; Offaly who had won the crown in 1994 and lost the final of 1995; Wexford who surprised everyone in 1996 with a great All-Ireland win and who retained their Leinster crown in 1997.

In the end it proved to be Offaly's year. It was a long adventurous journey. It was a campaign in which they played eight games – the most any county ever had to play to capture the blue riband. 'We were up and down. There were stages when we didn't know where we were. The pinnacle of the year was the final whistle on All-Ireland day – a very tight game – you need a bit of luck, no matter what.' And the game he enjoyed most? 'It has to be the third game against Clare in Thurles – it was unbelievable that day.'

Let's now take a look at the Offaly hurling odyssey of 1998.

v Meath (4:28 to 0:8)
v Wexford (1:15 to 0:17)
v Kilkenny (1:11 to 3:10 (lost))
v Antrim (2:18 to 2:9)
v Clare (1:13 to 1:13)
v Clare (1:16 to 2:10 (lost) but replayed due to short time played)
v Clare (0:16 to 0:13)
v Kilkenny (2:16 to 1:13)

'We were without the Birr players for the league of that year until March because they were involved in the club championship. I was captain for the league and I just happened to be left there.'

The campaign was not a tour-de-force performance of displays by Offaly – rather an up and down graph that reflected the strange character and temperament of hurling's most enigmatic team.

Their manager, Babs Keating, dissatisfied with the Leinster final display against Kilkenny, departed the scene. Recalling the occasion Tom Humphries wrote as follows in *The Irish Times* of 14 September '98: 'He resigned before he was impeached. He was replaced by a man with no reputation. Michael Bond, Double-Oh-O, as the little joke went. We imagined the scenes as the hapless Mr. Bond walked in for his first night amongst the most difficult hurlers in the country. The gentlemen of Offaly putting down their cocktails, extinguishing their cheroots. 'Ah, Mr. Bond, we've been expecting you.' They seemed neither stirred nor shaken by Bond's arrival. They played Kilkenny in a challenge two weeks later and lost by 20 points . . . '

In Kilkenny, when they came off that evening, having humiliated their most passionate enemies, they should have listened to the winds. That's all there was to hear. In the Offaly dressing-room it was quiet, too quiet. The boys of Summer were about to get serious.'

We saw them in earnest in the third game against Clare in Thurles on Saturday 29 August – a day in which Hubert Rigney and his team demonstrated what they were really capable of – a day when we saw hurling of rip-roaring intensity, glorious pace and fierce passion – a day when aggression tested sportsmanship to the limits, and sportsmanship prevailed.

Writing on the game in the *Sunday Tribune* Kevin Cashman had this to say: 'Offaly's defence was probably tighter than it was even in the most Alcatraz days of its long experience. . . . Hubert Rigney had his best game ever at centre back. He was at the side of every colleague in the slightest difficulty. His striking was conciseness embodied, and, *mirabile dictu*, he probably pucked more ball than Whelehan. Kevin Martin was tremendous too.'

And so to the final against Kilkenny. Hubert and his men had a tentative start. They had luck when Brian Whelehan cleared a certain goal off the line and more luck when Stephen Byrne saved a rasper that had goal written all over it. Most importantly of all though they had misfortune that turned to gold. A 'flu-stricken Brian Whelehan left the right half wing of the Offaly defence creaking. Michael Duignan moves from attack to defence to seal the gap. Brian Whelehan goes to full forward and proceeds to score 1:6 and emerge as Man of the Match.

As the game progressed, a superb Offaly defence marshalled around an increasingly effective Hubert Rigney, tightened their grip on proceedings and like a collection of clams sealed the road to goal.

A contest to savour ended Offaly 2:16 Kilkenny 1:13. Hubert Rigney had captained Offaly to their fourth All-Ireland success. It was easily Offaly's All-Ireland win of greatest splendour.

Tom Humphries summed it up well in the opening paragraph of his report in Monday's *The Irish Times*. 'Ripping yarns and tall tales. This was a hurling summer to tell the grandchildren about, won in the end by a team whose legend needs no embellishment. Offaly. It ain't what they do. It's the way that they do it.'

Anthony Daly
CLARE
1995 & 1997

'On the windswept Hill of Tulla
Within whose breast so deep
With dreams of Resurrection Morn
A thousand hurlers sleep,
And with them Tommy Daly
Four yews above his head
On the windswept Hill of Tulla
Where the Claremen place their dead.'

(Bryan McMahon)

15

It was a day full of sorrow for Clare hurling and its loyal supporters when, after great victories over Limerick and Cork, they slumped to humiliating defeat at the hands of Tipperary in the Munster final of 1993 with a scoreline of Tipperary 3:27 Clare 2:12.

Anthony Daly played at corner back that day.

> I walked from the pitch after the final whistle feeling numb and dismayed. The team had lost badly and played badly and after twenty minutes the game was a lost cause. I was very disappointed with my own display – felt stuck to the ground – couldn't get going. I felt ashamed too, ashamed for my brother who had come home to see the game and for all the family who were there as well – and of course for our supporters.'

Anthony felt even worse after the defeat by Limerick the following year. At the time he saw little future for the county team.

> My club was doing well, however, and I began to think in terms of winning county and provincial and maybe All-Ireland titles with Clarecastle.

Yes indeed, after the defeats of 1993 and 1994 Clare's hurling future did look grim. The county felt shattered. A dense, dark cloud descended on Clare hurling. But phoenix-like they were destined to rise from the ashes of defeat.

The Resurrection Morn – hurling-wise – referred to in Brian McMahon's poem dawned in 1995 under the managership of the indefatigable Ger Loughnane. Clare were on the march. Captain Anthony Daly was at the helm.

Anthony, born in 1970, played his club hurling with Clarecastle and won county honours and captained them in one of those successes. He won a Harty Cup and All-Ireland Colleges title with St. Flannan's in 1987. And in 1989 he donned the Clare senior jersey for the first time in a National League game against Waterford.

He became part of a great Clare halfback line – Liam Doyle, Sean McMahon, Anthony Daly – that represented the county from 1995 to 2000 – a halfback line that will go down in the annals of the game as one of the great halfback lines of hurling.

Anthony's own performances earned him All-Star awards in 1994, 1995 and 1998. He captained the men of Dal gCais from 1992 to 1998 and led them to two memorable All-Ireland triumphs in 1995 and 1997. In doing so he joined an elite band that had the glory of leading their county to All-Ireland victory on two occasions.

Clare's opening game in the 1995 championship was against Cork and they came through with a point to spare. Their next encounter was against Limerick – reigning provincial champions and All-Ireland finalists of 1994 – in the Munster final. Playing brilliantly, Clare ran out winners by nine points. The celebrations that followed buried all the frustrations of a sixty-three year gap of unrewarded endeavour. Next to fall were Galway. Clare then faced Offaly, reigning All-Ireland champions, in the All-Ireland final. They won a heart-stopping encounter by two points. The results of the 1995 campaign read as follows:

v Cork (2:13 to 3:9)
v Limerick (1:17 to 0:11)
v Galway (3:12 to 1:13)
v Offaly (1:13 to 2:8)

The final was watched by two surviving Clare veterans, Tom McInerney and John Joe Doyle, from the 1932 final – a game Clare lost to Kilkenny by 3:3 to 2:3. Their presence added a touch of nostalgia to a day of sunshine and glamour when a unique pairing contested an absorbing final. For Clare and their loyal followers the pre-match parade 'was but the prelude to that glorious day'.

Anthony Daly delivered a wonderful winning speech from the Hogan Stand – one of the finest heard on final day. It was comprehensive, dignified and thoughtful – a credit to him and the team he represented. 'This was as close as All-Ireland-winning captains come to a Gettysburg Address,' wrote Enda McEvoy in the *Sunday Tribune* of 24 February 2002. In mentioning team manager Ger Loughnane, Anthony said 'his obsession has become a reality'. Writing long after the game in the *Sunday Tribune*, Kevin Cashman beautifully described a key point scored by Anthony in the second half:

> After that racking, interminable delay, Anthony Daly, mere feet in from the sideline, lifted and struck the seventy toward the canal goal. Trajectory and velocity told instantly that he had applied the truest spot of his timber to the ball. But direction?

17

The ball was heading heavily wide of the Corporate Stand post; the natural bend of Daly's right-handed stroke would bring it back some. But never enough!

Then, the zephyrs of Croke Park, or the destiny that shapes our ends, or the shades of all the warrior heroes of Dal gCais, intervened. The natural bend became unnatural; a ball that – from any team at any time, except The Banner in The Year of The Banner – deserved to go a yard wide, soared blithely a foot inside that upright.

Passion and emotion and celebration had still to be given their due. But the summit of that rapture had been attained during the fierce, sweet hours of July 9 (Munster final) when The Banner resumed her place amongst the nations of the earth, and in the following days. That, being unique, could not be recaptured or repeated in September.

The year of 1995 was exclusively The Banner's.

The Irish Times ran an editorial:

The All-Ireland hurling final was a victory for the brave: for Clare, a county long accustomed to defeat, which showed more resilience than most observers thought possible . . .

The circumstances conspired to make the occasion memorable. Here was a county whose last appearance in a hurling championship final was in the 1930s, whose last success coincided with the outbreak of the First World War. Yet its teams had never lacked enthusiasm or courage and their followers invariably travelled in hope, even when the odds against them seemed overwhelming.

Ironically, the county from which Clare derived fresh encouragement and not a little satisfaction was Offaly, champions until Sunday and clear favourites to retain their title. In fifteen years, Offaly had come from nowhere to take a place, if not with Cork, Tipperary and Kilkenny in the first rank of hurling mastery, at least in that honourable company which includes Limerick, Galway and Wexford.

If most neutrals supported Clare on Sunday it was not that they failed to appreciate Offaly's contribution to hurling, or hurling's contribution to Offaly's identity and pride; rather that Clare, as well as being challengers to champions, held the affections of many who had taken to heart the vivid colours of its music and folklore long before they came to recognise the colours of its GAA teams.

It was the celebration of neutrals on the journey home which delayed a long procession of Clare cars at towns and villages in the midlands – even before the team's plane landed at Shannon Airport and the county's own celebrations, at Newmarket-on-Fergus, Clarecastle and Ennis, began in earnest.

In 1996 in the Munster semi-final, Clare with Anthony Daly still at the helm fell to Limerick in the sweltering heat of a June afternoon – fell in particular to Ciaran Carey's winning point after a sixty yards solo run – 'the greatest winner ever scored'.

However, Clare were back in 1997 with a bang and intent. They indulged in practice shooting in their opening game with Kerry. Then one by one the three superpowers of hurling, Cork, Tipperary and Kilkenny, fell before the awesome might of Clare hurling – full of power, passion and precision.

Clare's 1997 programme read as follows:

v Kerry (3:24 to 1:6)
v Cork (1:19 to 0:18)
v Tipperary (1:18 to 0:18)
v Kilkenny (1:17 to 1:13)
v Tipperary (0:20 to 2:13)

Victory over Cork confirmed Clare's 1995 superiority over the Rebel County. By defeating Tipperary for the first time in the Munster final, Anthony Daly and the men he captained dismantled a huge psychological barrier. They captured the scalp of the third hurling superpower when they triumphed over the men from the Noreside.

The All-Ireland final brought Clare face to face with Tipperary for the second time in the 1997 championship. Tipperary as defeated Munster finalists re-entered the championship and worked their way to the final. It was a clash of neighbours, a clash of clans, and a clash of Titans. Victory for Anthony Daly and the men of Clare would carry with it a seal of greatness. Defeat would leave question marks.

The game was a stirring contest. It built up into a gripping climax. Early Tipperary dominance left them four points to the good at half time. Clare dug deep in the second half and led by five points with a quarter of an hour left. They were playing with such precision and purpose that they looked set to add much more to a scoreline that read Clare 0:17 Tipperary 0:12.

Everything that makes a contest memorable was packed into the closing stages. Tipperary got a goal. It left them one point behind; nine minutes to go. Then another goal. Tipperary one point up; five minutes to go. Pandemonium. Tipperary followers go wild. All Clare hearts miss a beat. In a flash Ollie Baker equalises for Clare and Jamsie O'Connor with a truly smashing point gives Clare a one-point lead. Now, maybe three minutes to go. Even neutrals can feel the tension of an electric atmosphere. Suddenly it's a contest between John Leahy – menacingly alone inside the Clare defence and less than twenty yards from goal – and facing him with concentration written across his face is Clare custodian Davy Fitzgerald. The Clare man wins glory with a fine save. The Banner triumphs by one point. The seal of greatness is theirs.

In 1996 Anthony Daly captained Munster to Railway Cup honours with a convincing 3:20 to 0:10 win over Leinster. In so doing, he joined the select company of a few players who had the privilege of captaining club, county and province to ultimate honours. The 1990s finished up a wonderful decade for Anthony. The dust of the early years of the decade turned to gold as the decade advanced – county titles, Munster titles (3), All-Ireland medals (2), Railway Cups (2), All-Stars (3), Munster club title.

After the Munster defeats of 1993 and 1994, to have aspired to such awards would have been tantamount to dreaming the impossible dream.

Martin Hanamy
OFFALY
1994

'The tumult and the shouting dies;
The Captains and the Kings depart.'

When Eamon Cregan undertook the management of the Offaly senior hurling team in 1994 he never for a moment thought that the paths

20

of Offaly and his native Limerick, with whom he won many honours, including an All-Ireland medal in 1973, would converge at Croke Park in the afternoon of 4 September to decide the destiny of the MacCarthy Cup. Irrespective of who won or lost that day he would be left with mixed feelings.

There was a wonderful atmosphere in the stadium as spectators looked forward to a first ever All-Ireland final contest between the two counties. Limerick, with their green jersey and white collars and cuffs, were appearing in their fifteenth All-Ireland final and their first since defeat by Galway in 1980. Offaly, the Faithful County, with the horizontal hoops of green, white and gold were contesting their fourth All-Ireland decider and their first final since they won their second crown at the expense of Galway in 1985.

Offaly were captained by Martin Hanamy from the St. Rynagh's club on the banks of the Shannon. Martin was one of the finest cornerbacks in the game during his hurling days. He possessed an uncanny sense of position. He gave consistently good performances and was a commanding figure in the fullback line, difficult to outwit, always effective, tight in his marking, authoritative without being flamboyant.

Both teams had impressive paths to the final and had many quite talented hurlers in their ranks. Offaly travelled as follows:

v Kilkenny (2:16 to 3:9) – All-Ireland title holders 1992 and 1993
v Wexford (1:18 to 0:14) – Leinster finalists 1992 and 1993
v Galway (2:13 to 1:10) – defeated All-Ireland finalists 1993

Limerick had a longer passage:

v Cork (4:14 to 4:11)
v Waterford (2:14 to 2:12)
v Clare (0:25 to 2:10)
v Antrim (2:23 to 0:11)

As a matter of interest, Tipperary, the third of the 'Big Three' were eliminated by Clare on the score 2:11 to 0:13 – sweet revenge for a humiliating defeat in the Munster final of 1993.

Now to the game itself. On Sunday 4 September Martin Hanamy presided over one of the most astounding and remarkable All-Ireland hurling victories ever.

In the course of the game he was switched from the left corner to the right corner to curb the wiles of the rampant Damien Quigley who contributed 2:3 of Limerick's total. 'I hate the right corner but I had to try and do a marking job on him and I did O.K. in the end.' Journalists were at a loss to describe and analyse what had happened. All kinds of adjectives were used – unbelievable, mind-boggling, sensational, incredible, miracle.

Donal Keenan writing in the *Irish Independent* the following Monday had this to say: 'They (Offaly) had reserved their worst performance of the championship for the biggest game. They also met a Limerick team playing its best hurling since they beat Cork in the first round last June . . . The victory, Offaly's third senior hurling success, was the result of a miracle of such proportions that it defies Biblical analogy. Damn it, it almost defies description.'

The result sent Con Houlihan scurrying down memory lane in his article in the *Evening Press* headed 'Faithful and Fateful Day'.

I have never known such an evening for comparisons – in the Shakespeare and in Mulligan's and in Hourigan's they floated in the air. We heard about Kerry and Roscommon in the All-Ireland final of 1946 – that too had a mellow dramatic climax.

The Western champions led by two goals with four minutes to go; twice Kerry put the ball into their net and drew. They won the replay. And of course we heard about Kerry and Offaly in the All-Ireland final in 1982 – the year of a five-in-a-row that never was. Kerry led by five points with about that many minutes remaining – the rest is history.

And of course there was the All-Ireland semi-final in 1977. Kerry seemed to be coasting to victory: two goals in as many minutes wrote a new scenario. I remember all those romantic codas – but for me yesterday afternoon's score-quake recalled a game not in Croke Park but in Anfield.

It happened on a May evening, a few years ago in the last game in the topmost division of The Football League. Arsenal came to Lancashire in what seemed a hopeless position – they needed not only to win but to win by two goals to take the title. With five minutes to go their cause seemed hopeless; Liverpool were coasting home. And then came a goal; within a minute there came another goal – the home team hadn't time to recover.

And we remember how Jersey Joe Walcott was cruising past Joe Louis but ran into a late punch-storm.

Yes, indeed, 'a late punch-storm', surely the most apt description of all. For with five minutes remaining Limerick led by five points and seemed to have their hands on the MacCarthy Cup, in a game where they had outshone and in general outplayed the men of Offaly. 'They were quicker, stronger, more eager and more composed,' wrote Donal Keenan in the *Irish Independent*. The scoreboard read Limerick 2:13 Offaly 1:11. And yet despite all their superiority Limerick had been very wasteful. With 18 wides to their discredit their dominance was not reflected in a five-point lead. Five minutes remained. Con Houlihan observed Martin Hanamy and subsequently wrote 'Martin Hanamy is an inspiring captain but even he seemed resigned to playing out time doggedly. I had a ringside view of him in the second half – as the clock on the canal terrace showed a quarter to five, his face seemed devoid of hope.'

Suddenly, like a clap of thunder, the Offaly resurrection came out of the blue. Johnny Dooley ignored sideline instructions to take a point from a 21 yards free. He sent it to the net. Its impact was lethal. Limerick froze. Thirty-five seconds later the sliotar was in the Limerick net again via Pat O'Connor. Now it's a punch a minute as points follow from Johnny Dooley, John Troy and three from Billy Dooley.

Martin Hanamy climbed the Hogan Stand. One journalist commented that he seemed dazed – dazed in disbelief as he took to hand the famed MacCarthy Cup. 'Sometimes victory is as bewildering as defeat,' wrote Tom Humphries in *The Irish Times*.

In victory, the Offaly players displayed a dignity and chivalry we have come to associate with them. Their centre-forward, Jim Troy, said 'a horrible way to lose' and Martin Hanamy in his greatest sporting moment had a profound thought for the vanquished – 'Christ, you'd have to feel sorry for them.'

A French journalist, Nicholas Beuveret of *L'Equipe,* said 'It was so unique, so fast and so tense too. I think that the players in this game seem to be very humble; proud and skilled but not arrogant.'

Martin retired from inter-county fare after the championship of 1999 by which time he had left a lasting impact and garnered many honours – chief among them being a National League (1991), Railway Cup (1993), All-Ireland titles (1994, '98), three All-Stars (1988, 1994, '98).

Declan Carr
TIPPERARY
1991

'But tho' my bundle 's on my shoulder,
And there 's no man could be bolder,
Tho' I'm leavin' now the spot that I was born in;
Yet someday I'll take the notion
To come back across the ocean
To my home in dear old Ireland in the mornin'.'

Declan Carr, standing at 6'1" and turning the scales at 12st. 7lb. at the height of his hurling career, was born a 'Dub' of Tipperary parents on 30 July 1965. In 1980 at the age of 15 he moved to Tipperary where he played his club hurling with Holycross-Ballycahill.

It is interesting to note that his brother Tommy played football with Dublin, although he did wear the blue and gold of Tipperary in that code on a few occasions. Tommy made his All-Ireland début in 1985 when he came on as a sub in the final against Kerry, only to taste defeat. He was captain of the Dublin team in 1992 but again, defeat was the lot of the metropolitans in the final against Donegal.

In Tipperary Declan progressed from under-21 level to senior ranks and played in the league campaign of 1988–'89 at midfield. They lost to Galway in the final by two points. He lined out at midfield again in the league final of 1991–'92 against Limerick at the Gaelic Grounds on a wet, miserable and windy May afternoon. In the dying seconds of the game, to Declan's dismay, Ray Sampson put Limerick ahead for the first time in the hour with a superbly taken point that heralded defeat for Tipperary. Following a sojourn in America in the '90s Declan was back on the Tipperary team at midfield for the league of 1999. It was a case of third time lucky. Tipperary avenged the defeat of 1988–'89 with four points to spare over Galway.

Declan played in two All-Ireland finals. The first was in 1989. Tipperary emerged from Munster for the third year in a row with a very convincing win over Waterford, followed by a close encounter with Galway in the All-Ireland semi-final – winning in the end by three points. That was on 6 August at Croke Park. On the same day in the other semi-final Antrim created a mild surprise when they defeated Offaly by 4:15 to 1:15.

Fans now faced a unique pairing on Sunday 3 September at Croke Park in the All-Ireland final. Tipperary v Antrim. It would be Antrim's second time in the history of the championship to contest a final. Their first appearance in a final took place almost half a century earlier in 1943. They had performed gaiscí in disposing of Galway and Kilkenny at Corrigan Park, Belfast. But dreams of fame and glory died against the might of Cork in a very one-sided final.

Now in 1989 supporters of both sides and neutral spectators – although it must be said that the hearts of all neutrals lay with the men from the Glens – having enjoyed a fine minor final between Clare and victorious Offaly, eagerly awaited the senior contest. There was a carnival atmosphere, a great contrast in colour – the saffron and white of Antrim, the blue and gold of Tipperary. The pairing created a sense of the romantic.

The exchanges of the first twenty minutes were fairly even. At midfield, however, Declan Carr was having a magnificent game. He and his partner Colm Bonner broke Antrim hearts and gave Tipperary a decisive pull in that sector of the field. Declan's play was stylish, energetic and intelligent. His probing shots opened the way for Tipperary scores. In the course of the hour he contributed two points to Tipperary's total of 4:24 – half of which, incidentally, came from the camán of that classy wizard of the ash, Nicky English.

Victory that day, which left Declan with enduring memories, brought him his first All-Ireland medal and his adopted county their 23rd title, after an inordinate lapse of 18 years. His performance at midfield throughout the championship brought its own personal award when he was selected for the All-Star team of 1989.

Two years later Declan was back again in Croke Park. This time he was skipper of the side. On the way they met Cork in a Munster final that went to a replay. The game carried a script that would have done justice to a Hitchcock thriller. Picture the scene. As the clock ticked towards the quarter hour of the second half, Kevin Hennessy scored a goal to put Cork nine points clear – Cork in the ascendancy on a day when the afternoon heat and fierce physical exchanges soaked up energy.

Tipperary made several switches. They cut the Cork lead to three points. Now came a moment to savour for Declan who had moved to the forwards. John Leahy sent a ball goalwards. Declan was there to finish it to the net. Tipperary level. Their supporters ecstatic. A famous victory beckoned. It came. Tipperary 4:19 Cork 4:15.

In the final against Kilkenny Declan was back in his favourite position at midfield, partnered by the speedy and elusive Aidan Ryan. Tipperary were firm favourites. But the pundits didn't get it quite right. This was a close run encounter. The only goal of the game had a telling impact. It came after ten minutes of the second half had elapsed, at which time Tipperary led by just one point. A foul on Nicky English saw Michael Cleary – a brilliant marksman – step up to take a free about thirty yards to the left of the goal. A stroke intended for a point was mis-hit and the sliotar deflected off a Kilkenny defender's hurley into the net. Tipperary four points up.

Declan was having a fine game and his second half performance in particular was inspirational. He was one of the leading contributors to a 1:16 to 0:15 win. His was the MacCarthy Cup to take back once more to the Premier County. Tipperary's 24th title. Declan's second success. It had been a good year.

Further honours came his way at Kilkenny on 15 March 1992 when he captained Munster to Railway Cup honours, defeating Ulster 3:12 to 1:8.

Tomás Mulcahy
CORK
1990

Coming from a family background of 'hurling madness' my late father was a staunch member of Glen Rovers Hurling and Football club and I suppose it was inevitable that at an early age I would be the recipient of a new camán and sliotar to follow in his footsteps.

Having brothers who were also very keen on the game, my early memories of matches up and down the street in Boyces Street with our neighbours, was the start of greater things to come. Nothing else mattered in our lives but to follow and emulate our heroes on the playing fields of Ireland. Those early years at school and under-age level with Glen Rovers brought great success and gave me the ambition and the drive to achieve more.

The tradition and folklore of Glen Rovers is now household in GAA circles and to meet and get advice and encouragement from stalwarts such as Jack Lynch, Christy Ring and Jim Young will long stand in my memory.

To me hurling is a game of 'passion and skill' or else it is nothing and to represent your county and achieve the success I had was a great privilege.

I remember travelling to Thurles for Munster finals and to Croke Park and the pride in wearing the famous red jersey will be with me forever.

My wish for hurling in the future is that we go back to basics and concentrate more on the skill levels than the physical side of things and promote the game even further in the so called 'weaker counties'.

> 'An tríocha fear ag rith is ag léimneach,
> Buillí á mbualadh le neart is le héifeacht,
> Tapúlacht coise is oilteacht láimhe,
> Ar dhroim an domhain níl radharc is áille'
>
> (Sean Ó Finnéadha)

Tomás played minor for Cork for two years without success. He was rewarded, however, in 1982 at the age of 19 when he came on as a sub in the under-21 All-Ireland final against Galway. He made his senior county début at Jack Barrett Park in Kinsale in a tournament game against Waterford in 1983. That day the full forward line read:

Seanie O'Leary   Jimmy Barry Murphy   Tomás Mulcahy

Three great men, I suggested. 'Two great men and a little greenhorn.' From then until 1995, when he retired, Tomás gave many outstanding performances for club, county and province. Nowadays, he gives a very erudite analysis of hurling games, as a panellist on T.V.

In the Munster final of 1992, against Limerick, he gave evidence of his quick thinking. He lost his hurley around the 21 yards line – 'it was pulled from me' – but unfazed, he put the head down and with his back to the referee headed for goal, hopping the ball on his hand before despatching it to the Limerick net. The green flag waved and many saw it as a turning point in the game.

He won all the major honours the game had to offer: a county title with Glen Rovers in 1989; a National League title in 1993 after a three games marathon with Wexford; All-Star awards in 1984 and 1986; Railway Cup medals in 1984 and 1985; six Munster titles that led to five All-Ireland finals (Galway beat them in the All-Ireland semi-final of 1985); All-Ireland victories of 1984, 1986 and 1990.

Football success eluded him. He played minor at county level and 'was sent on as a sub in the 1985 Munster senior football final against Kerry in Killarney to mark Páidí Ó Sé and try to get a goal'. There have been easier tasks on the football field.

Tomás's love for hurling began at an early age. 'It was a tradition in our house on Saturday and Sunday mornings to go and watch street leagues in Blackpool. I was always captivated by the depth of enthusiasm shown by my father and my older brother, Liam, who went on to play minor and under-21 for Cork. My father had played hurling with Glen Rovers and football with St. Nicholas's and was a great enthusiast.'

Ray Cummins was his hero. 'I watched him a lot – a dual player, a good leader, a great presence of mind and a great distributor of the ball – a star man.'

Tomás never saw Christy Ring play but he grew up hearing about the legendary figure. 'I played with Christy Jnr. in under-age matches and often talked with his father who was always there to watch his son and encourage us all.'

Any special wishes for the game?

- I would love to see a situation arrived at where players only practised two nights a week and played one match at the weekend.
- I would like a special effort to bring the standard in the weaker counties to an acceptable level.
- I'd like a return to concentrating on basic skills and letting the ball do the work.

On lying on the ball – a habit creeping into the game. 'Very dangerous, should be penalised immediately.'

From many memorable moments the following ones will always have a special place in Tomás's thoughts. His days in North Mon were very rewarding.

'It was a haven of hurling. There was a half-day on Wednesday – not to go home – when everyone went to the Old Mon field to play hurling and football. It was part of the curriculum. 1980 was a great year for the school. We won the Dean Ryan Cup and the Frewen Cup – the junior competitions in hurling and football. The senior team won the Harty Cup – we beat St. Colman's, Fermoy, in the final and then went on to beat St. Kieran's, Kilkenny, in the All-Ireland colleges final.' Tomás felt very honoured to have participated in all those successes and he recalled that Tony O'Sullivan of future Cork fame was on the Mon senior team and that Ken Hogan, who would later star in goal for Tipperary, was on the St. Kieran's team.

In 1989 Tomás was captain of Glen Rovers when his club won the county title after a lapse of 13 years. 'We were the first team to bring the Cup across the Christy Ring Bridge. The first man to meet us at the Bridge was Jack Lynch. He was a hero for me off the field as well.'

Tomás will always remember the Centenary hurling final in Thurles in 1984. Cork lost the 1982 final to Kilkenny. The following year Tomás, playing at right full forward, was in his first year in senior championship hurling. But Cork went down for the second year in a row to the Noresiders. Victory in 1984 under the captaincy of John Fenton was special for Tomás in a number of aspects. It halted a Cork losing sequence. It was victory in the Centenary year. It was his first All-Ireland senior medal. 'It was a success that gave you the ambition to do more.'

1990, the year Tomás captained Cork, probably holds pride of place in his hurling heart. 'Cork City witnessed great celebrations that year. After 100 years, Cork again won the football and hurling double. Not too many have the chance. When the footballers returned on the Monday after the final we were there on the platform. Larry Tompkins and myself exchanged the Sam Maguire and Liam MacCarthy Cups. It was a good moment for sport.'

Tomás's father, Gerald, now gone to God, was at the hurling final – and an exciting and hectic one it turned out to be. 'He had a heart complaint and was advised not to go to the match.' However, go he did. Maybe it helped relieve the pressure that Cork, with victories over Waterford, Tipperary and Antrim, were underdogs while Galway who were carrying the scalps of London and Offaly were firm favourites.

In any event, Gerald was treated to a thrilling spectacle – an exhilarating contest in which all the skills and thrills of our ancient game were in evidence – a game for the gods.

At half time Galway led by five points and it could have been more. Joe Cooney, their centre forward, was in devastating form and had scored 1:5 from play and one point from a free to leave the score 1:13 to 1:8. Within five minutes of the restart Galway had stretched their lead to seven points and appeared to be in the ascendancy.

But the Cork mentors had made a second half switch that was to prove vital. Tomás Mulcahy was moved from right full forward to centre forward. In the seventh minute he scored a goal that cut the Galway lead to four points. That coupled with a fine overall performance from Tomás – supplemented by attention to the games basics and the use of ground strokes by the Cork team in general, paved the way to a surprise victory in which Lady Luck and the gods also played a role.

The game produced 43 scores – Cork 5:15 Galway 2:21. And really from the moment the ball was thrown in – Kevin Hennessy netted for Cork after 40 seconds – to John Moore's final whistle, this thrill-a-minute contest was no place for weak hearts – be they neutral or partisan. Great, therefore, must have been the strain and pressure on the heart of Gerald Mulcahy as he watched his son Tomás captain Cork, in glorious weather conditions, to the county's 27th title.

'When the game was over I said to myself, I hope he is alright. After the presentation of the Cup I was in the dressing-room in a

30

corner after interviews. There were fellows beating down the door trying to get in but there was high security keeping them out. Again I was thinking of my father and hoping he was all right. The next thing I saw was my father coming through the door. There were tears in his eyes. He came over and put his arms around me and hugged me.' A special moment, an enduring memory.

Bobby Ryan
TIPPERARY
1989

'Onward they press with might and main!
Onward, backward, on again!
Here they rush, there they meet,
Centremen, backmen, forwards fleet.
Then list to the click and creak and crash
As hero meets hero, ash to ash.'

(Sliabh Ruadh)

Having been born into a family that was steeped in hurling, I always felt that I would someday play with Tipperary. When that day finally arrived it was one of the proudest days of my life.

As a young boy growing up in Borrisoleigh hurling was almost like religion. Everything revolved around the game. Our family were very involved in the game locally. All my brothers would have played for our club, my sisters would wash the togs and my mother used to pray!! My mother in particular played a huge role in my development as a player and a person. She taught us how to accept defeat as well as victory.

My greatest disappointment has got to be the Munster final of 1984 v Cork. I was captain of the team and it was also Centenary year. Cork stole the game on Tipperary in the final minutes and I ended up with a broken leg.

Winning the All-Ireland in 1989 and captaining the team was for me the biggest thrill in my sporting career. To captain your county to All-Ireland success is the greatest honour any player can get.

I have many great memories from my years of hurling with Tipperary and Borrisoleigh and indeed Templemore CBS. But what I treasure most is the friendships that I have made from both inside and outside the county.

I have many reasons to be grateful. I played a game I loved at the highest level. I hope in years to come I will be remembered as a great sportsman rather than a great player.

The thought of not playing county senior hurling for his native Tipperary never entered Bobby Ryan's head. 'It was always a case of when will I play for Tipperary – never would I play for Tipperary. It was the same with my brother Aidan. My other brothers Pat, (who won a minor All-Ireland in 1976), Tim (dec'd), John and Eamon never thought like that and never played for Tipperary.'

In a way it is easy to understand Bobby's line of thinking. His late father, Tim, played left half forward on the victorious All-Ireland Tipperary team of 1951. Right half forward on that team was his uncle Ned. In the centre was Mick Ryan of Roscrea – no relation – making it an all Ryan half forward line.

Centre back on that team was his uncle on his mother's side, the great Pat Stakelum from Thurles, one of the game's greatest defenders, who in 1951 won his third All-Ireland medal in a row. He was captain of the 1949 team.

Bobby proceeded to remind me that the concept of professionalism wasn't necessarily a thing of the present day. He enjoyed recalling that 'my father Tim, while working in west Cork, travelled on his motor-bike one Sunday in the late forties to play with St. Finbarr's in the Cork championship. He played under an alias and was paid – (a brief silence from Bobby) – he was given a half a crown' – two shillings and six pence at the time, later converting to twelve and a half new pence and in today's euro currency 16 cent.

Bobby grew up in Borrisoleigh. It was a parish that produced great hurlers such as Philly, Sean and Pat Kenny, Jimmy Finn, Noel O'Dwyer and Liam Devaney – players that Bobby could aspire to emulate. And add to those the hurling heroes of his youth, Tadhg O'Connor and Francis Loughnane, whom he idolised.

Bobby went to Secondary School at Templemore CBS and was part of a great team that won the school's only Harty Cup triumph to date in 1978 and went on from there to win All-Ireland honours. After that honours flowed in abundance to this versatile performer from the time he joined the county senior panel around 1981 to his retirement from inter-county hurling in 1993.

His major honours include:

- All-Ireland senior hurling successes in 1989 and 1991 when he played at centre back;
- Munster titles in 1987, '88, '89, '91 and '93;
- National League success (1987–'88) at right halfback;
- county titles with Borrisoleigh 1981 (centre forward) 1983 (centre forward) 1986 (left halfback);
- All-Ireland under-21 titles 1980 (centre forward) 1981 (centre forward);
- All-Star awards 1986 (left halfback) 1988 (left halfback) 1989 (centre back);
- All-Ireland club title 1987 when he gave an outstanding display at left halfback, his favourite position, against Rathnure in the final.

It was around this time 1986–'87 that Bobby was playing his best hurling – even allowing for a brilliant display against Cork in the Munster final of 1984 – until he retired injured. 'In 1986 I was playing very well with Borrisoleigh. In the Munster championship against Clare in Ennis we were beaten. I had a pain in my hand from pucking back the ball.' The All-Star award of 1986 meant a U.S. tour in May 1987. '"Babs" (Keating), for whom I have the greatest admiration, was then manager and I know he didn't want me to go on the tour. It nearly cost me my place on the team. He replaced me. I found myself among the subs. With the defence playing so well without me I was glad to be eventually handed the No.14 jersey. At full forward my displays were not very colourful or productive. In the All-Ireland final of 1988 I ended up at wingback and didn't play full forward again for Babs.'

Bobby's mother, Bridget, never went to watch her sons play. But she did instil in her sons a great sporting philosophy – a great attitude to both victory and defeat. 'It takes a great man to accept victory but an even greater one to accept defeat,' she said to Bobby after the heartbreaking Munster final defeat of 1984 at the hands of Cork.

Before a game we would be told never do to somebody what you wouldn't like to have done to yourself. We would be mortified if we had done anything we shouldn't have. In all my years playing I was never sent off and I am proud of that – although I did have my name taken a few times – if I had to I could give and take it with the best. With my mother the important thing was that we didn't get a belt and that we didn't hurt anybody – well and good if we won. Before a game we used have to kneel down in front of the Sacred Heart picture and say a decade of the rosary – three Hail Marys if time was against us. Mother gave us great values. I am trying to get a Sacred Heart lamp for the house at present but I am finding it impossible.

In 1973 Limerick defeated Tipperary at Thurles in the Munster final by 6:7 to 2:18. Tipperary didn't contest another Munster final until 1984 when under the captaincy of Bobby Ryan they faced Cork in Semple Stadium, Thurles. 'Here we were in 1984 hoping to make history like the men of 1949 to 1951, having been drip fed about them from the family as we grew up. Nothing can prepare you for a Munster final in Thurles. The tension is terrible. There we were in the Pallotine Convent. The nuns made tea for us. We heard massive cheers from the minor match. Some felt sick with the tension. We said what are we letting ourselves in for. Nothing prepares you for it.'
  Bobby will never forget that 1984 Munster final.

It was about half way through the second half. I contested a high ball with Tim Crowley about forty yards out near the Old Stand. I don't know who won the pull but I fell and Tim fell on top of me. Tim got up. When I went to get up I couldn't. I must have cramp I thought – I'll be able to run it off. I got up but fell again. I had broken the fibula bone. Even then I didn't want to go off. For me it was a terrible tragedy, a terrible disappointment. I wanted to hurl on but I couldn't.
  'With about six minutes to go Noel O'Dwyer struck over a point to put us four points up. He danced a jig. There I was on the sideline lying down injured. I couldn't imagine a worse nightmare – only 22, Centenary year, captaining Tipp., playing Cork in Semple Stadium. I won't be able to accept the cup – not with this leg, I thought to myself. The honourable thing would

be to ask Noel to accept it. After all he won an All-Ireland away back in 1971. Why I was chosen over Noel I don't know. Those were my thoughts. Then, bang, bang. If I live to be a thousand I won't forget that day – my worst day, my greatest disappointment.

Yes, it was bang, bang alright. In the minutes that remained Cork scored 2:2 to win by four points and scatter to pieces Bobby's dream of leading Tipperary, not only to victory, but to a hurling revival as well.

However, in 1989 there was compensation – but not sufficient to erase the memories of 1984 that still linger to this very day – when Bobby captained Tipperary to an All-Ireland title with success over Antrim – their 23rd title and first since 1971.

By nature, Bobby was gentlemanly and sporting on the field of play. His style was brave, dashing and spirited. Due a great extent to the influence of his mother's sporting philosophy he was equally gracious in victory and defeat.

Despite many disappointments Bobby ended up winning two All-Ireland titles. Those victories made him remember the many great players who never won an All-Ireland. He instances 'Sean Stack of Clare, Jimmy Brohan of Cork who was in the wrong place at the wrong time and Ciaran Carey of Limerick, with loads of heart, who still lives in hope.

'The best player I ever marked – I played a lot of hurling as a forward – was Sean Stack of Clare; the way he could read a game; could hurl left and right. And such a clean hurler. You knew when you went for a ball with him there would be no early or late pulling.'

He regards the modern game as brilliant. For Sean McMahon of Clare he has special words of praise, who during the nineties gave several magnificent displays at centre back for his county. 'It must put him up there with the great ones like Pat Stakelum.'

Bobby's last game with his native Tipperary was in the 1993 All-Ireland semi-final against Galway when he was called upon, following an outstanding display for Borrisoleigh in the Tipperary championship, to replace Michael O'Meara at centre back. Tipperary lost by 1:16 to 1:14. 'I knew walking off the pitch at Croke Park that day that I would not play with Tipperary again. It hurt deeply. The legs were gone for play at that level.'

35

Bobby was sitting in the stand with his wife Elaine as the Tipperary and Clare teams paraded around Croke Park prior to the All-Ireland final of 1997. He watched them go by. For him it was an emotional moment. He saw the No. 7 jersey – the jersey of his favourite position, left half back. He said to himself 'I should be out there.' He was now within two months of his 36th birthday on 23 October. But the legs were gone. He would never again wear the blue and gold of Tipperary. Tears filled his eyes and a few flowed down his cheeks. Tears for an era ended. 'Elaine said I understand – I said you don't, you couldn't.'

> *'Ease thee! Cease thy keening! Cry no more!*
> *End is! And here is end! And end is sore!'*

Ní bhíonn in aon rud ach seal.

Tom Cashman
CORK
1986

> *'So long and so unsullied has the game been handed down from sire to son that the very parish soil is permeated with the hurling spirit.'*
>
> (Carbery)

Coming from a hurling family, hurling was my hobby and love. As I look back I was very lucky to come on to a great Cork team. However, playing the game was so important. Meeting and playing with so many great players brings back so many memories. I remember advice from my father Mick, Fr. Michael O'Brien – what a coach! Hurling is a joy. Best game in the world, producing great players every year, new names to take over from yesterday. Long may it continue.

Tom Cashman descended from a great sporting background. His father, Mick, had a brilliant career with Blackrock, Cork and Munster. He starred as a centre halfback and goalkeeper through the fifties and into the early sixties. 'My father was born in 1931 the year Blackrock won something like its 20th county title. They didn't win again until 1956 – 25 years later – when my father captained them to victory over Glen Rovers.'

Did you ever see him play? 'I saw him play in goal for Blackrock Seniors and in inter-firm matches towards the end of his career, but never with the county.'

Was he an influence on your own career? 'Yes, he was. He was a big influence. But he wouldn't say too much – only what needed to be said. And any advice was short – a one liner – but it would be important.'

Tom's mother, Ann, is a sister of Jimmy Brohan, another great Cork stalwart in the era 1954–1964, who gave wonderful service to club, county and province. And during his days his many regal displays at cornerback entitled him to rank as one of the all-time greats in that position. Two other brothers, Bobby and John, excelled at soccer for Evergreen United and Cork Hibernians respectively. Tom's aunt Maureen, on his father's side, played camogie for Cork.

So Tom had much to live up to. Live up to it he did. He faced the challenge and excelled.

Success came at an early age to him. The Féile na nGael competition was initiated in 1971. Blackrock won through in Cork and advanced to represent the county in the All-Ireland series. 'We beat the representatives of Kilkenny, Tipperary and Dublin and were crowned champions in Thurles on Sunday 18 July 1971. I played in goal and Finbarr Delaney was captain. Half the team were underage for the following year but I couldn't play because the age was brought down from under 15 to under 14. I will always remember the enthusiasm of those running the team, their appetite for the game – so excited to see us winning, rushing onto the field delighted and then hugging us. They would take it to heart more than we would if we lost. Tom Clancy was always there with the hurlers and Connie Keeffe with the footballers.'

Each of the team received a wooden plaque – a trophy Tom still cherishes. Those who saw Tom in action in the final considered his splendid goalkeeping to be on a par with the great displays of his father.

Underage success continued for Tom. A rare double came his way in 1974, when he won All-Ireland minor hurling and minor football titles with wins over Kilkenny and Mayo respectively. Two years later he won an All-Ireland under-21 hurling medal with a decisive victory over Kilkenny.

In his early tender years Ray Cummins was his hero. 'To me he was a god at the time. He was a thinking hurler – always looking around to see what was the best thing to do. I had great admiration for Gerald McCarthy too. He was a great player – a fine midfielder – the kind of player you'd love to have on your side'.

Tom first sampled senior county fare at 19 in the National League campaign of 1976 and called it a day after defeat by Tipperary in the Munster final of 1988. The intervening years are strewn with success. He played in six All-Ireland finals and won on four occasions. The details are as follows:

1977 centre field v Wexford (won by 1:17 to 3:8)
1978 centre field v Kilkenny (won by 1:15 to 2:8)
1982 centre field v Kilkenny (lost by 3:18 to 1:13)
1983 left halfback v Kilkenny (lost by 2:14 to 2:12)
1984 right halfback v Offaly (won by 3:16 to 1:12)
1986 centre back v Galway (won by 4:13 to 2:15)

From 1977 to 1986 inclusive, the only years Cork failed in Munster were 1980 and 1981, and in those years they won the National League title.

But the medals and trophies coming Tom's way didn't stop at that. There were county titles with Blackrock in 1976, '78 and '79; an All-Ireland club title with Blackrock in 1979; Railway Cup wins in 1978, '81 and '85 with Munster; All-Star awards in 1977, '78 and '83. 'I think my two best games were the Munster finals of 1977 and 1978 against Clare – especially 1978, when we played with a strong wind in the first half. We were only two points up at half time and won in the end by 13 points to 11.'

However, even the most successful players have their moments of regret. 'The All-Ireland defeats of 1982 and 1983 at the hands of Kilkenny after going through so easily in Munster and at a time when I was still playing some of my best hurling were disappointing days. But sometimes a name is on the cup just as it was for us in '99 and for Tipperary in 2001.' Tom would love to have won a Cork senior football title with St. Michael's – the Blackrock football team. 'We contested three finals in a row but lost each time; beaten twice by Nemo and once by the Barrs. It was more or less the same bunch of players as those playing the hurling. Football wasn't to be for us.'

Being captain of the county senior team in 1986 stands out as the highlight of a wonderful career. 'To captain your county to an All-Ireland title is something you never forget. We had a close call against Clare in the Munster final – winning by three points. We scraped through against Antrim in the All-Ireland semi-final. We went into the final as complete underdogs.'

Galway were firm favourites to take the All-Ireland crown. They had trounced a fancied Kilkenny side by 11 points in the All-Ireland semi-final in Thurles. And the previous year they had beaten Cork at the same stage of the championship. *Ach ní mar a shíltear a bhítear*. Cork played against the wind in the first half. They whipped in two early goals. It left Galway chasing a losing cause. Johnny Crowley in the Cork defence was playing the game of his life. It ended Cork 4:13 Galway 2:15. Tom Cashman had led Cork to their 26th All-Ireland crown and took the Liam MacCarthy Cup to the Leeside for the 19th time. His younger brother Jim, playing at midfield, shared in that success and he too was a majestic giant of the hurling scene.

Tom retired from the county scene in 1988 at the age of 31. I couldn't help asking if it was a little premature. 'I had been playing for fifteen seasons – hurling, football and a bit of soccer too. Even by the time I was 21 I had played a lot of games at underage both for club and county. At 31 I found the training more demanding – it was getting tougher and harder.' Time to quit!

On Tom's desk, in his office, rests a photograph of Cork's three most recent winning captains. The smiling, happy trio are Tom Cashman (1986), Tomás Mulcahy (1990) and Mark Landers (1999).

Tom was an exceptionally talented and versatile sportsman. In his time he played in 13 different positions for Cork, missing out only in the goalkeeping and fullback berths. His favourite position was centre halfback – yet he starred wherever he played. Those who saw him play, witnessed a great stick man – a player of style and quality, equally adept left and right, a master of every stroke.

One journalist summed him up as follows: 'Sweetest and most stylish of hurlers. Perfect sportsman. Usually first to be called upon when an emergency arises, as against Nicholas English in the 1985 Munster final.'

In *A Centenary Year Publication* of the Blackrock Club Tom is described as follows: 'The true ball-player, lightning fast striker of the sliotar, left or right, on the ground or in the air. Some of his classic points from mid-field, shot from his hurley as bullets from a gun and with the same accuracy. A sportsman supreme, Tom Cashman adorns the game of hurling.'

Pat Fleury
OFFALY
1985

'Is binne glór mo chamáin féin
Ná guth na n-éan is ceol na mbard.
'S ní binne fuaim ar bith faoin ngréin
Ná poc ró-thréan ar liathróid ard.'

It would have been inconceivable, when my senior inter-county career began in the 1975 championship, that by the time I would decide to retire after the Leinster final of 1986, Offaly hurling would have reached levels which were beyond our wildest dreams.

One sentiment which remains constant is of being fortunate enough to be part of a great team which made the breakthrough in Leinster in 1980, won our first ever All-Ireland senior hurling title in 1981 and was equally fortunate to captain that team in two successive All-Ireland finals – 1984, when we lost the Centenary final to Cork, and 1985, when we overcame an emerging Galway side to win our second title.

While there were many great occasions and great memories, pride of place must go to the Leinster final of 1980. On the basis that something can only be won for the first time once, it will always be special.

The Centenary final must rank as the greatest disappointment but, happily, we compensated our supporters in 1985.

My club, Drumcullen, supplied me with my childhood hero in the shape of the incomparable Paddy Molloy and wonderful encouragement and support throughout my playing career and during my term as Offaly senior hurling manger. My single greatest regret is that we failed to win an Offaly senior championship during my time with them.

Pat Fleury was born in 1956 and grew up in the parish of Drumcullen. In his hurling days he stood at 6ft. and weighed 12st. 7lbs., 'but there were days when I was sorry I wasn't a stone or more heavier'. The local hurling hero was Paddy Molloy of Offaly and Leinster fame. 'He was our Cú Chulainn and when you saw him walking or cycling down the road you felt like genuflecting. I was fortunate to get on the local team, where it all starts and ends, at an early age and had the privilege of playing with Paddy. He played all over the field for the club. Then there was Tom Dooley who came of a great hurling family. He used to organise young teams and bring us to matches.'

Pat made his county début in 1975 in a Walsh Cup game against Kilkenny at Kilkenny. His task that day was to mark Pat Delaney. He got his baptism to championship fare in a drawn game with Kildare – a replay that was won – and a Leinster semi-final against Wexford that was lost.

At Presentation School in Birr, Pat came under the influence of Brother Denis, Brother Cronin and Michael Queally. There was a lot of underage success and in 1973 the school won the All-Ireland Senior B Colleges title. Pat then progressed to county minor and county under-21 with Offaly.

His university days were spent at UCG. In 1977 the college won the Fitzgibbon Cup competition with a famous victory over Maynooth on the score 1:14 to 1:12. It was Galway's ninth success in a competition that was dominated by UCC and UCD since its inception in 1912 by a Capuchin Priest, Dr. Edwin Fitzgibbon. Great hurling names featured in that UCG team. 'You had Conor Hayes, Tom Cloonan (father of Eugene), Niall McInerney, Joe McDonagh, Frank Holohan, Cyril Farrell (who was a powerful centre forward), Kieran Brennan and Joe Connolly. Three of those players went on to captain All-Ireland winning teams – Conor Hayes in 1987 and '88, Joe Connolly in 1980 and myself in 1985.'

Pat has been dedicated to coaching all his life and in this regard has put a lot back into the game. 'It began in my second year at UCG when I trained the first-year team and (they) won a league and championship. When I qualified I came to Limerick CBS and started training Harty Cup teams. We reached the final in 1984 but lost a replay to Farrinferris. Success was slow in coming but perseverance paid off in 1993 when the school won the trophy for the tenth time. Earlier successes were in 1920, 1932, three in a row in 1925–1927 inclusive and a great four in a row from 1964–1967 inclusive.' Pat gave one term at county management when he was in charge of his native Offaly in 2000.

Pat quit the county scene in 1986 after losing the Leinster final to Kilkenny. "Twas a big decision. It was hard to leave. You leave a big part of your life behind. But there were a few injuries. As well as that all my training had been done from a distance – from Galway during Uni days, from Limerick once I began working.'

Hurling was always strong in Offaly but it was weakened at county level by a fierce parish rivalry. So when the breakthrough came it was really an emergence rather than a renaissance.

Pat remembers well the lead up to the days of Offaly success. 'In 1975 we played Wicklow in a National League game in Aughrim on a dreadful day. At half time the score was Offaly 1 point Wicklow nil. At full time the score was Offaly 3 points Wicklow 1 point. Lots of teams came a cropper in Aughrim. Our objective of getting into Division One A of the National League in the second half of the seventies was achieved. It was a big thing for us. We met Clare in the league semi-final of 1977 and went into the game with optimism. One hour later we had lost by 2:15 to 7 points. 'Twas a rude awakening.

'In 1979 the two Leinster semi-finals were played in Athy. It was Dublin v Kilkenny and we lost to Wexford by one point. For us that was real progress. Then in the autumn of 1979 the county board brought in Dermot Healy. He made a big impact. His contribution was enormous. Success came earlier than people anticipated.

'Dermot placed emphasis on doing the basics well – tight marking, blocking, hooking and direct hurling. These became the trademark of Offaly hurling.' In 1980 an open draw was introduced in Leinster. It led to a provincial final meeting of Offaly and Kilkenny. In almost all eyes Offaly were perceived as sacrificial lambs. Only 9613 turned up to witness the slaughter.

But Dermot Healy had prepared them well. He covered much detail. He dealt with the mental as well as the physical. It was, after all, only Offaly's sixth Leinster final with no success to date.

1901 v Wexford (7:6 to 1:3)
1924 v Dublin (4:4 to 3:1)
1926 v Kilkenny (3:8 to 1:4)
1928 v Dublin (9:7 to 4:3)
1969 v Kilkenny (3:9 to 0:16)

Dermot's words rung in every Offaly ear. 'At no stage look into the stand at the crowd. In the parade just keep your eyes on the man in front of you. Either get the ball or stop your man scoring if you're a back – stop him clearing effectively if you're a forward. Eradicate frees. Close-in frees should all be scored.'

Despite a few errors, induced by the big occasion, Offaly, after a first half of much quality hurling mingled with grim resolve, were only two points – a little unluckily perhaps – behind at half time. The score stood at 3:6 to 1:10.

For over twenty minutes of the first half we had played a good game and made Kilkenny come from behind. But at times in that half we saw all the hallmarks of the same old story. We were behind at the break, yet we knew we should be ahead. Dermot didn't come into the dressing room until a little while after us. There was a big smile on his face. He said he was delighted the way things were going. He was using psychology. He pointed out we had been ahead in the first half so why couldn't we do it again. We could now accept what used to be inevitable defeat in the past or go out and do something about it.

The second half was enthralling. It was fast and furious as the ball moved to and fro about the pitch. With ten minutes to go the pressure was unreal.'

The final whistle presented the incredible scoreline of Offaly 3:17 Kilkenny 5:10. A new hurling force was on the march.

Unfortunately, the famous victory became overshadowed by sadness. A cloud descended on the occasion when it was learned that Tommy Horan – father of Padraig, one of Offaly's heroes of the day – had died in a car while listening to the match.

Offaly lost the All-Ireland semi-final to Galway by two points but a year later they defeated the Tribesmen in the All-Ireland final by three points. Glory days had begun. The victory qualified Offaly for an All-Stars trip to America. 'It was very beneficial to the team. It was our first time away as a group. We were relaxed. There was a togetherness. It got us through our Leinster championship game against Wexford. Then came one of my greatest hurling disappointments. We faced Kilkenny in the Leinster final in optimistic mood. There was a great sense of unity in the panel. We lost a great game by two points. But you don't like losing to events outside your control.' In a tight close-marking game only one goal was scored. It came Kilkenny's way, but only after a 'wide' ball had been flicked back into play by a Kilkenny forward and then finished to the net. Sometimes the Fates are unkind.

Pat's hour of captaincy glory came in 1985 when he displayed great leadership qualities in leading Offaly to a two-point victory over Galway in the All-Ireland final.

> *'I was for that time lifted above earth,*
> *And possessed joys not promised in my birth.'*

'It was a very tense game. Pat Cleary's goals – about seven minutes to half time and immediately after half time – were vital. They put us five points up.'

Pat felt that they owed that All-Ireland victory to their supporters after the homecoming reception they received the previous year, despite failing to Cork at Thurles in the Centenary final of 1984. 'The journey home from Thurles was difficult in 1984. We were very disappointed. We didn't play well. Yet it was a game that could have been very different and even though Cork dictated the second half, I didn't feel the gap between us was as great as the final score of 3:16 to 1:12 might suggest. The reception that awaited us in Tullamore was unbelievable. The crowd was as big as when we won in 1981. We were blown away by the reception. We were so moved and so shocked by it all. As Captain I had to make various speeches. I found it hard to compose myself – the emotion of it all. I had a lump in my throat. There was the crowd gathered en masse in O'Brien Park. It was deeply emotional. All that was missing was the Cup. It made a huge impact on the players. They resolved to deliver in '85.' And they did.

However, the All-Ireland success of 1985 was another great Offaly victory that was tinged with melancholy. 'In 1985 we travelled to Armagh to play Antrim in the All-Ireland semi-final. It was Pat Carroll's last game. He was unwell. When we won the All-Ireland title we visited Pat in hospital and brought the Cup. He was delighted. But he would hurl no more. For us all there was sadness amid the happiness. Pat died the following March. The funeral was enormous.'

Pat Fleury was a stalwart defender – staunch and uncompromising. At corner back he was like a sentry on duty. He cleared his lines with speed and without ceremony.

His hurling career brought lots of honours – the major ones being two All-Ireland titles, two All-Star awards and four Leinster successes.

The following is an excerpt from a 'This is your Life' presentation made to Pat by his club Drumcullen.

Pat Fleury, hurling supremo, sportsman sublime, loyal friend, husband and father, the pages of this book can never adequately record the depth of appreciation and goodwill felt for you by the officers, committee, members and friends of Drumcullen GAA club and true sportspeople everywhere. Your service to this club and the honour your success has brought is a source of great pride for which we will always be grateful. We hope you will always stay with us. May you have a happy, healthy retirement from the game you adored as a player.

May you live as long as you want and never want as long as you live.

Brian Cody
KILKENNY
1982

I don't really remember a time when hurling wasn't a part of my life. My parents had a real interest in hurling so from an early age I was forever pucking around. I come from a place called Sheestown, four miles from Kilkenny city, and the teacher in the local school, Joe Golden, helped to nurture the love of hurling in all the pupils. Brother Basil O'Brien of the De La Salle Order played an important part in my development too, as our school played with St. Patrick's De La Salle in the local schools competitions.

I was very lucky to belong to the James Stephens Club and I went on to win many juvenile honours with the club. My father was heavily involved with James Stephens and went on to serve as chairman for many years. St. Kieran's College also played a big part in my development. I was a boarder in S.K.C. and just about all our spare time was spent in the hurling pitch. I was a fellow student of many great players and as a result enjoyed success on the playing fields there, culminating in All-Ireland success in 1971.

In 1972 I had the honour of captaining Kilkenny minors to All-Ireland success and went on to make my début for the seniors in the league of that year. My first game was against Limerick in Nowlan Park. This was a golden era for Kilkenny hurling and I consider myself very lucky to have an involvement in it.

I went on to enjoy good success over the following number of years with Kilkenny and most importantly as well with my club James Stephens. I won my first senior county championship in 1975 and went on to become the first team from Leinster to win the All-Ireland club championship. That was a real highlight of my career as we beat a brilliant Blackrock team in the final in Thurles. We were captained by the outstanding Fan Larkin who was the real driving force of that team. We went on to retain our own county championship in 1976 also. We had to wait until 1981 to win our next county title but we also went on to win the All-Ireland club championship again, beating Mount Sion. That golden era for our club was all achieved under the chairmanship of my father, Bill.

I suppose I mention my club so much because I got wonderful enjoyment from just playing at every level – be it club or county and I suppose my biggest worry for hurling at the moment is that the club player is probably losing out because of the greater emphasis on inter-county training and preparation.

A major highlight of my career obviously came in 1982 when I captained Kilkenny to win the senior All-Ireland. It was a great team with a great spirit and we had a great victory over Cork in the final. On the day we were total underdogs but we prepared well under Pat Henderson and on the day turned in a great performance. It was indeed a special moment.

I could not finish without paying tribute to Fr. Tommy Maher's contribution to Kilkenny hurling. He was in charge of the team during the 70s when I first joined the panel and was a major influence on us all.

In conclusion I will just say that I don't look back on my career and think in terms of what I won. I recall the great enjoyment I got from the game over a long period of time and can honestly say that playing for both James Stephens and Kilkenny was always a source of pride for me.

'I am the master of my fate:
I am the captain of my soul.'

Brian's late father Bill was a native of Thomastown. 'All his life he loved, and lived for, the game of hurling. In his time he was a county minor and senior selector. He was chairman of James Stephens club for 17 years – it coincided with the club's great days.'

Brian's mother Annie (née Hoyne) was also a native of Thomastown. Growing up in that parish she spent her spare time 'playing camogie and revelled in the game'.

Little wonder then that their son Brian has a profound love and passion for hurling. At present he is Manager of the Kilkenny senior hurling team. He lives and breathes the game. Its presence in his daily life is oxygen to his very being. As you talk with Brian, you realise that his hurling days merge into a panorama of moments that brings to the surface his love for, and devotion to, hurling that transcends trophies and victories – although he does admit that they too are necessary and at times essential.

He played in the black and amber jersey 'for the last time against Westmeath in either the 1985 or '86 championship. I was a sub against Galway in the All-Ireland semi-final of 1986 in Thurles. I didn't retire – I'm still available – I'm waiting for the call.'

And he tells you that with a smile that reveals the magic and nostalgia that memories of the past conjure up for him. For even to this very day there is nothing he enjoys more than just to puck the ball around – sometimes with his son Donnacha who was part of the St. Kieran's College senior hurling panel that recently (April 2002) won the Leinster Colleges title.

Brian made his mark on the hurling scene at an early age. With St. Kieran's College he won Leinster titles in 1971 and 1972. The 1971 team, captained by Brian playing at centreback, went on to win the All-Ireland title.

In the same year he was centreback on the county minor team that lost the All-Ireland final to Cork by just one goal – 2:11 to 1:11. The following year, however, with Brian as captain they avenged that defeat with an emphatic 8:7 to 3:9 scoreline. Many contend that the 1972 minor team was arguably the best ever to represent the county and that Brian at centreback gave classic displays. Others who progressed to senior fame from that team were Kevin Fennelly, Ger Fennelly and Billy Fitzpatrick.

Brian's career at county senior level lasted from 1973 to 1986. Despite a knee injury earlier in his career, which interrupted his playing from time to time, his achievements were many and varied – All-Ireland titles in 1974 (sub), 1975, 1982, 1983; Leinster titles; National League (1976 and 1982 and 1983 (sub)); All-Ireland minor (1972); All-Ireland under-21 (1974 and 1975).

Any success with one's club is always special. But All-Ireland victory with your club represents an Everest of glorious attainment that stirs all hearts in the parish and generates widespread reflected glory. Such was the case in the James Stephens club in 1976. Victory in the county in 1975 led to the following All-Ireland club campaign:

v St.Rynaghs (1:14 to 2:4)
v Ballygalget (4:15 to 1:7)
v Blackrock (2:10 to 2:4)

The defeat of Blackrock, with such household names as John Horgan, Dermot McCurtain, Frank Cummins, Pat Moylan, Ray Cummins and Eamon O'Donoghue, represented the zenith of the club's many great achievements and without doubt its proudest moment. Brian, playing in his favourite position at centreback, gave his usual rock-like performance.

In his years playing with his club he often had to face the challenge posed by the experienced and great Pat Delaney playing at centre forward for The Fenians. And at no stage was Brian ever found wanting.

In 1982 Brian was honoured with the captaincy of the county senior team. A narrow two points victory over Offaly in a thrilling Leinster final, followed by a ten point win over Galway in the All-Ireland semi-final brought the Noresiders face to face with the men from the Lee on final day 5 September at Croke Park. On a day when Cork were firm favourites, Brian led Kilkenny to one of their biggest victories ever over the Rebel County. The game ended 3:18 to 1:13. Brian's late father Bill was on the Hogan Stand to relish the occasion. GAA President, Paddy Buggy, himself a former Kilkenny All-Ireland hurling star, proudly handed the MacCarthy Cup to Brian. Later in the year an All-Star award followed for Brian.

Brian finds it difficult to single out any one success above another. Instead, he picks the year 1975 as having special significance – a year when a lot of honours came his way – and he just 21 years old. 'I won my first All-Star – a second under-21 All-Ireland – a senior All-Ireland on a team that had five players from "The Village" (James Stephens) – myself, Fan Larkin, Mick Crotty, Liam O'Brien and Tom McCormack. That was special. I also won my first county title with James Stephens – that too was very special. It led on to our All-Ireland club win the following March.'

Proinsias Ó Donncha, Cigire Scoile, ó Ghleann Fleisce i gCo. Chiarraí, wrote a very fine article in the *Kilkenny 1996 Yearbook* recalling his memories of 40 years of Kilkenny hurling beginning with 1957 when he first saw Ollie Walsh in action. Proinsias picked a team from that era – a fascinating one well worth recalling here:

Ollie Walsh

Paddy Prendergast   Brian Cody   Jim Treacy

Joe Hennessy   Ger Henderson   Seamus Cleere

Frank Cummins   Liam O'Brien

Sean Clohessy   Pat Delaney   Eddie Keher

Billy Fitzpatrick   Mick Crotty   D.J. Carey

In selecting his fullback Proinsias said 'Brian Cody is simply the best.'

Joe Connolly
GALWAY
1980

'Camáin á luascadh ar fud na páirce,
Is an sliotar ag imeacht ar luas in airde.'
(Sean Ó Finnéadha)

Due to a bad knee injury, my career finished when I was just 28. However, I can honestly say that I had a wonderful hurling career and finished up winning nearly everything there was to be won. I won county and All-Ireland medals with my club Castlegar, All-Ireland and Oireachtas medals with my county Galway and Railway Cups with my province Connaught. I also won a Fitzgibbon medal in 1977 with UCG. In fact, the greatest sadness of my hurling career is that I never won a Connaught medal with my school St. Mary's, Galway. We lost three Connaught finals in a row – v Gort by one point, two points and one point. I missed the final of the last one through having broken my ankle just the week before the game. The two greatest disappointments of my hurling career were losing that 1974 Colleges final and of course the 1981 All-Ireland against Offaly.

Today a great deal of the contentment that I have in my life comes from my past experiences as a hurler. I consider myself to be so unbelievably lucky that I finished my career with All-Ireland medals with both my club and my county. Bill Gates can have his wealth, but I honestly wouldn't swop my All-Ireland medals for all the Microsofts of the world. I am married to a Limerick woman, Cathy, and my five sons, Paul, Brian, James, Barry and Joseph all wield the camán at underage level for Castlegar. Tá súil agam go mbainfidh siad an sult agus an aoibhneas as a gcuid saol iománaíochta is a bhain mise.

My national school teacher Micheál McSweeney was a huge influence on my early hurling career as a teacher in Briarhill N.S. John, Michael and myself visited him in hospital a few months ago. All four of us in the room knew that he was dying of cancer, and had only a short while to live. I am glad I told him the great influence he had on my life.

Jim Stapleton, the first
All-Ireland winning captain
from Tipperary in 1887.

Mikey Maher (Tipperary) with his granddaughters,
Margaret and Ann Casey.

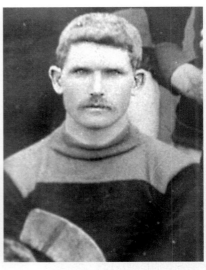

Jer Doheny, captained Kilkenny to their first All-Ireland crown in 1904.

Sim Walton (Kilkenny) captained the last 17 a-side in 1912.

Richard 'Dick' Doyle, Wexford's first All-Ireland winning captain, 1910. *(Courtesy of Ibar Carty, Enniscorthy).*

nny Leahy, Tipperary All-Ireland
ain 1916 and 1925.

Limerick's second All-Ireland winning
captain, Willie Hough, with the Great
Southern Cup in 1918.

Father J J Meagher, Chairman, Tipperary County Board, Jim Lanigan, Captain
1937 All-Ireland team and Captain Johnny Leahy, Secretary County Board.

he only Laois team ever to win an All-Ireland title - the hurlers of 1915. *Back row*: Paddy Lee, J
arroll, Jim Deegan, J Loughman, Rev J Kearney (CC Portlaoise), Paddy Ryan, Joe Dunphy, John Phela
addy Campion, John Higgins. Middle: Joe Phelan, Tom Finlay, Jack Walsh, Jack Finlay (capt) B
'Keeffe, Ned McEvoy, Jim Carroll. Front: Jim Hiney, Jack Daly and Jack Carroll.

Cork All-Ireland champions 1928. Dinny Barry Murphy
(centre front row) led Cork to victory in 1929.

In 1922 Wattie Dunphy (*top right and left*) was the first man to bring the MacCarthy Cup to Kilkenny. Later he captained Leinster to their first Railway Cup victory in 1927.

Eudie Coughlan who led Cork to victory after a historic three final games in 1931, kissing the ring of Rev. Dr. Hayden, Archbishop of Hobart, before the first replay. Lory Meagher, the Kilkenny captain, is on Eudie's right.

Timmy Ryan, following his last championship game with Limerick in the Munster final 1945.

The legendary Lory Meagher who led Kilkenny to a famous victory over Limerick in 1935, score 2:5 to 2:4.

Mick Mackey (*left*) with his brother John at the Limerick Gaelic Grounds in 1934.

Cork team 1942 (*captained by Jack Lynch*): Back (*left to right*): J. Buckley, P. O'Donovan, C. Tobin, J. Lynch, C. Murphy, J. Barry (*trainer*). Centre: E. Porter, M. Kenefick, W. Murphy, S. Condon, J. Young, D. J. Buckley. Front: J. Quirke, D. Beckett, C. Ring, B. Thornhill, C. Cottrell. Missing from this picture of the Munster champions is A. Lotty who took part in the All-Ireland final.

I admire great hurlers hugely. I would have given anything to have had the first touch and vision of my brother, John, for instance. I never had it myself, but I used to try to make up for it by being as determined as possible. The two greatest hurlers of the modern era I consider to be D.J. Carey and Brian Lohan. One from the hurling county I admire most, Kilkenny, and the other from the hurling county I like most, Clare. The greatest hurler I ever saw was Eddie Keher and I would love to have seen Christy Ring. He must have been something really special. I love the company of people who really love their sport, whatever it may be. Give me a few hours in the company of the regulars in Jimmy O'Brien's pub in Killarney for instance, and there is no one happier in the world.

Fr. Michael O'Grady from Kildysart in West Clare, where my wife's family are from, has been a priest in Phoenix, Arizona, for over forty years. For a few weekends a year, he heads for the hills around Phoenix with a small bottle of Paddy and about 20 videos of hurling and football matches. If there's heaven on earth . . .

As a youngster, Joe remembers directing a car into a parking space at his home during race week. It was worth a half a crown to him. 'Well, who stepped out only Jim Treacy of Kilkenny, an All-Ireland medal holder. I was in awe. I ran in and told Michael and Ger to come out. Mother invited Jim and his wife in and gave them tea. We looked at the mug he drank from afterwards and held it. Imagine, we thought, an All-Ireland medal holder drinking tea in our house and parking in our grass. It shows you where we were coming from as regards winning All-Ireland medals.' For Joe the winning of an All-Ireland medal became an ambition and a daily dream.

Hurling was central to the Connolly household. All the boys played. Joe's father was a great enthusiast. Their mother was a great supporter. But she never saw them play. Instead she stayed at home and prayed. 'She went once to watch John at underage in a club game. She left at half time. She spent the half hour with the rosary beads, head down —' *Sé do bheatha, a Mhuire . . . A Naomh Mhuire, a Mháthair Dé* . . . an occasional quick glance up . . . *Guígh orainne peacaithe* . . . She had unhappy memories of a serious injury a neighbour had received in a club game. She died at 82. She was a

51

wonderful woman. She had her priorities right in life. She died of cancer.'

Listening to Joe talking about his mother you gathered very clearly the depth of love and affection both he and all the family had for her.

All her sons knew that she worried and prayed when they played. And on occasions with good reason. 'Always when we came back from matches we would shout before we went in – we're back, we're alright. I remember one day coming back after a game. I had an ugly cut on my face. So before I went in I knocked on the door and said I have a cut on my face, but it's not bad. I remember another day when John and Michael and myself were playing a club match. John and Michael were injured and taken to hospital as a precaution. I went home and didn't say anything. Both Father and Mother were asking what was delaying John and Michael. Then Paddy Molloy, a club officer, knocked on the door and came in. "The lads are not bad at all," he said, "but they are being kept in." No wonder she prayed.'

A series of injuries, culminating in a bad knee injury that damaged the ligaments in a club game in 1984, brought Joe's hurling career to an end. He was just 28. His inter-county career began in the National League of 1975–'76 and he made his championship début in the All-Ireland campaign of 1976. He remembers well the All-Ireland semi-final of that year against Wexford at Pairc Uí Chaoimh in Cork. And he recalls how close it was – a draw on the 15 August, a one goal defeat one week later: 5:14 to 2:23 for Galway the first day, 3:14 to 2:14 the second day. It reminded Joe, just then 20 years of age, of the many stories he had heard growing up of great Galway teams being pipped at the post and their dejected and crestfallen supporters cycling home from venues such as Ennis and Birr – journeys made longer by the burden of defeat.

But all that was about to change. Not since the championship of 1923, when Galway won their first All-Ireland title with a victory over Limerick, had the men of the West been victorious on All-Ireland final day. The disappointments, disillusionments and frustrations of decades would be buried on the first Sunday in September 1980 when Joe Connolly, potent and prolific in the art of score-getting, would lead a great Galway team to a thrilling victory over Limerick.

Let's now reflect on 1980 from a Galway standpoint. On St. Patrick's Day, Connaught, represented by an all-Galway selection and captained by Joe Connolly, defeated Munster in the Railway Cup final on the score 1:5 to 7 points. Earlier in the semi-final they had defeated Leinster by 1:13 to 1:10 after extra time. It was Connaught's second Railway Cup title – 33 years after they first won the trophy in 1947. Joe identifies as passionately with Connaught as he does with Galway and would never wish to see Galway participate in either the Munster or Leinster championship. The Railway Cup success was a tonic victory for Galway that boded well for the days ahead, particularly after the disappointing 1979 All-Ireland defeat at the hand of Kilkenny.

Galway hurling got a further shot in the arm when on the 25 May Castlegar defeated a star-studded Blackrock (Cork) team by 2:9 to 9 points in the All-Ireland club semi-final. On 1 June Castlegar won the All-Ireland club title with a 1:11 to 1:8 victory over Ballycastle (Antrim) at Navan. The Connolly family figured prominently, as shown hereunder, in that historic win.

Padraic – full back
John – centreback
Joe – centre forward
Gerry – right full forward
Michael – (captain) full forward
Tom – a sub
Murth – a sub

With a Railway Cup and club title under their belts, Galway faced the championship with confidence. They reached the final against Limerick as follows:

All-Ireland quarter-final v Kildare (5:15 to 1:11)
All-Ireland semi-final v Offaly (4:9 to 3:10)

'The intensity of the effort put into the preparation for the final was fantastic. In the dressing-room on final day there was no screaming or roaring before the game. I was six months injury free. I worked hard at training. On the day I felt totally in control. I knew I was right. There was a feeling of confidence – a feeling it could be our day. We looked on Limerick as equals.' Mentally, Galway were free of the baggage associated with the hurling tradition and successes of the 'Big Three', Cork, Tipperary and Kilkenny.

Galway got off to a dream start. A delivery from Joe Connolly reached Bernie Forde who made ground before kicking the sliotar to the net. A second goal by P.J. Molloy after ten minutes sent Galway into a 2:1 to nil lead. Thus was the foundation of victory laid. Galway withstood a series of furious Limerick assaults in the final stages of a hectic game. 'Not until the last ten seconds could we say we were going to win.' At the call of time the scoreboard read Galway 2:15 Limerick 3:9. Joe Connolly (All-Star 1980) at centre forward played a valiant captain's part and contributed four points. His brother John at full forward (Hurler of the Year 1980), Michael at midfield and Padraic on the substitute bench made it a very special day and year for the Connolly family.

Winning an All-Ireland medal in 1980 made Joe feel very proud – proud because it represented reaching the Everest of the hurling world. And as each year passes nostalgia adds a deeper glow and lustre to that cherished medal. The success also made Joe feel humble – humble because he often thinks of the many great players who aspired to hurling's Everest, only to be denied by fate and circumstance.

The jubilant scenes that greeted the Galway triumph defy description, as euphoric supporters basked in the glory of victory – real and reflected. Joe delivered the finest post-match victory speech that Croke Park had ever heard. The Irish language part of his speech was as follows:

A mhuintir na Gaillimhe, tar éis seacht mbliana is caoga tá Craobh na hÉireann ar ais i nGaillimh. Is mór an onóir domsa, mar chaptaen, an corn seo a ghlacadh ar son an fhoireann uilig.

Ba mhaith liom buíochas a ghabháil le cúpla duine a chabhraigh go hiontach linn ar feadh an ama. Tá triúr roghnóirí – Cyril Farrell, Bernie O'Connor agus go mór mhór, Cyril Farrell, a chuidigh linn an corn seo a bhaint amach. Freisin cé a dhéanfadh dearmad ar Inky Flaherty a rinne a lán oibre ar son an fhoireann.

Bhí beirt eile, Willie Bennett an masseur agus an Dochtúir Mary McInerney, a thug cabhair iontach duinn é seo a bhaint amach.

Agus ba mhaith liom fáilte agus buíochas faoi leith a chur roimh bheirt a bhí ag imirt le Gaillimh leis na blianta agus mar gheall go raibh siad gortaithe nach bhféadfadh leo a bheith linn inniu. Sin iad Jack Lucas agus an tAthair Iggy Clarke.

Is iontach an lá inniu a bheith mar Ghaillimheach. Ta daoine ar ais i nGaillimh agus tá gliondar ina gcroíthe, ach freisin caithfidh muid cuimhneamh ar dhaoine i Sasana, i Meiriceá, ar fud an domhain agus tá siad b'fhéidir ag caoineadh anois faoi láthair.

Le críochnú suas ba mhaith liom buíochas a ghabháil le foireann Luimní as ucht an chluiche iontach a thug siad dúinn inniu agus ba mhaith liom ar bhur son trí scréach anois a thabhairt do Luimneach.

The following day the *Irish Press* ran an editorial on the game.

Yesterday's All-Ireland Hurling Final, apart from being one of the best, most thrilling, and most sporting played at Croke Park, will go down in the annals of the GAA as triggering off one of the greatest celebratory outbursts that Galway or the West has ever witnessed.

For not alone will the West be awake, both in the spirit and terms of the extemporary version of the song, rendered by the Galway player who seized the microphone for a delightfully impromptu moment during the presentation ceremony after the match, but to invert Galway captain Joe Connolly's borrowing of the Pope's memorable phrase about the young people of Ireland, to bestow it on his native Galway, it is true that today both the young and the old people of Galway love their team.

Not alone can one be assured that the West's awake, there's very little fear of its going to sleep, or of anyone connected with the winning team being allowed to sleep for the next few days.

It wasn't only a triumph for a marvellous Galway side, which had distinguished itself at every conceivable level throughout the year, it was a triumph for that peculiarly Western spirit of conferring almost a cultural stamp on an occasion. With typical Western panache, Galway got in first, got in often, almost invariably got in sportingly, and in the last few minutes held on, very courageously, to prove yet again that if the experts all say a thing is going to happen, then one can be absolutely certain that the opposite will occur.

And so Limerick, the almost universal favourites, lost. It's too bad there had to be a loser and a winner, because although the men from the West undeniably got the drop on the Shannon-siders, Limerick played fine hurling, and on almost any other day against any other side would certainly give a better account for themselves.

This was so generally recognised that one of the more pleasant aspects of the game was the generous tributes which several of the Galway officials, as well as the Galway captain, paid to Limerick. It was typical of the splendid sportsmanship that a bloodstained Galway captain, asked by an interviewer about his injury, should volunteer: "I must have hit myself some-where!"

In such a game it is almost invidious to single out individuals, but if skill and heart could have done it, Eamon Cregan, the top scorer of the match, would have single-handedly won the trophy.

In the event, facing a Galway team which contained a forward like Bernie Forde, and an incredible goalkeeper like Mike Conneely, no one man or team could have been expected to do better.

Certainly one man who could not have been improved upon was the referee, Mr. Noel O'Donoghue, who handled the tension-laden occasion with discrimination and determination, so that the game was neither held up by excessive whistling nor marred by petty fouls.

All in all, it was a great day for Galway, a wonderful shot in the arm for the game of hurling, and a sporting occasion in which the country as a whole could truly rejoice and to which, incidentally, RTÉ's excellent coverage greatly contributed. May Galway and the GAA go on to contribute to many more like it.

As always Joe's mother didn't go to the game, nor did she watch it on T.V. Instead she walked the nearby Ballybrit Racecourse – and prayed, rosary beads in hand, *'Sé do bheatha, a Mhuire . . . a Naomh Mhuire . . . anois agus ag uair . . .* Sara, her daughter, hailed her at full time. It was time to conclude with *Fíor na Croise* and hurry in to celebrate.

Ger Fennelly
KILKENNY
1979

'Of late they are giving a deal of attention
To physical culture with every invention;
Without being too bold I would just like to mention
That hurling's the manliest art of them all.'

(Sliabh Ruadh)

Born in Piltown. My earliest memories are of my father, Kevin, bringing home four or five new hurleys from Henry Giles who was a working colleague of my father's – a rent collector – and taking great pride in that hurley; after playing a game with the brothers, hiding the hurley and cleaning it. Moved to Ballyhale at seven years of age where my father bought a farm. Have great memories of our underage hurling days at Ballyhale N.S. where we had two great teachers in Peadar O'Neill and Joe Dunphy. Have great memories of Ballyhale minor team winning three county titles which included Frank Cummins and Maurice Mason. Winning four county under-21 championships which were the foundation of our great senior team.

My mother was big into the hurling – worrying about us a lot of the time in case of injury. But she had many great days.

Living in Castlebanny it was hurling for breakfast, dinner and supper when we were young. It was hurling every evening of the week. Three or four families lived near our house. One man was Maurice Mason who was a few years older than us. He was an inspiration to us all with his will to win. My father was a great inspiration to me. Work finished on the farm at six o'clock and then off to the training field with the whistle in his pocket as referee. Them were the days that made us so successful.

My memory of great players I came up against would have been many – men like Mick Jacob of Wexford, John Fenton of Cork, Pat Delaney of Offaly, Sean Foley of Limerick, the Connollys of Galway and of course Tony Doran.

My memory of outstanding players I played with would be Fan Larkin, Liam O'Brien, the Hendersons, Billy Fitz., Joe Hennessy, Mick Crotty and many more.

Outstanding games I played in would be the 1975 All-Ireland under-21 against Cork in Dungarvan; 1982 against Cork in senior All-Ireland. Great memories too of three club All-Irelands – big one against St. Finbarr's with seven or eight Cork county players.

Ger Fennelly, son of Kevin and Teresa (née Hoyne), comes from a great hurling family. Seven brothers – listed from eldest to youngest – Michael, Ger, Kevin, Brendan, Liam, Sean and Dermot – all played the game and all wore the black and amber jersey of Kilkenny at some grade at county level. And of course we mustn't forget their first cousin Mary, who won All-Ireland camogie titles in 1974, '76 and '77. Hurling was Ger's passion. A cool calm exterior camouflaged the internal nervousness that preceded every game. A man of quiet disposition, he always gently encouraged those around him.

Inspirational figure in the household was their late father Kevin whose whole life revolved around the game of hurling and its promotion. He played a key role in 1972 in getting the two teams in the parish of Ballyhale to unite under the new name of Shamrocks.

Another great son of that parish also played a role in that amalgamation. He was Father Sean Reid of the Order of Carmelites. Here is an excerpt from a letter he wrote me following publication of *Giants of the Ash* in 1991.

I have been in the United States for 59 years, mostly in New York city. I was Chairman of the Kilkenny hurling club for 25 years until the time of my retirement. I was President of the New York G.A. for two terms. I helped reorganise the Kilkenny hurling club in New York and even played for a time until we were able to get some good hurlers. In 1970 I got leave of absence to go back to Ireland where I worked for three years in my old parish of Ballyhale. At that time I was able to persuade the two teams in Ballyhale parish to come together and form the Shamrocks club.

It was a move that brought hurling riches to Ballyhale parish and Kilkenny county.

Ger Fennelly first tasted All-Ireland success in 1972 when he played centre field on the Kilkenny minor team that overwhelmed Cork in the final by 8:7 to 3:9. His brother Kevin was in goal that day.

Further honours came to the Fennelly household in 1974 and 1975 – a double each year via Ger and Kevin – when Kilkenny defeated Waterford (3:8 to 3:7) and Cork (5:13 to 2:19) respectively, in the under-21 finals of those years. Kevin was captain in 1975. Ger had the honour in 1974. 'Two weeks earlier I won an All-Ireland senior medal as a sub on the panel. Two weeks later I was off on a trip to America – all in the space of four weeks.'

As the years sped onwards the success rate gathered momentum. Honours and bouquets came from every quarter. And the Fennellys shared liberally in them.

Ger won three National League titles in 1982, '83 and '86. Liam participated in all those victories and was captain in '83. Sean was on the winning teams of '83 and '86 and Kevin was in goal in '86.

Sunday 2 September 1975 was a proud day for Kilkenny and a special day for Ger Fennelly. 'It was a great honour to be captain – my first full year in championship hurling – coming from a small club – playing in a game that was being covered all over the world – playing on All-Ireland day was big in itself.'

Following the final whistle against Galway, Ger held aloft the MacCarthy Cup in the Hogan Stand – a proud captain signalling Kilkenny's 21st All-Ireland senior hurling title. His brother Kevin came on as a sub that day. Two more senior titles came Ger's way in 1982 and 1983. Liam shared in those successes and was captain in 1983.

The performances of Ger and Liam in the 1983 campaign brought them All-Star awards – a rare honour for family members in the same year.

Let us now look at the three All-Ireland club titles won by Ger's club Shamrocks.

1981

v Coolderry (Offaly) 3:10 to 1:8 at Athy
v Ballycastle McQuillans (Antrim) 2:11 to 0:12 at Ballycastle
v St. Finbarr's (Cork) 1:15 to 1:11 at Thurles

Interestingly, it was Richie Reid, nephew of Fr. Sean, who captained the winning Shamrocks team.

1984

v Kinnity (Offaly) 3:6 to 0:9 at Athy
v Ballycastle McQuillans (Antrim) 3:14 to 2:10 at Navan
v Gort (Galway) 1:10 to 1:10 at Birr
v Gort (Galway) 1:10 to 0:7 at Thurles

His brother Liam played a hero's part in the games against Gort. On the Wednesday before the drawn game he removed the plaster from his leg – he had broken a bone in a league game. He came on in the closing stages of the drawn game when his club was four points down. He played the full hour in the replay but the damage he did his ankle lasted for quite some time afterwards.

1990

v Cuala (Dublin) 2:11 to 0:7 at Athy
v Sarsfields (Galway) 2:8 to 0:12 at Ballinasloe
v Ballybrown (Limerick) 1:16 to 0:16 at Croke Park

It was Ger who scored the all-important goal against Ballybrown in the 1990 final. 'I got a shoulder and got a free – about fifty yards out. I was probably going for a point but it ended up in the net – badly needed at the time. I played that game with five stitches in my finger – injured it the week before the game, kept it quiet, thought I wouldn't make it – but I did.'

These club victories represented for Ballyhale parish and the Fennelly family a coup de grace, a pièce de résistance.

It brought the parish on level terms with Blackrock of Cork – three titles each.

It brought the Fennelly family a unique honour that we can safely bet will never be equalled, not to mind surpassed. All seven brothers played in each final. The family collected 21 All-Ireland senior hurling club medals.

The All-Ireland final of 1987, when Kilkenny lost to Galway (1:12 to 0:9), represented a swansong for the Fennelly family hurling dynasty at county level. Kevin, Sean, Liam and Ger all played that day.

Liam, however, flew the flag once more for the Fennelly family. That was in 1992 when he captained Kilkenny to their 24th All-Ireland crown and following which he bowed out from the county scene.

Ger called it a day in 1989. But the lure of the game lingered on and in retirement he has found fulfilment in coaching the local juvenile teams.

Charlie McCarthy
CORK
1978

'When Time who steals our years away
Shall steal our pleasures too,
The mem'ry of the past will stay
And half our joys renew.'

(Tom Moore)

Charlie McCarthy of the St. Finbarr's club was one of the great corner forwards in the history of hurling. He generally played at right full, but there were occasions when, as the late Micheál O'Hehir would have described it, he played top of the left.

Charlie made his All-Ireland début at minor level in 1964. In the final against Laois he gave evidence of his future potency by finishing with 3:1 to his credit. A year later he was on the Cork county senior team and in 1966 he had the rare distinction of winning All-Ireland medals at under-21 and senior level. Wexford were defeated in the under-21 final. Kilkenny fell in the senior encounter.

Charlie was a player whose hurling style portrayed smooth, sweet, silken skills. Total concentration on what was going on around him created an alertness which, allied to speed of thought and action, made him one of the most dangerous corner forward men of his time. Lightly built and standing at 5'7", he relied on pure skill and opportunism to outwit opponents and register telling scores.

In a long and illustrious career he won every honour in the game. The year 1978, deep in the autumn of his playing days, must surely stand out as being particularly memorable. Let's examine that year. It began well when, on St. Patrick's Day at Thurles, he captained his club St. Finbarr's to All-Ireland victory in a campaign that read as follows —

v Tulla (3:5 to 3:5)
v Tulla (2:8 to 0:6)
v O'Donovan Rossa (6:12 to 1:16)
v Rathnure (2:7 to 0:9)

It was Charlie's second club title, having been on the team that defeated Fenians (Kilkenny) in 1975.

The success story continued on 7 May when he captained his province to Railway Cup success in the following campaign –

v Connaught (0:20 to 1:11)
v Leinster (2:13 to 1:11)

This was Charlie's second Railway Cup medal. The occasion was unique because for the first time in the history of the competition, the final was played at Páirc Uí Chaoimh.

Sunday 3 September saw a dream come true. He captained his native Cork to All-Ireland senior honours with a four-point victory over great rivals Kilkenny on the score 1:15 to 2:8.

It was his seventh All-Ireland final. He was the leading scorer of the day with seven points to his credit. The win brought Cork their 24th title and Charlie his fifth All-Ireland medal – a win that carried with it an added glow. Let's see why.

Three-in-a-row successes, or better, in the history of the hurling championship, have been few. Kilkenny did it once, although their first of three titles in 1911 resulted from a walkover from Limerick.

Tipperary achieved the honour on two occasions – 1898, '99, 1900 and again in 1949, 1950, '51.

Cork, however, lead the field. They were the first to achieve the hat-trick away back in 1892, '93, '94. Half a century later they made it four in a row – 1941, '42, '43, '44 – the first and only time to date by any county in hurling. Their latest success of this nature was in 1976, '77, '78. As we have already noted Charlie McCarthy was captain in 1978. To add to his day of triumph, with Cork holding on to a precarious one-goal lead, he scored the last point of the game in injury time, thus ensuring victory.

The year ended in a blaze of personal glory when he was chosen for the third time at right full forward on the All-Star team of 1978.

1975–1961

Billy Fitzpatrick
KILKENNY
1975

'Buail an liathróid ar an gcéad luascadh.'

Back in the early sixties growing up in Johnstown, hitting the ball against the gable end of our house you dream of playing in Croke Park, of winning All-Irelands for Kilkenny. I was lucky enough to achieve all those things. I was lucky enough to be part of a great Kilkenny team in the early seventies – and a great Fenian team in that era. The experience I gained from that time was to stand me in great stead in following years. Hurling was a great and enjoyable part of my life. Friendships were made that have lasted a lifetime. While the 1983 All-Ireland was probably the pinnacle of my career, I get as much satisfaction from the four county titles with the Fenians as anything else in my career. I came across so many great players that it is nearly impossible to single a few out. I would like to think that I gave my family and friends some happy memories during my career and that my own kids will be proud of my achievements in the years ahead.

Billy Fitzpatrick – son of John and Bridget (née Farrell), an aunt of Pa Dillon of Kilkenny hurling renown – was only 21 years old when he led the men in Black and Amber around Croke Park prior to the All-Ireland final against Galway on Sunday 7 September 1975. It would be the first seventy minute final in the history of hurling.

Though young in years Billy had many hurling hours put up on his camán. Many victories and much success had come his way.

In 1971 he won an All-Ireland Colleges hurling title with St. Kieran's College. The following year he was captain when they lost the final to Farrenferris – one of his great disappointments. However, there was compensation. He won an All-Ireland minor medal when Kilkenny had a resounding victory over Cork. In that game he gave evidence of his scoring potency and potential with a personal tally of 3:4 from the left half forward position.

County titles with his club Fenians were won in 1972, '73 and '74. All-Ireland senior and under-21 titles were won in 1974. 'It all seemed so simple.' As a consequence the significance of the glory associated with being captain in 1975 passed Billy by. 'It would have meant a lot more if it came after a lean spell.'

In 1975 Billy was playing with a great Kilkenny outfit – a team with a remarkable forward unit, one of the greats of hurling – Crotty, Delaney, Fitzpatrick, Brennan, Purcell and Keher. Kilkenny were contesting their fifth All-Ireland final in a row and were about to win their third out of five appearances. From training and together-ness each player was programmed to respond effectively to the movements and actions of all colleagues. They functioned as of one mind and as a consequence were capable of breaking down the sternest opposition. And so it was in 1975. After leading by 9 points to 1:3 at half time they ran out comfortable winners in the end with 12 points to spare over Galway. GAA President Donal Keenan of Roscommon presented the MacCarthy Cup to Billy. Another triumphal hurling return to the Marble City was under way.

Billy played in six All-Ireland senior hurling finals and was success-ful on five occasions. It was a remarkable success rate. And yet, before each final he experienced the 'butterflies'. 'The worst time of the day for me was always around 12.30. You had that sinking feeling. Things improved after that, although watching the minors didn't do you any good either. You saw them sending over points from seventy yards and thought, I'll be expected to do that too.'

Billy was a classical hurling forward – skilled, speedy, sporting, consistently accurate, a clinical finisher, often Kilkenny's leading marksman. He made everything about the game look simple and effortless for he played with an art that concealed art. His repertoire was vast and was displayed to the full in the All-Ireland final of 1983 against Cork.

Kilkenny won by 2:14 to 2:12. Victory was largely due to a tour-de-force performance by Billy. He finished with a personal tally of ten points (five from frees). Over the hour he caused havoc in the Cork defence. Playing with élan and abandon he gave a dream performance – deft touches, delightful artistry, classical skills, a master craftsman. He was voted Man of the Match.

His was a display to proudly recount in years to come for his grandchildren – a story he can tell with lots of superlatives. And no doubt, the passage of time will add a glitter of nostalgia to his recollections.

Billy's career at senior county level started in 1973 in a league game against Cork. It ended in Thurles against Galway in 1986 'when I came on as a sub'. During those years the defensive hurling of Eamon Cregan (Limerick), Denis Coughlan (Cork), and Joe Hennessy (Kilkenny), made a deep impression on him.

His career was richly rewarded – a Colleges title, five All-Ireland senior titles, three National Leagues, one Railway Cup, seven Leinster titles, four county titles, two All-Stars, a minor All-Ireland, two under-21 All-Ireland titles. The good days were many, chief among them being 'the All-Ireland Colleges title of 1971, my first county title with Fenians in 1972 and the All-Ireland victory of 1983'. Disappointments were few, the two biggest being, 'the lost Colleges title of 1972 and the All-Ireland club final defeat of 1975 at the hands of St. Finbarr's of Cork'.

To watch Billy Fitzpatrick in full flight, displaying all his artistry and wizardry, was a hurling delight. Kevin Cashman, sports journalist, had this to say of Billy: 'Indeed it is arguable – and some Cats do so argue – that, for sheer skill and scoring potential Billy Fitzpatrick was Keher's equal. But Fitz. had a relaxed and whimsical soul which would not drive him to the top of the inter-county heap.'

Billy was one of the all-time greats. Carve his name with pride among the hurling immortals.

Eamon Grimes
LIMERICK
1973

'Now like hare by greyhounds chased,
That nimble ball is pressed and paced,
Whilst thousands watch, with hearts a-beat,
The fortunes of that contest fleet –
From some a shout, from some a moan,
As the leather enters the danger zone.'

(Sliabh Ruadh)

Eamon Grimes was a born athlete and almost from his cradle days he was swinging a hurley.

He was a native of Donoughmore. He hurled with South Liberties club and went to school at Sexton Street CBS Limerick – a famed hurling nursery.

On the hurling field Eamon was a schoolboy wonder – a blonde youngster, now tussling for possession, now pulling first time, now streaking away on a lightning solo run.

He was on three Harty Cup winning teams, as follows:

1964 v St. Flannan's, Ennis (6:10 to 4:7)
1965 v De La Salle, Waterford (4:6 to 1:5)
1966 v Thurles CBS (6:5 to 5:3)

Two of those successes were converted into All-Ireland titles as follows:

1964 v St. Peter's College, Wexford (6:7 to 4:5)
1966 v St. Mary's, Galway (8:9 to 2:2)

In 1966 Eamon had the honour of captaining the team.

During those successful years with Limerick CBS team mates included Seamus Shinnors, Noel O'Gorman, Donal Manning, Eamon Cregan, Pat Doherty, Liam Moloney, Pat Hartigan and Sean Foley.

Eamon made a successful début at county senior level in 1966 when Limerick defeated Tipperary – reigning All-Ireland champions of the two previous years – by 4:12 to 2:9. 'I took an awful chance. It was the day before the Leaving Cert exam.' Outstanding man on the field that day was Eamon Cregan who scored 3:5.

Eamon Grimes's county career lasted from 1966 to 1980 inclusive. During that time he was one of the game's great players. In 1973 the mantle of captain of Limerick was bestowed on him and at the end of the season he was awarded the Texaco Hurler of the Year trophy.

Uppermost in Eamon's mind would have been the galling one-point defeat – 4:16 to 3:18 – by Tipperary in a gruelling 80-minute Munster final at Killarney in 1971. He would have been very conscious that Limerick hadn't won an All-Ireland title since 1940. He would have been aware of the near misses and might-have-beens, especially in the 40s when there were many and to a lesser degree in the 50s and 60s when the whims of the gods and the quirks of fate were particularly unkind on a few occasions.

Dates with destiny were in Eamon's hands and the men he captained when the All-Ireland championship of 1973 began. The first outing was against Clare. All through the seventies Clare were good – at times very good. They caused a shock and surprise by defeating Limerick in 1972. In a torrid clash Limerick just survived in 1973 – a two-point cushion at the final whistle. Limerick sharp shooter Richie Bennis said it was the toughest game he played in.

The next game was against Tipperary in the Munster final in their own backyard – Semple Stadium, Thurles. It was a sweltering hot day. The attendance was around 42,000. The atmosphere throughout was tense and electric. The contest was gladiator-like. The finish was straight from a Hitchcock thriller. With time up scores were level. Limerick forced a seventy. Referee Mick Slattery of Clare told Richie Bennis he must score direct. And score he did and the white flag waved and Limerick were Munster champions and their fans went wild – a first Munster crown since 1955. Eamon Grimes was returning in triumph to the Shannonside with the Munster Cup.

The All-Ireland semi-final against London at Ennis carried a banana-skin warning. Galway had already fallen to London. But all went well as Limerick took victory by 11 points.

In Thurles, before Limerick took the field, Eamon Grimes had urged and exhorted his colleagues. Now in the dressing-room at half time in the All-Ireland final against Kilkenny he is doing the same. Limerick are ahead by two points. 'In forty minutes I'm going across for that cup and I want you behind me.' He held up his speech and then placed it inside his sock.

Victory came with a seven point margin. Eamon, giving a great display, had been a magnificent captain. Tirelessly he rampaged the field and inspired his colleagues, with some rising to exceptional heights. Sean Foley at left halfback gave a regal performance that matched any display seen in that position. Eamon Cregan was majestic at centre halfback. Richie Bennis was superb at midfield and was top scorer of the day with ten points. In goal, Seamus Horgan brought off some miraculous saves. But overall it was a team performance – a great cohesive effort that produced passages of elegant hurling. Eamon Grimes had led Limerick to a 13th Munster title and 7th All-Ireland crown. It was glory days again by Shannonside. Mick Mackey had worthy successors.

The Limerick heroes of 1973 lined out as follows:

Seamus Horgan

Willie Moore   Pat Hartigan   Jim O'Brien

Phil Bennis   Eamon Cregan   Sean Foley

Richie Bennis   Eamon Grimes

Bernie Hartigan   Moss Dowling   Liam O'Donoghue

Frankie Nolan   Ned Rea   Joe McKenna

Tom Ryan replaced Bernie Hartigan.

Eddie Keher
KILKENNY
1969

'Nuair is mó an spórt is cóir stad de.'

It was well into the spring of 1969 before Eddie Keher knew that he would captain Kilkenny in the championship of that year. Following a league encounter with Tipperary the previous year, the great Ollie Walsh was handed down a very controversial six months suspension. As a consequence, he would have been unavailable to his team, Thomastown, for the 1968 county championship, until the term of his suspension ended. Accordingly, the Rower-Inistioge, Eddie's team, very sportingly agreed to defer their semi-final game against Thomastown until Ollie was eligible to play.

The game was won by the Rower-Inistioge and they then beat a highly talented Bennettsbridge team – going for three in a row – in the final. A game in which 'our goalkeeper Donal Kavanagh gave an inspired display'. Victory led to Eddie being nominated and chosen as captain of the county senior team for 1969. 'I am acutely aware of the great privilege. I know only too well that relatively very few hurlers in the history of the game have had the honour of being a winning captain.'

Eddie recalled for me his recollections of 1969, a year in which I saw the All-Ireland final through the eyes and voice of the late Micheál O'Hehir, as I listened intently from my home in Tralee.

We were very fortunate against Offaly in the Leinster final. Paddy Molloy played a stormer that day for Offaly. For most of the game we were playing catch-up. Only for Pat Delaney we would have lost. He got our three goals – he palmed the third to the net to give us the lead towards the very end.

There was a buzz in the Kilkenny camp from early in the year. Any year it was like that we won. It would start with Paddy Grace the county secretary although I must say we didn't make a great start to the year, we didn't do well in the league.

Cork were favourites in the final. But our defeat in the final of 1966 at the hands of Cork was a real motivator. We wanted to avenge that.

There was panic in our dressing-room before the game when we learned that our midfielder Paddy Moran had the 'flu. He wouldn't last the hour. He was replaced by Mick Lawlor who played a blinder.

The game started badly for us. A mix-up among the backs let Charlie McCarthy through for a goal after two minutes. Coming up to half time Cork were seven points up. Mick Lawlor got a point for us. Then Mick took a 45 yards sideline cut. It was blocked by Paddy Barry in the Cork goal but Martin Brennan was there to send it to the net. We were only three points down at half time. We had been outplayed but the defence held firm with Ted Carroll outstanding.

Charlie McCarthy got a point for Cork at the start of the second half. Soon after Joe Millea got a goal for us. Around the tenth minute Pat Delaney was stretchered off with what looked a very serious head injury. I pointed the free. It was then we really began to hurl. Paddy Moran came on at left half forward. I moved to centre forward. Pat Kavanagh came on as a sub and scored a point immediately. The half back line of Billy Murphy, Pat Henderson and Martin Coogan was clearing everything. We won by 2:15 to 2:9.

Eddie was Kilkenny's top scorer with a contribution of eight points.

What made the day special for you?

'There were a number of things:

- the prematch parade, leading the team;
- being presented with the Cup and holding it up to delighted supporters;

- the fact that four players from the Rower-Inistioge took part in the win – Billy Murphy, Fr. Tommy Murphy, Pat Kavanagh and myself;
- the celebrations when we returned to Kilkenny and especially when we took the Cup to our parish.'

When Eddie reflects on a hurling career that stretched at county senior level from 1959 to 1977, three All-Ireland day occasions stand out.

- 1963 against Waterford when I won my first medal.
- 1969 against Cork when I was captain.
- 1972 against Cork because it was such a great game to play in.

When I put it to Eddie that he had achieved everything, and that all that was left to win was more of the same, and in many cases, more of lots of the same, he responded by saying that prior to his senior days he had won four Leinster minor medals and not one of them was translated into an All-Ireland success.

Fleeting moments from games listened to and watched tend to stay in one's mind. Such is the case with me. I can still hear the closing minutes of the 1946 All-Ireland football final between Roscommon and Kerry with the score standing at 1:7 to 0:4 in Roscommon's favour. And then, suddenly, Kerry have the ball in the Roscommon net – not once, but twice in a bewildering finish that takes the game to a replay.

When I think of Eddie Keher, four such memories from finals remain etched in my mind.

It was the 1959 replay against Waterford. In the second half of the game I scanned my programme as I watched a youthful figure come on as a sub – Eddie Keher. I knew he had played a month earlier in the minor final against Cork. Little did any of us realise that day in Croke Park that we were witnessing the entry to senior ranks of a player who would make a lasting impact on the hurling scene and join the all-time immortals of the game.

I will never forget his scoring performance in 1963 against Waterford – 14 points (ten from frees) – leading scorer. He scored from all angles and distances, a flawless performance. It was neither a freak nor a once-off. It was the product of patient and painstaking practice. It was the stuff of perfection – the stuff that spawns success. It was the hand of a master at work.

His goal in the 1972 All-Ireland final in the second half from a high probing shot from the Hogan Stand side, about fifty yards out near the sideline, that deceived Paddy Barry in the Cork goal, is as vivid in my mind as I write, as the moment it happened. Eddie was again top scorer of the day with 2:9 to his credit. 'That was an eighty minute final and I remember feeling drained after it.' Later that year he received the Texaco Hurler of the Year Award.

Finally, there was 1975 against Galway. It was shortly after the second half started. A Kilkenny movement saw Eddie drift unmarked to the left. A perfect pass from Mick Crotty and you knew the minute Eddie grabbed the sliotar that it had goal written all over it. Again he was top scorer of the day with 2:7.

Eddie had a phenomenal scoring record right through his career and with the exception of 1961 was at all times among the leading scorers – heading the charts in 1965, '66, '68 and from 1970–'76 inclusive.

He played in an era when Kilkenny contested eleven All-Ireland finals. He participated in ten of those and was successful on six occasions.

He retired in 1977 from inter-county hurling.

> I remember the Leinster final against Wexford. Normally when I got possession I could lose my man in the first ten yards of the sprint. That day I got the ball but couldn't shake off my man. As I ran I knew I was being shadowed. So as not to be hooked I had to shorten the hurley. My attempt for a goal went over the bar. I knew then the legs were gone. I played on for a couple of years at club level and was playing very well. People were saying to me that I shouldn't have retired. Maybe so. But I used think to myself that it was nicer to hear that, than to have people saying that I stayed on too long.

Gerald McCarthy
CORK
1966

'But his Captain's hand on his shoulder smote –
Play up, play up and play the game!'

It was famine times in Cork hurling when Gerald McCarthy, the St. Finbarr's man, arrived on the scene in 1966 to captain Cork. The county hadn't won an All-Ireland title since 1954. The last time they contested a final was in 1956 when they lost to Wexford. The previous barren periods existed between 1903 and 1919 and later between 1931 and 1941.

The outlook for Cork's prospects in 1966 looked bleak when Kilkenny overwhelmed them in the League semi-final on the score 4:11 to 1:8.

It was a time, too, when they were still haunted by the Munster final results of the two previous years against Tipperary which were as follows —

1964 (3:13 to 1:5)
1965 (4:11 to 0:5)

Then came good news for Cork. A young, fast Limerick team out-hurled Tipperary in the first round of the Munster championship and won by 4:12 to 2:9. A new star of the future, in the person of Eamon Cregan, scored 3:5 that day for Limerick. For Cork, the Tipperary obstacle, psychological and otherwise, was gone.

The Munster semi-final of 1966 between Cork and Limerick at Killarney was the best game of the year. Despite wretched weather conditions and a greasy sod, the teams served up vintage hurling — fast, crisp and exciting. Two goals to Cork, via Charlie McCarthy and Seanie Barry, in the last ten minutes of the game and a disallowed Limerick goal, via Tom Bluett, in the dying moments gave Cork a place against Waterford in the Munster final on the score 2:6 to 1:7.

Victory over Waterford brought Cork face to face with firm favourites Kilkenny in the All-Ireland final. It was the counties' first such meeting since the classic All-Ireland final of 1947.

Gerald McCarthy with a week to go to his 21st birthday led a determined young Cork team around Croke Park on final day. At the final whistle he headed for the Hogan Stand where he took possession of the MacCarthy Cup from GAA President Alf Murray of Armagh.

Cork had won against the odds — goalkeeper Paddy Barry was outstanding, full forward Colm Sheehan scored all three goals and Justin McCarthy received the Caltex Award Trophy for 1966. Probably the proudest man in Croke Park that day was Cork trainer Jim Barry. He was jubilant after the win: 'This is one of the proudest moments of my history. It is the fourth generation of Cork teams I have trained to win All-Ireland finals. The players did everything I asked of them during the year and made many sacrifices.' Jim died two years later.

This was the campaign Gerald McCarthy captained.

v Clare (5:11 to 1:7 after a replay)
v Limerick (2:6 to 1:7)
v Waterford (4:9 to 2:9)
v Kilkenny (3:9 to 1:10)

Gerald also captained the Cork under-21 hurlers to All-Ireland honours in 1966. I am not sure whether this dual captaincy was unique or rare. Whichever, it was very special for Gerald.

He was the kind of player you would wish to have on your team. He was strong, aggressive, determined and skilful. He had tremendous utility value – was equally at home and commanding whether as halfback, half forward or midfield. In the 1977 All-Ireland final against Wexford, playing at centre forward, he was Cork's leading scorer with six points out of a total score of 1:17. Ground play and overhead striking came naturally to him.

The laurels of 1966 pointed the way to a highly successful hurling career that was festooned with honours. Eleven Munster titles were translated into five All-Ireland successes that included a three-in-a-row from 1976 to 1978 inclusive. A remarkable feature of those successes is the fact that twelve players including Gerald participated in all three finals – Martin Coleman, Brian Murphy, Martin Doherty (1977 captain), Johnny Crowley, Denis Coughlan, Pat Moylan, Jimmy Barry-Murphy, Charlie McCarthy (captain 1978), Ray Cummins (captain 1976), Seanie O'Leary and John Horgan. As well as county titles Gerald won Railway Cup glory with Munster on four occasions and in 1975 an All-Star came his way.

In retirement Gerald remained close to the game and in recent years as manager of Waterford he came, on occasions, tantalisingly close to a successful breakthrough. But the gods were unkind. Success was not fated.

Jimmy Doyle
TIPPERARY
1962 & 1965

'A thing of beauty is a joy forever:
Its loveliness increases, it will never pass into nothingness.'
(John Keats)

Meet Jimmy Doyle, a master of his craft. Hurling immortality is his.

I met Jimmy Doyle of Thurles town in the summer of 1993 following which I profiled him in considerable depth in my publication *Hurling Giants*, so let's now take another look at this gentle genius of the hurling world.

Jimmy began hurling at the age of eight. That of course wasn't surprising. His father Gerry hurled with Tipperary and was on the county panel as sub goalie on the victorious All-Ireland sides of 1937 and 1945. His uncle Tommy was one of Tipperary's greatest players and over a playing career of sixteen years won many honours including five All-Ireland titles.

Such was the hurling brilliance of Jimmy Doyle that at 14 years of age he played in goal for Tipperary minors in 1954 but lost the All-Ireland final to Dublin. For the next three years he played in the half forward line on the county minor team – winning three All-Ireland titles at the expense of Galway, Kilkenny and Kilkenny respectively. In 1957 he had the honour of being captain. His scoring feats in those tender years presaged what was to come in senior ranks. Jimmy set a unique record in Gaelic games when he became the only player to take part in four successive All-Ireland minor finals.

On a July afternoon in 1957 at Limerick Gaelic grounds, Jimmy played minor and senior for his native Tipperary. It was the launch of his senior career.

His career at county level in the blue and gold jersey spanned twenty years. Every honour in the game came his way and he set all kinds of scoring records. He took part in nine All-Ireland finals and was on the winning side on six occasions. In 1962 he captained the team and led them to victory over Wexford in one of the truly great, and most memorable of, All-Ireland finals. In 1965 he joined a small band of players who had the distinction of captaining victorious All-Ireland teams on two occasions. Wexford again fell victim.

In Jimmy's hands the hurley was a magic wand – an extension of himself, an expression of his personality.

He was also a superb marksman, technically brilliant and skilful almost to the point of hurling perfection.

He stood out as a hurling craftsman of the highest order – a player of rare class, a hurler of vision. A friend of mine who knows his hurling and hurling men well often talks about coming out of Croke Park after the All-Ireland finals in the 1960s that Jimmy Doyle played in, his mind still focused on Jimmy's performance, his style, his grace of movement – making it all look so simple and effortless. Yes, that's it, simple and effortless; but only made to look so as a result of countless hours spent fine-tuning and studying and perfecting – in so far as it is possible to perfect – every skill and swing and swerve and motion associated with the artistry that sets the sublime hurler apart from the useful and the good.

Jimmy's hurling career coincided with a golden era in Tipperary hurling. It was a time when the name of the Premier County was synonymous with hurling glory. Every honour in the game flowed Tipperary's way. In captaining his county in 1962 and 1965 Jimmy was presiding over, not only two of Tipperary's greatest teams ever but, two of the finest teams in the history of the game to grace the green sward of any hurling arena.

In 1962 Tipperary defeated Wexford in a classic contest 3:10 to 2:11. During the course of the game Jimmy had to retire with a broken collarbone but not before he had contributed four valuable points.

In 1965 Jimmy's team proved too experienced for a young Wexford team and won comfortably on the scoreline 2:16 to 10 points with Jimmy scoring six of Tipperary's points.

The Tipperary team 1965:

John O'Donoghue

John Doyle   Michael Maher   Kieran Carey

Mick Burns   Tony Wall   Len Gaynor

Theo English   Mick Roche

Jimmy Doyle   Larry Kiely   Liam Deveney

Donie Nealon   John McKenna   Sean McLoughlin

Eleven of the team were there in 1962. Newcomers were John O'Donoghue, Len Gaynor, Mick Roche and Larry Kiely. Gone were Donal O'Brien, Matt O'Gara, Tom Ryan and Liam Moloughney.

As a person Jimmy was shy, quiet, retiring and modest. On the hurling field he was a gentleman and a sportsman – a model for youth to emulate.

A brilliant and memorable county career ended in 1973, where it had started in 1954 – in goal.

Mick Murphy
TIPPERARY
1964

'The joys I have possessed, in spite of fate, are mine.
Not Heaven itself upon the past has power,
But what has been, has been, and I have had my hour.'
(John Dryden)

Mick Murphy played at county minor level for his native Tipperary for three years and was on the winning team of 1957, captained by the great Jimmy Doyle.

Mick and Jimmy grew up together in the same street in Thurles and were schoolmates in Thurles CBS. 'We were seated beside each other – we weren't great at the books. Even at that early age of 12 and under-14 you could see the range of skills Jimmy had. He was uncanny whether in goal, corner forward or wing forward – wherever you wanted to put him. We lived in the hurling field day in day out – we had nothing else to do – we had no money.

> I won a Dean Ryan and Croke medal with Thurles CBS and had the misfortune of missing out on a Harty Cup medal because I went working and hadn't time to come back and sit at the back of the class and read the papers.

Having finished in minor ranks, Mick played county junior in 1959 and progressed to the county senior panel in 1960, where he remained until 1964. In that year, in the county championship, in a game against Roscrea he picked up an injury. 'I fell and hurt my knee – no

76

one hit me – I just came down awkwardly – injured the cartilage. Despite every effort, medical science of the day couldn't repair the damage.'

Yet, in a career of short duration, Mick had many memories to reflect on. In his early days in senior ranks Tipperary were playing Waterford in a league game. Mick was playing on veteran forward Johnny Kiely – 'a real gentleman'. Early in the game they both chased a ball to the wing and the incident which followed brought no retaliation from Johnny, just a paternal-like reprimand. 'I, bould as could be, gave Johnny the handle of the hurley. Johnny, having got the ball – I think he scored a point – came back to me and said you're too young for that young man.'

In the Oirechtas final of 1961, Tipperary faced Wexford in the late autumn of that year. The game went to a replay. In the drawn encounter, Mick gave a vintage performance in the halfback line. 'It was dressing-room choice Mick Murphy who most frequently caught the eye.' (Mick Dunne – *Irish Press* – 23 October 1961.)

'It still mystifies me that a team which had such celebrated figures as Wexford had yesterday in Rackard, English, Lynch, McGrath and Mitchell did not win against opposition who could parade only Tony Wall and Mick Murphy as men of equal calibre.' (John D. Hickey – *Irish Independent* – 23 October 1961).

The replay, two weeks later, on 5 November was won on the score Tipperary 2:13 Wexford 3:4. John D. Hickey writing in the *Irish Independent* the following day had this to say 'Murphy's striking of ground balls, when the situation screamed for Tipperary's most favoured of all approaches, won the hearts of supporters of the winners.'

At the opening of the GAA grounds in Tipperary town we were playing Cork. I was about 20. Paddy Leahy came and said to me, Murphy go in there and hurl centreback and hurl the way you hurl for your club Sarsfields. Lo and behold who was I marking but the maestro himself, Christy Ring. During the course of the game a row broke out. I stood back. Ring turned around with fire in his eyes and said to me – what's wrong with you. He must have been 40 years of age. I had so much admiration for the man on the one hand and on the other hand felt so much in awe, that I simply said – 'nothing sir'.

A great sense of comradeship existed between Glen Rovers of Cork and Thurles Sarsfields of Tipperary since the days of the Church Tournament games. So on the occasion of the opening of the Glen Rovers Pavilion an 'old' Sarsfields team was invited to play the Glen. 'I played fullback that day. After the game we were invited back to Glen Rovers for two hours for free drinks in the company of such a distinguished gentleman as Jack Lynch. He drank porter and sang songs with us. I spoke to him about my uncle Flor Coffey, a brother of my mother Nan (Annie), who won All-Ireland medals with Tipperary in 1945 and 1949. Jack said Flor was one of the finest stick-men he ever hurled on. My uncle John Coffey was also on the 1945 team. There was no hurling tradition on my father's (Michael Snr.) side.'

One of the very special treats of Mick's hurling career was the trip to New York in 1964 to play New York in the National League final. 'We barely won. It was 4:16 to 6:6. It was a brilliant game. New York had a mighty good team. Gaelic Park was full to the seams. Great players from the New York team included Brendan Hennessy (Kerry) Jim Carney (Clare), Brendan Kelleher (Limerick), Pat Dowling (Cork) and that famous handballer Pat Kirby (Clare).'

Many players have a few amusing anecdotes to relate and Mick is no exception. On the county team he had as a team-mate Sean McLoughlin – a corner forward with a penchant for scoring goals. 'I remember how he would attempt to intimidate Ollie Walsh in the Kilkenny goal by shouting at him from time to time – I'm coming, I'm coming.' Those were the days when forwards could charge the goalkeeper – echoes of earlier decades when Micka Brennan of Cork, with the black togs, would parade along the square and turn occasionally to the goalkeeper and say 'I'll pay you a visit soon.'

But the story I liked best was the one about his club colleague Mickey Byrne, star Tipperary defender and wit personified. Mickey was on his way out of Thurles cemetery after a funeral and remarked to those around him that the Bishop had taken steps to ensure that he (Mickey) wouldn't be buried there. The knowing ones would have had a fair idea of what was coming but the innocent ones might have pondered on what unconfessed reserved sin rested on Mickey's soul that had yet to be atoned for. Mickey, in as serious a tone as he could muster, announced to all that the Bishop feared he might start an underground movement.

When Thurles Sarsfields won the county title it was their custom to rotate the captaincy of the county team. Following a proposal by Paddy Maher and seconded by Martin Troy, Mick was elected captain for 1964. 'It was a mighty honour – in your wildest dreams to think you would captain an All-Ireland winning team. We prepared well and trained three nights a week. Ossie Bennett was our masseur at the time. Our first match was against Clare. I was pitted against Pat Hinchy, a man I thought was a brilliant wing forward but he got very little recognition. He was switched off me that day and I sighed relief when I saw him going.

'We went on to play Cork in the Munster final and won handsomely. I was on Patsy Harte – we had it fairly tough, and tough too in club games when we played the Glen. When it came to collecting the Cup they had no cup to give me. It wasn't there. They brought it down to the hotel and when we were finished the meal they brought it in and handed it to me.'

The victory over Cork booked Tipperary a place in the All-Ireland final against reigning All-Ireland champions Kilkenny. At the time Mick was working in a pharmacy. With him was John Dwyer a friend and colleague who was very fond of the Irish language and was known as 'Seán Ó Duibhir an Ghleanna'. 'If you go up to collect the cup, said John to me, have you an Irish speech ready. I had to admit I hadn't and was unlikely to have. Surely he said you're not going to say everything in English.' The result was that for several days at lunchtime John put Mick through a crash course in Irish to prepare him for the big day – and on the big day Mick duly delivered from the Hogan Stand.

An attendance of 71,282 watched the final in ideal weather conditions. Tipperary led at the break by 1:8 to 6 points. There was every indication it was going to be a close, tight affair to the final whistle. And so it seemed early in the second half when Kilkenny narrowed the gap. But it was mere deception. Tipperary went into overdrive. Their backs stood rock solid. The forwards moved in a manner that Carbery would have described as 'like mowers in a meadow'. They were prolific in their scoring with Jimmy Doyle having ten points and Donie Nealon three goals over the hour. It ended 5:13 to 2:8. Mick had captained Tipperary to their 20th All-Ireland title. They now led the field followed by Cork and Kilkenny with 19 and 15 titles respectively.

Mick recalls that Eddie Keher said in an interview that 'it was the greatest Tipperary team I have seen in my lifetime'. It is hard to disagree with that comment when one considers that Liam Devaney wasn't selected in the starting forward line-up. However, he did come on as a sub in the second half.

The autumn of 1964 saw the end of Mick's hurling career. He was only 24. 'It was short and sweet. But there was ten more years in me.' Mick cried when he realised he could play no more. 'Hurling was all we had in those days.'

Mick captained one of the great teams of hurling history in 1964. The team lined out as follows on All-Ireland final day.

John O'Donoghue

John Doyle Micháel Maher Kieran Carey

Mick Burns Tony Wall Mick Murphy

Theo English Mick Roche
(0–1)

Jimmy Doyle Larry Kiely Michael Keating
(0–10)   (0–2)

Donie Nealon John McKenna Sean McLoughlin
(3–0)   (1–0)   (1–0)

Matt Hassett
TIPPERARY
1961

My earliest memory of hurling was playing on the road leading from Limerick to Dublin during the Second World War. The first competitive games were as an under-15 player with Toomevara but without any success. I became secretary of Toomevara in 1954 when hurling was at a low ebb, but with the late Michael Bourke we started to organise the juveniles and minors with some success. The club entered a senior hurling team in the Tipperary championship in 1956 and eventually succeeded in winning the county final in 1960. My earlier years were as a forward of little note but when I moved to corner back in 1958 I started to enjoy my hurling.

My greatest memory was the Munster final v Cork in Limerick in 1961 when I was captain. I played on Christy Ring that day, which I think was his last Munster final. My career with Tipperary was short – 1960 to 1962 – but very successful. Michael Maher had a great influence on me and all the Tipp. players of that time. I recall playing on a number of great players – Donal Whelan and Phil Grimes of Waterford, Christy Ring and Paddy Barry of Cork, Dermot Kelly of Limerick, Tim Flood and Padge Kehoe of Wexford – all great hurlers and sportsmen.

Stephen Hackett, Toomevara and Tipperary, had a great influence on my early hurling career. He was a neighbour and I remember listening to him as a young boy, sitting in the haybarn smoking his pipe and talking about the "Greyhounds", and then having a few pucks in the yard.

I remember Matt Hassett from his hurling days with Patrician College, Ballyfin, in Co. Laois, in the early fifties. In those days he played at full forward. He was always a leading light on the college team – a skilled opportunist who played with a quiet authority – a true hurling sportsman with a sweet, silken style.

Matt was born into the legendary hurling parish of Toomevara in 1932. Stephen Hackett was a neighbour. He had hurled with Tipperary from 1917 onwards – losing the All-Ireland finals of 1917 and 1922 to Dublin and Kilkenny respectively, winning the 1925 title at the expense of Galway. As a youngster Matt would drop in to Stephen's house – it was an era when neighbours dropped in and out of each other's houses regularly. 'Stephen had a wireless, one of the few in the parish. We'd listen to that for a while. Then we'd drink a cup of tea. Stephen would tell hurling stories. Then we'd go out the back and have a few pucks together.' Those 'few pucks' made Matt feel special.

Hurling blood flowed in the veins of both of Matt's parents. His father Pat, 'who did a little hurling and did cross country running' was a first cousin of the famed 'Wedger' Meagher who captained Tipperary in 1913 – only to fail to Kilkenny in the final. 'I only met "Wedger" twice – when he was on visits from America where he emigrated in 1926.'

81

Nora O'Meara was Matt's mother's name. Her uncle, Jim O'Dwyer, won an All-Ireland title with Tipperary in 1887, the inaugural year of the hurling championship. The renowned Tipperary custodians, Jack 'Skinny' O'Meara and Tommy O'Meara were second cousins.

In 1958, Matt, who to this very day loves going to matches – 'some weeks I might see five matches, juvenile, camogie, senior, any match' – thumbed to Buttevant to watch a game between Tipperary and Cork for suit lengths and finished up playing cornerback for Tipperary. After that he played other tournament games and in 1960 was selected at right fullback for his native county following the retirement of Mickey Byrne.

His task in the Munster final of 1960, played at Thurles, was to mark Christy Ring. How did you feel about the prospect? 'Terrified!! I stood on the embankment in Thurles in 1956 and watched the Limerick v Cork Munster final. I saw what Ring did to Limerick that day in the closing stages – scored 3:1 in about five minutes – at a time when Limerick seemed to have the game won. I said to myself there's only one way to play him – don't let him get the ball. I had played against him in a challenge game, so I knew what to expect. My plan was to play him from the front. I weighed under 11 stone but in a five yards burst I wouldn't be beaten.' Matt did well. Tipperary won by two points and out of Cork's total score of 4:11, Ring over the hour was held to three points from play by Matt.

The game itself was a furious, gruelling, physical encounter – a hurling frenzy played in an atmosphere and with an intensity that at times was almost alarming.

In the All-Ireland final Tipperary caught a tartar in a sparkling Wexford performance that produced a major shock with a 2:15 to 0:11 victory for the Model County. 'We did some very heavy training that year. I'd have been better off at home drinking a pint of milk.'

In 1960 Toomevara won the Tipperary county senior title for the first time since 1931. As a result Matt became the Tipperary captain for the 1961 All-Ireland title race. As in the previous year they came face to face with arch rivals Cork in the Munster final at Limerick. 'I got up early and cycled to 9 o'clock Mass in Moneygall. On the way streams of cars were passing me heading for the final in Limerick.' It was the biggest attendance ever for a Munster final. The official figure is 60,177. However, in the interests of safety the gates to the Gaelic Grounds were opened. No one knows how many really watched the game. Some place the figure as high as 70,000. Matt had another good day on Christy Ring. Tipperary won well (3:6 to 0:7). Matt was now playing on a great Tipperary team and in the company of many of the game's greatest exponents. Beside him at fullback was the ever-reliable Michael Maher. 'If you caught the ball in the fullback line you'd hear a loud whisper from Michael – hold on to it, hold on to it.'

Tipperary met Dublin in the All-Ireland final, the first meeting of the counties at that level since 1930. Tipperary were firm favourites. Strangely, Dublin were undervalued and under-rated. Difficult to tell why. After all, in the Leinster final of 1959 against Kilkenny it took a goal, from a sideline puck, to deprive them of the Leinster title by one point. The puck out brought the final whistle. In 1961 Dublin defeated Wexford, reigning All-Ireland champions, in the Leinster final by 7:5 to 4:8. And in the Railway Cup final of 1962 Leinster with eight of the 1961 Dublin team defeated Munster by 1:11 to 1:9. Without a doubt the Dublin hurling team of 1961 was a very fine team.

Sunday 3 September 1961 turned out to be a memorable day for Matt. Victory went to Tipperary by one point over a gallant Dublin team led by Noel Drumgoole. Matt knows it might have been different. 'We were lucky to win, but we did and I suppose that's what counts.'

In the Hogan Stand GAA President Hugh Byrne of Wicklow presented Matt with the MacCarthy Cup. The triumphal return home would follow. It was his proudest moment – the first man from Toomevara to captain Tipperary to All-Ireland victory.

Matt's reign at top level hurling was relatively short. 'I know I was lucky and fortunate to achieve what I did' – captain in 1961 when he led Tipperary to National League, Oireachtas and All-Ireland honours; Munster titles in 1960 and '61; county title 1960; two further Oireachtas titles; three county Tipperary senior football titles (1958, '59 and 1961) 'for which we did no training at all – we were fit from the hurling'.

Reporting on an Oireachtas final against Wexford on 6 November 1961 John D. Hickey wrote as follows in the *Irish Independent* –

Team captain Matt Hassett, who had what was easily his best game in the county jersey, and played with an astuteness

that nullified Padge Kehoe's marked weight advantage . . .
also contributed regally to the success.

Unfortunately, Matt's county career came to a rather abrupt end in
1962 at a time when he was hurling very well. Playing against
Limerick he broke and severely damaged a finger. It confined him to
the subs' bench for the rest of the season. John Doyle dropped back
to cornerback. Matt never regained his place. Quietly, he drifted
into the hurling sunset.

1960–1946

Nick O'Donnell
WEXFORD
1955–1960

*'Full many a gem of purest ray serene
The dark unfathom'd caves of ocean bear;
Full many a flower is born to blush unseen,
And waste its sweetness on the desert air.'*

When I think of Nick O'Donnell, I always wonder if the above lines from Thomas Gray's 'Elegy in a Country Churchyard' would have applied to him if he had not come to reside in Co. Wexford. For it was with the St. Aidan's, Enniscorthy, club that his hurling potential and talents were spotted by the Wexford selectors.

Nick O'Donnell, a native of Graiguenamanagh, Co. Kilkenny, was born in 1925. By nature he was shy and retiring. He was a man that shunned the limelight. He preferred to leave whatever speech-making there was to be done to others. I had the pleasure of visiting Nick in 1981, but only after the good offices of hurling colleague Padge Kehoe had prepared the way and cleared the ground. And even after that it took the gentle promptings of his wife, to get him to write a paragraph in the leather-bound journal in which I was recording the personal written contributions of many of the great men of hurling.

In Nick's early hurling days he played with Eire Óg, a club based in Kilkenny city. He was a member of the panel of the Kilkenny junior team that won the All-Ireland title in 1946 – beating Galway (4:2 to 2:3) in the Home Final and London (5:4 to 2:2) in the final. He was 21. Team-mates on that occasion who later figured prominently at senior level were Mark Marnell, Paddy 'Diamond' Hayden, Peter Prendergast and Willie Cahill. Interestingly, in the game against Galway, the western goalkeeper was none other than Tony Reddan who would subsequently star with his adopted Tipperary.

Nick was a sub on the Kilkenny team of 1947 that defeated Cork in a thriller by 0:14 to 2:7 – an occasion that gave immortality to Terry Leahy. Only twenty medals were presented. Nick got none. Ever after the disappointment niggled.

He came to Co. Wexford in early 1950. He became an employee of Roadstone Ltd. in Enniscorthy and a playing member of St. Aidan's, the local senior hurling team.

By that time 'Diamond' Hayden had established himself as the Kilkenny and Leinster fullback. There appeared to be no place in the Kilkenny defence for Nick. He threw in his lot with the Model County and having been adopted by them, there was no going back.

He became eligible to play for Wexford in the 1951 championship. Thus began a glittering hurling career that reached the pinnacle of stardom over the next dozen years. His displays in the No. 3 jersey of his adopted county caused him to be regarded as one of the great fullbacks of hurling. This was borne out when he was honoured in that position by the Centenary team selectors in 1984 and the Millennium selectors in 2000.

Nick had a great sense of position. His reading of a game was sharp. He had the strength and skill to course a ball out of defence. His clearances were long and effective. His style of movement suggested he was slow, but that was a deception. In an era when many fullbacks played a stopper role, Nick played a lot of hurling. It made him stand apart.

He made his début in the purple and gold against Dublin in the championship of 1951. In that game he nullified the threat and wiles of the highly talented Tony Herbert.

When the 'Diamond' Hayden retired from the hurling scene, Nick became the established Leinster fullback in the Railway Cup competition from 1956 to 1961 inclusive. Munster dominated the competition in those years and Nick O'Donnell's only success was in 1956 when he captained the side. It contained nine Wexford men.

In the 1954 All-Ireland final against Cork, Nick had to leave the field in the second half with an injured collar bone, following a clash with Christy Ring. Wexford responded by moving Bobby Rackard from centre back, where he was playing brilliantly, to fullback where he gave a superb exhibition of defensive play. Wexford lost by 1:9 to 1:6. Whenever the game is debated there are critics and pundits who argue that if Bobby had been left at centre back the game would have been won. I have always viewed the debate as a side issue. Wexford could have won with a good margin to spare if their forwards hadn't wasted so many golden opportunities.

In 1955 Wexford gave their adopted son the great honour of being their captain. Despite all the valiant efforts since 1950 the MacCarthy

Cup had eluded them. Many in the county felt that failure in 1955 could spell the end of the line for a great team.

Up until then Wexford's only hurling title was won in 1910, when they defeated Limerick by 7:0 to 6:2. Their last appearance in a hurling final was in 1918 when they failed to a great Limerick team. Accordingly, in 1955 Wexford hurling men led by Nick O'Donnell, managed by their dedicated mentors and spurred on by thousands of loyal supporters, were on a mission.

The campaign began with a good, if slightly flattering, win over Westmeath by 5:9 to 3:4. Indeed, so heroic was the Westmeath effort that the crowd rose at the final whistle to applaud them off the field. The next hurdle was the Leinster final against Kilkenny on Sunday 17 July. Wexford were favourites; yet lingering doubts persisted. Wexford had never beaten Kilkenny in a Leinster final. Laois, Offaly and Dublin, yes. The Cats, no. Perhaps the presence of Kilkennyman Nick O'Donnell at the helm for Wexford would change the fortunes of the Model County. Time would tell.

Came the day. And a sweltering July day it was. From the throw-in it was nip and tuck for the entire hour – gripping and exciting, but not classical. At fullback Nick O'Donnell gave a performance that was inspirational. In the dying seconds he averted a certain goal after Padge Kehoe had levelled the score for Wexford with a point. The game ended at 2:7 each. Wexford players, mentors and supporters breathed a collective sigh of relief. The 'Indian Sign' of Kilkenny had yet to be erased.

The teams lined out for the replay on 31 July. The pitch was rock-hard. At half time the score was Wexford 3:3 Kilkenny 2:6. Still level! What, if anything, would separate them. And then out of the blue came the answer in sensational fashion. From the throw-in for the second half (it was the time when only the backs went back into position and forwards and midfielders – all sixteen of them – lined up at midfield for the throw-in) Nicky Rackard gained possession about sixty yards out from the Kilkenny goal and sent a speculative shot goalwards. It hopped on the hard ground in front of the Kilkenny goal and then hopped again to deceive the Kilkenny custodian and crossed the goal line without reaching the net. Reality only dawned on the crowd when the umpire waved the green flag.

That goal divided the teams at the final whistle when the score-board read Wexford 5:6 Kilkenny 3:9. The Kilkenny barrier had been breached. Nick O'Donnell and his men were on the march.

It was another scorching summer day when Wexford faced Limerick in the All-Ireland semi-final at Croke Park on 7 August before a record semi-final attendance, officially recorded as 50,840. Limerick, young, fast and skilful, led at the break by 2:2 to 1:3. Wexford, strong, composed and very experienced, dominated the second half to win comfortably by 2:12 to 2:3.

Now only Galway, who got a bye into the final, stood between Nick O'Donnell and the gallant men he captained and glory. They faced the Tribesmen for the final showdown on 4 September, cautious, yet confident. They were cautious because they had failed to the men of the west in recent years as follows:

1950 Oireachtas final (2:9 to 2:6)
1951 National League (6:7 to 3:4) Home Final
1952 Oireachtas final (3:7 to 1:10)

At half time the caution was justified. Galway led by 2:5 to 2:3. However, in the second half the power and experience of the Wexford men paved the way to a great victory. Here is how Nicholas Furlong in his book *The Greatest Hurling Decade* described the aftermath:

> We didn't know whether to go mad, to stand on our heads or burst forth into violent song. In the general mayhem others had certainly gone mad or half-mad. Nicky Rackard later wrote that he made for the dressing-room as hard as he could and sat in a corner, head in hands, in dazed realisation that at the end of his playing career he had achieved an All-Ireland medal; one gold medal, a concept once regarded as an absurdity to all save himself. The rest of the day and night is confusing, for it was only the first night of abandon, of celebration and banquets, team visits and team canonisation. It must have taken five hours to get to the new bridge at Wexford, for the bonfires and crossroad dancing had to be sampled. The journey featured long, slow caravans of cars, since no one in the night's delirium was in a hurry. Hundreds of cars did not go home at all but stayed in Dublin or Bray to accompany the team back to Co. Wexford the following night . . .
>
> Our own region's emotional moment was well observed. The Piercestown Parish reception for the St. Martin's Club members who had won All-Ireland medals was held in Murrintown hall

a little later on, early in the New Year. In that small but important hall there shone brightly on a table the massive Leinster Cup, the Oireachtas Cup and the All-Ireland Cup. Clocks were presented to each of the club members who had gold All-Ireland medals on their persons; Ned Wheeler, Jim Morrissey and sub goalie Chris Casey . . . The traditionally well-dressed farmer and cattle dealer, Phil Berry, tipped his felt hat to the back of his head on contemplation of the tables shimmering contents. 'God Almighty,' he declared in a loud voice, 'isn't it great to be alive.'

Nick O'Donnell had the honour again in 1960 of leading the men in purple and gold. His performances in the championship of that year earned him the 'Texaco Hurler of the Year' award.

The campaign that registered Wexford's fourth All-Ireland title brought the following results:

v Dublin (3:5 to 2:8) a draw
v Dublin (4:6 to 1:7) replay
v Kilkenny (3:10 to 2:11)
v Tipperary (2:15 to 0:11)

The defeat of Tipperary was certainly the hurling upset of the decade. Tipperary had reached the final in convincing fashion.

v Limerick (10.9 to 2:1)
v Waterford (6:9 to 2:7) (reigning All-Ireland champions)
v Cork (4:13 to 4:11)

Mick Dunne, writing in the *Irish Press* on the Monday morning after the game, captured the magnitude of the Wexford win by quoting, as his opening, the first two lines from the poem, 'The Destruction of Sennacherib' by Lord Byron.

> *'The Assyrian came down like a wolf on the fold*
> *And his cohorts were gleaming in purple and gold.'*

Nicholas Furlong in his book *The Greatest Hurling Decade* eloquently described the performance of Nick O'Donnell. 'We were leading by 2:11 to 0:9 . . . but there were fifteen minutes to go and there was not, could not be a cave-in by Tipperary; but what last-ditch assaults there were broke down against one mighty man and his corner back support. Nick O'Donnell team captain, was that man, and his corner supporters were John Mitchell and Tom Neville of the Hook Peninsula.

'O'Donnell at fullback resembled nothing so much as a massive digger with a boom that advanced, retired and grated to left or right as required. He caught balls in the middle of flailing hurleys. He moved out as if he were six feet in breadth to cover and quell danger. Nothing lower than twenty feet got by him. . . The pitch was invaded. The Wexford no-hopers were submerged. I saw a rare sight, the usually solemn Nick O'Donnell laughing, and he was later seen laughing in conversation with President De Valera as the MacCarthy Cup with gold and purple ribbons was presented.'

Mairfidh ainmneacha iomráiteacha iománaithe Loch Garmain na gcaogadaí i mbéaloideas na hiománaíochta, go deo na ndeor.

The men of '55.

Art Foley

Bobby Rackard	Nick O'Donnell	Mick O'Hanlon
Jim English	Billy Rackard	Mick Morrissey

Jim Morrissey   Seamus Hearne

Paddy Kehoe	Ned Wheeler	Padge Kehoe
Tom Ryan	Nicky Rackard	Tim Flood

Subs: Oliver Gough for Ned Wheeler, Ned Wheeler for Oliver Gough and Dominic Aherne for Tom Ryan.

The men of 1960.

Pat Nolan

John Mitchell	Nick O'Donnell	Tom Neville
Jim English	Billy Rackard	John Nolan

Ned Wheeler   Jim Morrissey

Jimmy O'Brien	Padge Kehoe	Seamus Quaid
Oliver McGrath	John Harding	Tim Flood

Subs: Sean Power for Seamus Quaid, Mick Morrissey for Sean Power.

'Goodly news, goodly news, do I bring, youth of Forth;
Goodly news shall you hear, Bargy man!'

Frankie Walsh
WATERFORD
1959

'Oh for the clash of the ash so sweet,
The flying ball and the hurlers fleet'

(Carbery)

Frankie Walsh made his début at county senior level in a tournament game against Kilkenny. He was young and fit and energetic. It was an era when backs took up their positions prior to the start of the game. The centre field pair and forwards lined up at midfield for the throw-in.

With the game under way Frankie headed for the corner forward position where he would be marking Mark Marnell – now at the veteran stage. Frankie had decided to give Mark the run around. That was until he took up position beside him and 'he pulled my jersey and said you're not going far this evening'.

As Frankie reflects on that occasion he sees the humour in it and smiles. But he recalls one of his next games that could have left him maimed for life. It was his championship début against Cork in 1956. He received a fractured skull from a swinging hurley. 'I spent over a month in hospital. I was allowed no visitors, no papers, no nothing. As I lay on my back I wondered a lot about the future.'

Thankfully, Frankie made a good recovery and was in Dungarvan the following year for a training session with his colleagues for the 1957 All-Ireland campaign. John Keane – Waterford star of yesteryear – was there as trainer and selector. So too was Pat Fanning who spoke passionately to the players and told them he believed they had what it took to win an All-Ireland title.

As Frankie, then not yet 21, listened to those words his mind went back to when he was 12 years old. 'I was showing promise as a hurler. Brother Magill took me on a visit to John Keane's house. John was a distant relative of mine. He lived opposite Phil Grimes. We were given a cup of tea and biscuits. Then John said to me – "Did you ever see an All-Ireland medal?" I said I hadn't. He went upstairs and brought down the medal he won in 1948 when Jim Ware was captain. When I looked at it the first thing I said was – I want one of those.'

91

Frankie pondered Pat Fanning's words and saw no reason to doubt them. 'At the time Mount Sion had a strong team and were beating leading clubs outside the county.' It augured well.

> I remember travelling to Dublin for the 1957 All-Ireland final against Kilkenny. Tom Cheasty, Seamus Power and myself got out at Carlow to stretch our legs. Tom went to buy orange juice – he had a pain in his head. Seamus went to a bookie's office to check on horses. I went to a hardware shop to see if there were any new tools on the market – I was a welder.
>
> On our way back to the car Seamus saw a weighing scales outside a chemist's shop. He got up. It registered 12st. 7 lbs. He was delighted. 12st. 7lbs., and fully fit – a good weight. Then Tom got up. He weighed 13st. 5lbs. 'You get up,' said Seamus to me. 'No, no,' I insisted. 'Are you frightened to spend a penny?' said Seamus. I got up and turned the scales at 9st. 7lbs. Seamus looked at me and said 'you should be a feckin jockey on some of those horses I backed'. In time my weight went up to 10st. 2lbs.

The final of 1957 is one Waterford will always feel they let slip. They played great hurling and with about twelve minutes to go were six points clear – and looking good. And yet, when the final whistle blew they were a point in arrears. Supporters and neutrals were dumbfounded.

Carbery had this to say. 'Kilkenny's recovery was reminiscent of many other finals won by a point . . . Waterford have never hurled a better game than this. They had never faltered and their splendid exhibition surprised and pleased us all. My opinion is that a draw would be a true verdict.'

It was a case of so near and yet so far. However, a young Waterford team with a belief in the future and supported by enthusiastic management would no doubt have said to themselves after the disappointment of defeat had worn off, beidh lá eile ag an bPaorach.

The 1959 All-Ireland campaign began with Frankie Walsh as captain. It is likely that he would have reflected on 'the slings and arrows' of 1957. A closer memory still would be the 16-point hammering they got from Tipperary in the 1958 Munster final. Despite all Frankie felt the team was learning.

92

I realised that if we all struck form and played the kind of hurling we were capable of, that we were good enough to handle any of the teams and win a title.

It was Galway's first year in Munster. We met them in the first round and while we were confident we didn't expect to beat the Oireachtas title-holders by 7:11 to 0:8. The next match was against Tipperary at Cork athletic grounds. There was a wicked gale blowing. Tipperary won the toss and played against it. We ran up a huge first half score. I think it was 8:2 to nil at half time. I was the only forward to score in the second half. We won by 9:3 to 3:4. When the score was sent to Mícheál O'Hehir to announce it during his broadcast at another venue, he looked at it in disbelief and asked to have it checked. When he announced it half the country didn't believe it. The entire team was made Sports Stars of the Week.

I have personal memories of the Munster final at Thurles that year where Waterford faced Cork. I travelled to the game on the back of a motorbike from Wexford town – a round journey of 160 miles. It was a wet miserable trip. As Thurles came in view the sun broke through. The game was five minutes in progress by the time we squeezed our way in behind the town goal – just in time to witness an exchange between Christy Ring and Joe Harney as the Waterford man made a great clearance. Semple Stadium was packed like sardines – over 55,000 spectators – one of the biggest attendances ever in Thurles and 15,000 up on the 1957 gate when the same counties met at the same venue.

The game was won and lost when Waterford selectors switched Phil Grimes from midfield to centre halfback to curb a rampant Paddy Barry. Grimes was magnificent. He outplayed both Barry and Ring who alternated from time to time with a view to unsettling the Waterford defence – but to no avail. 'It was a difficult game. Ned Power in goal made great saves. We were glad when the final whistle blew – we won by 3:9 to 2:9.'

The next outing would be to Croke Park for the All-Ireland final on Sunday 6 September. Waterford's opponents would be Kilkenny – a repeat of the 1957 All-Ireland final. In the Leinster final of 1959 Kilkenny indulged in an act of grand larceny – as Mícheál O'Hehir would have described it – against Dublin. With seconds remaining

Dublin led by 1:11 to 1:9. Then came a sideline cut to Kilkenny. The sliotar floated goalwards. Sean Clohessy was on hand to guide it to the net. The puck out brought the final whistle.

Hurling fans looked forward to a quality final and hoped it would provide skills and thrills similar to that of the '57 encounter. Frankie Walsh remembers the occasion just as if it was yesterday – the honour of being captain, the thrill of leading the hurling men of the Decies around Croke Park. In particular, he remembers the closing moments when the scoreboard read Kilkenny 5:5 Waterford 0:17. 'It would take a goal to save the day. We won a sideline cut. Seamus Power moved forward from midfield and raised his hand. I took the sideline cut. I shouldn't have. It only went a few yards – you little so and so, Seamus shouted. He stayed forward. My memory is that Larry Guinan chased the ball and won possession. He passed it to Seamus – as you know, the rest is history.'

Well, history it certainly is for Seamus scored the equalising goal with a shot that deflected off the hurley of Kilkenny fullback 'Link' Walsh and passed his namesake Ollie in goal who up to that moment had kept a clean sheet with some superb saves that beggared description. 'When the final whistle blew Seamus thought we had won by a point – I thought we had lost by a point.'

Spectators had witnessed a magnificent game of hurling between two great teams. It was one of the great All-Ireland finals: a breathtaking contest, played at remarkable speed and full of intense exchanges where courage and skill and sportsmanship abounded. We looked forward to the 4 October and more of the same. On that October Sunday 77,285 spectators packed themselves into Croke Park bringing the combined official attendance to 150,992.

'Our backs were tighter the second day. We got off to a bad start – a bit nervous. I failed to lift a close-in free but whipped it off the ground over the bar. I think we were six points down after ten minutes – and we were playing with a strong wind. Then it all began to happen for us. Mick Flannelly, the lightest man on the team after myself, goaled. Tom Cheasty got two more. At half time it was 3:6 to 1:8. We only gave Kilkenny two points in the second half and they with the wind. We won by 3:12 to 1:10. Eddie Keher made his senior début as a sub that day.' In fact, he had played in the minor final that was lost to Tipperary.

Carbery had this to say. '. . . as fine a hurling team as ever won an All-Ireland final. And what a final it was . . . Fast and furious as

94

before, kept 78,000 enthralled in the exhilarating spectacle of 30 superb athletes battling with grim resolve to bring honour to the little village . . . every man in the Waterford side seemed to be on the move, and they moved at a sparkling rate . . . they hit ground balls from all angles . . . Frankie Walsh, the Decies captain, hit his most dazzling form in that winning second half. His left hand was meticulously accurate; he hit frees with rare accuracy from all ranges and angles; his play through the field was inspiring.'

It was Frankie's most memorable hour and year. In the five games of the championship he scored 2:28. Six of those points came in the drawn All-Ireland final and eight in the replay. His performance in the replay won him the 'Sports Star of the Week' award. He doesn't remember what he said in his speech. Indeed, he was so overcome with emotion and excitement that 'Dr. J.J. Stuart, President of the GAA, had to lift the Cup with me.'

The following St. Patrick's Day, Frankie captained a Munster team, that included seven Waterford men, to Railway Cup victory over Leinster on the score 6:6 to 2:7. It placed him among an elite that had the privilege of leading club, county and province to the ultimate prize.

In a career that spanned fifteen years 'my opponents included the following greats: Jimmy Finn and Mick Burns of Tipperary, Paddy Buggy and Seamus Cleere of Kilkenny, Jim English of Wexford and Paddy Fitzgerald of Cork'.

The great men he captained in the replay, lined out as follows:

Ned Power

Joe Harney   Austin Flynn   John Barron

Mick Lacey   Martin 'Óg' Morrissey   Jackie Condon

Seamus Power   Phil Grimes

Mick Flannelly   Tom Cheasty   Frankie Walsh

Larry Guinan   Tom Cunningham   Johnny Kiely

Mickey O'Connor and Donal Whelan replaced Mick Lacey and Tom Cunningham respectively.

Christy Ring
CORK
1946, 1953 & '54

'Toscanini for good music
Kathy Barry for crubeens
— and Ringey for goals.'

During my playing career, I met a lot of players that were faster, taller and better in several ways. But, to be a good hurler, you have to have something that the others have not got. I had that — strength. I never met anybody physically stronger than myself. I achieved this strength by hard physical training. Allied to this, I had fierce determination when going for the ball. I would go through a stone wall to get a 50/50 ball. I would stop at nothing. My strength was largely hidden, because I wasn't a big fellow. I never weighed less than 13 stone. I knew that weighing 13 stone and travelling at speed, I could take on any player. I only used my strength when needed. All-round physical strength was my best weapon. I never did weightlifting or anything like that to develop this strength. I had it automatically, and I'd say it was in the mind. Seventy five per cent of everything is in the mind, and it's the mind that counts.

When Christy Ring, the wizard from Cloyne, son of Nicholas and Mary, was chosen to captain Cork in 1946 he was a vastly experienced hurler.

A sub on the victorious Cork minor team of 1937, he went one better the following year when he played right halfback on the team that beat Dublin.

He was initiated into county senior ranks during 1939 with non-championship games against Limerick, Waterford and Kilkenny.

He got his baptism of fire to the heat of championship fare in the drawn and replayed Munster final of 1940 against Limerick. He described the intensity of the exchanges on the pitch as 'frightening'. And it was true, because Peter Cregan who marked him on both occasions and who had made his championship début two years earlier, gave exactly the same description when I spoke with him in 1981.

Christy grew up in Cloyne, where he was born on 12 October 1920, and spent his youth playing hurling. In 1941 he joined the Glen Rovers club in Cork city.

When he led the red-jerseyed men of Cork in the pre-match All-Ireland parade in 1946, he had as team mates five players who to him were God-like figures when he first played with Cork in 1940. They were Willie Murphy, Din Joe Buckley, Alan Lotty, Jim Young and Jack Lynch.

By All-Ireland day in 1946 Christy had collected four Munster titles ('42, '43, '44 and '46), four All-Ireland crowns ('41, '42' 43 and '44), three county titles ('41, '44 and '45), five Railway Cups with Munster ('42, '43, '44, '45 and '46). He was centre forward each of those years for Munster except '43 when he played right half forward. He had hurled with the cream of the province: Batt Thornhill, Johnny Ryan, John Keane, Peter Cregan, Christy Moylan, Willie Barron, Dick Stokes, Johnny Quirke, Jackie Power, Willie O'Donnell, Andy Fleming, Tommy Doyle, Mick Mackey, John Mackey, Jim Ware, Sean Condon, Tommy Purcell, Jim Devitt, Mick Hayes, Sean Herbert and P.J. Quane. He was not yet 26.

Now in 1946 in the eyes of many Christy was himself a God-like figure and was about to succeed Mick Mackey, who had played his last full championship match with Limerick in the Munster semi-final against Tipperary earlier that year, as the High King of hurling.

Cork's path to the final of 1946, under the captaincy of Christy Ring, yielded the following results:

v Clare (2:9 to 2:1)
v Limerick (3:8 to 1:3)
v Galway (2:10 to 0:3)

Now for a joust with Kilkenny!

Coming up to half time in the All-Ireland final, in a game that had been evenly contested, Kilkenny led by five points to three. Gerry O'Riordan got a Cork goal to put them one point up. It was now on the thirtieth minute of play. Paddy O'Donovan cleared for Cork. Ring, who had drifted out towards mid-field, displayed first touch perfection as he gathered. Away on a solo run, he dodged and swerved and slipped opponents until he was within scoring distance. He finished the defence-splitting move with a shot that gave Jim Donegan in the Kilkenny goal no chance. Half time, Cork 2:3 Kilkenny 0:5.

In a free-scoring second half, Cork finished the stronger. The scoreboard read Cork 7:5 Kilkenny 3:8.

Christy Ring was the hero of the hour and the idol of the crowd – particularly for Cork followers. He had captained Cork to their sixteenth All-Ireland title – three ahead of Tipperary, four ahead of Kilkenny. He had displayed skill and vision and craft and class. He scored 1:4 and made many more scores for his colleagues.

Writing on the game Carbery had this to say of the Cork captain. 'Christy Ring, the Cork skipper, excelled himself – his tireless elusiveness, his artistry, his bright good humour, his rapid, unselfish passes to a pal well placed – all make the Glen Rovers man an ideal leader, of whom I have often written in praise. That solo run of his near the end of the first half, following hot on Gerry Riordan's smashing 'netter' will live long in hurling memory, for it inspired his men and sent them to the dressing tent at half time with bubbling confidence . . . It proved the key score to the Championship golden gate.'

The following morning the *Cork Examiner* carried the heading 'Christy Ring's wonder goal was highlight of Cork's great win'. It wasn't his first time making the headlines. His last minute goal that beat Limerick in a replayed Munster final epic in 1944, prompted the following headline in a national daily – 'Ring's wonder goal keeps title in Cork'.

John Power, writer and journalist of those days, described the '44 goal thus: 'He is a pure skilful ballplayer, indefatigable and a trier all the way. For years to come his goal against Limerick in this year's Munster final replay will be spoken of with pride by grateful Cork followers the county over. It was the effort of an athlete who would not accept defeat. An effort, the like of which for sheer dramatic intensity, occurs only once, perhaps, in a lifetime. There were Limerick, winners it seemed, all the way. And Cork desperately battling against time to bring down that lead. Point by point Cork narrowed the score. There was brave Mick Mackey dashing from goal to goal, playing several men's parts to uphold their lead. Time was drawing out. Mick must have murmured "we must surely be winners this time".

Then, well back in his own half, this unconquerable Ring snapped up the ball. Tim Ryan went for him, Christy tapped the ball on his hurley and sailed around him.

On for twenty yards went the Cork man still tapping the ball on his hurley. Out came Jackie Power, then Cregan, then McCarthy, then Power again. Christy Ring still had the ball. Suddenly he stopped, steadied and swung his hurley. Like a bullet the ball flew, straight and true. Hurleys flashed to meet it, but there it was, dead in the back of the net. Tense and dramatic. It was seconds before the crowd had realised the truth. A few moments later the game was over – Limerick defeated. So there he is, hurling-lovers Christy Ring, hero of Cork's record breaking hurling championships and, in my book, anyway, the hurler of 1944.

This is how his team-mate and great Cork defender, Din Joe Buckley, recalled that winning goal for journalist Tom Morrison. 'Christy got the ball out on the right wing about twenty yards from the sideline and he must have travelled at least sixty yards before hitting his shot. Joe Kelly came thundering in and harassed the Limerick goalie Malone while the ball went directly to the net.'

In 1946 Christy was about a quarter way through his hurling career. A long odyssey of hurling fame lay ahead of him. In a career in which he played something like 1200 games he won:

- 18 Railway Cup medals
- 8 All-Ireland titles
- 9 Munster crowns
- 4 National Leagues
- 14 county titles
- Caltex Award 1959
- Hall of Fame 1971

Like us all, he had more than one persona. Two of them contrasted starkly. In social situations he displayed shyness and was retiring. On the hurling arena he was a phenomenon – assertive, determined and hortative. Kevin Cashman summed it up well in an outstanding article on the maestro in the *Sunday Independent* of 31 December 1995.

> He would have been 75 years old in this year of tremendous hurling happiness. His would have been the most profound – and most reserved – happiness; for, except among truest friends, the immensity of his generosity and intellect remained well wadded in reticence. I'm not much good at speeches, he told the spellbound thousands who welcomed him and the MacCarthy Cup home to Cloyne, in 1946 – and proved it by shutting up four sentences later.

That changed utterly at every throw-in of a sliotar. He would exhort and goad his own, and seek to disconcert and down-face the other lot, with trenchant wit and colour.

He was one of three hurling men to captain his county to three All-Ireland successes – the others were Mikey Maher of Tipperary and 'Drug' Walsh of Kilkenny. And Christy was the only man to take the MacCarthy Cup three times:

1946 v Kilkenny – his fifth All-Ireland medal (7:5 to 3:8)
1953 v Galway – his seventh All-Ireland medal (3:3 to 0:8)
1954 v Wexford – his eighth All-Ireland medal (1:9 to 1:6)

Little wonder then that in Cork city there is a bridge over the River Lee called the Christy Ring Bridge. There is also a Gaelic Grounds named after him in the city. And in Cloyne, his native place, a 9ft high bronze statue honours him – 'will stand in his native town for hundreds and hundreds of years, an eternal and everlasting tribute to this great hurler'.

Duine sainiúil ab eadh Christy i stair na hiománaíochta. D'éag sé ar an dara lá de mhí na Márta 1979.

> *'Like the dew on the mountain,*
> *Like the foam on the river,*
> *Like the bubble on the fountain,*
> *Thou art gone; and forever!'*

The Corkmen of 1946 lined out as follows:

Tom Mulcahy

Willie Murphy (0:1)   Con Murphy   Din Joe Buckley

Paddy O'Donovan   Alan Lotty   Jim Young

Jack Lynch (0:1)   Con Cottrell

Paddy Healy   Christy Ring (1:3)   Con Murphy (2:0)

Mossy O'Riordan (2:0)   Gerry O'Riordan (1:0)   Joe Kelly (1:0)

Sean Kenny
TIPPERARY
1950

'At evening time in the old kiln field, you can see the boys so bold
'Twould remind you of old Knocknagow, in Kickham's story told
To see them wield their camáns, so brave and manfully
There's many a Matt the Thrasher 'mongst the lads of Fair Ileigh.'

Borrisoleigh won the Tipperary county senior hurling title for the first time in the history of the club in 1949. That victory paved the way for their captain Sean Kenny to lead the men of Tipperary in the All-Ireland senior hurling campaign of 1950. Sean was in his 27th year. His position on the county team was left half forward.

The previous year, 1949, under the captaincy of Pat Stakelum, he won his first All-Ireland medal when Tipperary had a facile win over Leinster champions Laois on the score 3:11 to 3 points.

The hurling in Sean's genes came from the distaff side. His mother, Kate Harty, was a sister of Patrick Harty who captained the Tipperary junior team when they won the All-Ireland title in 1930. When Sean donned the captain's jersey in 1950 he had clocked up a lot of hurling hours and a lot of leadership hours too. 'All my life, since a chap, I was captaining teams. I won Dean Ryan (under 17) and Dr. Harty (under 19) titles with Thurles CBS in 1939. In 1941 I was captain of the county minor team – the year of the Foot and Mouth disease. Cork beat us in the Munster final. I was captain of the county senior team in 1950 and again in 1951 until a knee injury in the game against Waterford sidelined me – but I came on as a sub in the All-Ireland final against Kilkenny in 1950 to replace my brother Paddy. Jimmy Finn was captain that day. I was captain when we beat New York in New York in the National League final of 1949/50. We only barely got there in the end – two points, I think. And I captained Munster to a Railway Cup title against Leinster in 1951.'

As captain, Sean was a man who inspired and motivated those around him. His courage was limitless and he despised cowardice in any player. His performances on the hurling field typified and embodied the spirit and steel of Tipperary hurling. 'It was in my nature going out to want to win. I always tried to urge the rest to do the same. No matter who we were playing I would always say – we'll beat them.'

Jimmy Finn, a contemporary and team-mate, had this to say about Sean. 'He was a man for whom I had great regard – he was powerfully strong – in Borrisoleigh he was known as 'the bulldozer'.'

The commitment and discipline that Sean brought to his training and fitness schedule was punishing. It was a programme that often started at 5 a.m. No wonder he had the reputation of being an iron man on the field.

Did you have heroes in your young days? 'Mick Mackey – he was the greatest ever in my book. I went into Thurles to see him. I watched him at centre forward. I used say to myself, if only I could play like him, I wish I could imitate him.' Were there others? 'No, that's it, Mackey was the greatest. I played in a Thomond Feis tournament one day in Limerick against him. It wasn't easy get a place on the Tipperary team then – politics – you had to belong to certain clubs. It wasn't until Borrisoleigh made the breakthrough that I established myself.'

The 1950 All-Ireland campaign, in which Tipperary set about defending their All-Ireland crown, involved the following games and results:

v Limerick (4:8 to 0:8) at Limerick
v Clare (2:13 to 3:7)
v Cork (2:17 to 3:11) at Killarney
v Galway (4:7 to 2:6) at Tuam (opening day of Tuam Stadium)
v Kilkenny (1:9 to 1:8) at Croke Park

Limerick were team building at the time and Tipperary's victory was never in doubt. Against Clare they were pushed to the limit, but survived, on a day when star defender Tommy Doyle got a belt of the sliotar and had to retire injured. Sean will never forget the game against Cork in Killarney. It was tense and tough and torrid, with the rivalries spawned in the 150-minute marathon in Limerick the previous year, adding to the fury of the occasion.

> That day we had a heavy game. The crowd came in around our goal. They were interfering with play and annoying Tony Reddan in goal. I went in around the back line to defend. Bernie Murphy, a big man and a fine clean hurler,

came thundering through for Cork. I faced up to him. It was chest to chest. I went straight for him. He broke my hurley with his neck. The referee gave a free in. The incident sparked off a big row but it only lasted a minute.

Ring came up to take the free. He was starring in Thurles long before I got on the Tipperary team. I was taunting him, telling him he wouldn't score, saying I'd kill him if he scored. Ring said to the ref., put him off, he's mad. I looked like a madman. I kept taunting. He drove the free wide. If he had got a goal we'd have lost.

Victory over Galway paved the way for an All-Ireland final meeting with Kilkenny on the first Sunday in September. Traditional rivalry was very keen between these two neighbouring counties. To date Tipperary had won 14 All-Ireland titles. Kilkenny were close on their heels with 13. Tipperary hadn't put All-Ireland titles back to back since the three in a row of 1898, '99, 1900. Now they wanted to do that and at the same time widen the gap of titles with Kilkenny.

'I had a good game that day but it was very close in the end. We only won by a point.' Tipperary looked in trouble at half time when, having played with a strong wind, they trailed by two points. It was then that the Tipperary mentors made a vital switch. They brought Sean Kenny to centre forward to mark Peter Prendergast who had been playing a stormer for Kilkenny. Kenny's energetic style inspired his colleagues. After the defeat of Kilkenny in the final of 1950 Sean's performance won him the honour of 'Sports Star of the Week' award in the *Irish Independent*. The caption beneath his photograph read – 'He played a real Leader's part and a couple of his efforts were worthy of Mick Mackey at his best.' Interestingly, a year later his brother Paddy – one of the great corner forwards of hurling – won the same award after Tipperary's All-Ireland victory over Wexford.

Sean's career at top level didn't last very long – cut short in the end by a chronic knee injury. However, in that short time he won all the major honours in the game. Though the career was short, his impact was lasting.

Jim Ware
WATERFORD
1948

'Beyond this place of time and tide
Beyond this hour of woe,
There is a bourn in Paradise
Where all the hurlers go.
And there in pride they're goaling
As they race across the sod,
To thrill our dead forefathers
On the level lawns of God.'

(Bryan McMahon)

It isn't widely known that the Ware family – one of the great family names in hurling – had its roots in Cork city before moving to Waterford. There were four brothers. Listed alphabetically they read Charlie, Jack, Jim and Murty. All were fine hurlers. However, of the four Charlie and Jim scaled higher peaks.

Charlie made his name as a fullback where he excelled for his adopted county and played with the cream of Munster in the Railway Cup competition in the early thirties. So great was his love for the game of hurling that he was into his mid forties when he won his last county title with his club Erin's Own in 1947.

Jim had a long and illustrious career in hurling. He was a brilliant goalkeeper, renowned for his long puck out and dependability under the dropping ball. He ranks with the greatest the game has produced in that position. For a span of almost twenty years, stretching to 1949, he was the Waterford custodian. He was chosen by the Munster Railway Cup selectors in 1944, '45 and '49. The province was successful on each occasion. Jim had the honour of being captain in 1949.

I met Jim at his home in Waterford city in 1983. 'My first proud memory was in 1931 when I was picked as a sub on the Munster team, which included many of the best men I have seen hurling . . . A lifelong ambition was achieved in 1948 when we beat Cork in a Munster final thriller and then went on to win Waterford's first senior All-Ireland against Dublin.'

Let's now look at the 1948 championship campaign and the Waterford might-have-beens of earlier times. The paucity of trophies on the Waterford sideboard did scant justice to the county's contribution to the game. The success list is short – All-Ireland minor title (1929); All-Ireland junior titles (1931 and '34); Munster junior title (1936).

In 1931 Jim was in goal when Waterford played Cork in a drawn and replayed Munster final. On both occasions Jim was superb and displayed marvellous skill. It was the spring of Jim's career. Waterford lost. Jim didn't know it then but he would have to wait until the late autumn of his hurling days to taste the ultimate in hurling glory.

In 1938 he wasn't in goal when Waterford failed to Dublin by 2:5 to 1:6 in the All-Ireland final.

Came 1948. Waterford selectors came up with a great blend of experienced veterans and youth. Jim Ware was father of the side. Mick Hickey, who was captain in 1938 and who was only recalled for the 1948 All-Ireland final, together with John Keane and Christy Moylan, were survivors from 1938. Andy Fleming had years of Railway Cup experience with Munster. Mick Hayes and army-man Vin Baston were accomplished and renowned performers.

Clare fell by the narrow margin of two points (4:8 to 5:3), at Thurles in the first round to Waterford. Limerick who had accounted for Tipperary fell to Cork. It would be Lee versus Suir in the Munster final. The odds were heavily stacked against Waterford. Statistically, it was David against Goliath; Munster titles 25 to 1 in Cork's favour; All-Ireland titles 16 to nil in Cork's favour.

As Waterford prepared for the Munster final, Jim used reflect on the '43 Munster final. 'We very nearly beat a very good Cork team. We could have won. We led at half time by 2:5 to 1:6. I suppose you could say tradition won the game for Cork. We had lots of chances but we missed more than Cork. In the end it was a deflected goal that beat us.'

The attendance at that Munster final was 15,000 and gate receipts were £1040. The game was refereed by Mick Hennessy of Clare. Jim Ware was in outstanding form in the Waterford goal but unfortunately for his county his brilliance wasn't enough to save the day.

In 1948 Cork got off to a flying start and went into a five-point lead. However, good play by Waterford saw them ahead after fifteen minutes and they were a point to the good at half time.

Jim Ware was playing brilliantly. He made two really magnificent saves in the first half from close range. The first was from Jack Lynch. The range was so close and the speed of the sliotar so fast that Jim's reflexes didn't enable him to react with sufficient swiftness to keep the sliotar from hitting him on the chest before he cleared. Soon afterwards he saved a rasper from Con Murphy – not Con the defender.

Entering the last quarter Waterford were eight points clear. However, in hurling such a lead can very quickly disappear. And so it nearly happened. In injury time Cork had cut the lead to a point. Ring got possession at midfield. Over the hour he had been well policed and contained by Johnny O'Connor. Now as the sands of time were running out he made ground with a solo run. He made ready to strike. As he did, a timely and well-directed shoulder from Mick Hayes was sufficient to cause the sliotar to veer inches wide of the upright. The puck out from Jim Ware brought the final whistle. Waterford had beaten the favourites. They had won their second Munster crown and their first since 1938.

An interesting feature of that game was the fact that both captains Jim Ware and Tom Mulcahy were the goalkeepers and Cork-born. To add to Waterford's joy their minor team defeated reigning All-Ireland champions Tipperary in the minor final by 3:6 to 3 points.

On Sunday 5 September Waterford, having disposed of Galway in the All-Ireland semi-final, faced Dublin in the All-Ireland final at Croke Park. Dublin had beaten Wexford, Laois and Antrim on their path to the final. It was clear from early on that there was no doubting the better team. Waterford held all the trump cards. They were in command throughout the field. Victory came more easily than the final score of 6:7 to 4:2 might suggest. The attendance of 61,430 paid £5302. When Con Murphy, of Cork fullback fame, blew the final whistle, Mick Hayes took possession of the sliotar. However, it was Jim Ware who took possession of the Liam MacCarthy Cup and raised it aloft in the Hogan Stand to the delirium of every Waterford fan in Croke Park. For the fans had in fact witnessed a double. The minor team defeated Kilkenny on the score 3:8 to 4:2 – their second such crown.

Jim recalled the homecoming and the welcome the team received. 'It was unbelievable. They say there were 25,000 there to greet us. The bridge was decorated with blue and white flags. There were flags everywhere. And there were six bands.' Then his wife Alice, who was a lovely hospitable lady and a great enthusiast, added 'we got a great deal of letters from Waterford emigrants from all over the world. It is impossible to describe the sense of joy and elation the '48 victory brought to those emigrants overseas. They wanted to hear and read about the men who brought honour to Waterford. They felt a sense of loss that they were not at home to share in a great occasion.'

On the occasion of my visit in 1983 Jim picked a team for me. I have just perused it. What a hurling combination! It would rank with any all-time great selection. Each name spells skill and hurling mastery and conjures up deeds of romance that add a glow to nostalgia.

This is his team:

Jim Ware
(Waterford)

Mickey Cross	Charlie Ware	Willie Murphy
(Limerick)	*(Waterford)*	*(Cork)*

Jim 'Builder' Walsh	John Keane	Vin Baston
(Kilkenny & Dublin)	*(Waterford)*	*(Waterford)*

Christy Moylan   Jim Hurley
(Waterford)   *(Cork)*

Christy Ring	Mick Mackey	Dinny Barry Murphy
(Cork)	*(Limerick)*	*(Cork)*

Josie Gallagher	Martin Kennedy	Jackie Power
(Galway)	*(Tipp)*	*(Limerick)*

What amazed me was the speed with which he made his selection. And he was definite about each position. Would you put Mickey Cross corner back, I queried. Yes, he'd play anywhere, was the response. When it came to the fullback berth he said, I couldn't pass my brother Charlie. At left half forward he chose Dinny Barry Murphy. I was conscious that John Maher of Tipperary (*Giants of the Ash*) had placed him at right halfback. Was he a halfback, I asked of Jim. He was, said Jim, but he was just as good a half forward. The three Waterford men he choose, John Keane, Vin Baston and Christy Moylan, were all delightful stick men and accomplished hurlers.

Ta gach duine den bhfoireann a roghnaigh sé imithe ar shlí na Fírinne anois. Solas na bhFlaitheas dóibh go léir.

These are the heroes of '48 that Jim captained and that will always have a special place in Waterford hurling history.

Jim Ware

Andy Fleming   John Cusack   Jackie Good

Mick Hickey   Vin Baston   Mick Hayes

Johnny O'Connor   Eddie Carew

Kevin O'Connor   John Keane   Christy Moylan

Willie Galvin   Ed Daly   Tom Curran

Dan Kennedy
KILKENNY
1947

'Hurling at its best is a beautifully balanced blend of silken skills and fierce man-to-man combat, a spectacle of sport that beggars description.'

(Paddy Downey)

When Thomastown defeated Carrickshock in the Kilkenny county senior hurling final at Nowlan Park on 10 November 1946 by 5:4 to 4:5 it opened the door for Dan Kennedy to captain the men in the black and amber the following year. That was Thomastown's first county success. For Carrickshock it was the third in a row disappointing defeat.

Dan subsequently won county medals with Dicksboro in 1950 and with Bennettsbridge in 1952, '53, '55 and '56. Victory in 1952 brought Bennettsbridge a second county title after a lapse of 62 years. It was a victory that heralded a golden era for the club and within the space of two decades Bennettsbridge annexed the remarkable total of 11 county titles. In addition to Dan Kennedy the club gave other powerful names to hurling – among them Johnny

McGovern, Seamus Cleere, Martin and Jim Treacy, Pat Lawlor, Paddy Moran, Mickey Kelly and Noel Skehan who incidentally is a nephew of Dan Kennedy.

Dan was in his third year of inter-county hurling when he captained Kilkenny in 1947. It proved to be a wonderful year for Dan and his county. After the memorable one point victory over Cork in the 'thunder and lightning final' of 1939 Kilkenny lost the next three finals they contested:

v Limerick 1940 (3:7 to 1:7)
v Tipperary 1945 (5:6 to 3:6)
v Cork 1946 (7:5 to 3:8)

However, in 1947 they would make amends. In the first round at Nowlan Park they overcame Wexford in impressive fashion on the score 5:11 to 3:8. The Leinster final against Dublin was played at Portlaoise. Short Jimmy Langton and Jack Mulcahy the Noresiders were just one point to the good at half time. However, with Dan Kennedy and his partner Jimmy Heffernan in the ascendancy at midfield, Kilkenny forwards went into overdrive in the second half. They added 4:7 to their half time tally and took the Leinster title on the score 7:10 to 3:8.

The All-Ireland semi-final against Galway was played at Birr on 27 July before an attendance of over 23,000. It was refereed by D. Costello of Tipperary. The game turned out to be a thrilling and controversial encounter. Galway led at half time by 1:5 to 1:4. In injury time they were still ahead by the same margin. The referee whistled for a free and Galway supporters took it to be the final whistle. They surged on to the pitch to cheer their heroes. But it was a false alarm. Play resumed when the pitch was cleared. In more time added on Kilkenny were rescued by points from Terry Leahy and Jim Langton. The final scoreline read Kilkenny 2:9 Galway 1:11.

The All-Ireland final on 7 September attracted a crowd of over 61,000 who were entertained to a classic contest laced with excitement and superb hurling exchanges, especially in the second half and most particularly in the last fifteen minutes of play that included six and a half minutes of injury time.

The long hitting Dan Kennedy had a fine game throughout the hour at midfield where he held sway. I have youthful memories of

109

that remarkable final. I lost a bet of 6/- (34c). Not yet into my teens I listened enraptured to Micheál O'Hehir's broadcast. His every word painted a vivid picture of what was unfolding at Croke Park.

I remember in particular the magnificent display of Jim Donegan in the Kilkenny goal; the subdued hour that was the lot of Christy Ring; the closeness of the scores at all times, which of course added to the tension and excitement; Kilkenny's policy of taking every point opportunity in contrast to Cork who sought goals that didn't materialise; the closing stages when Cork with two goals – the second in injury time – edged ahead on each netting and seemed to have stolen the game; finally the overall performance of the ice-cool Terry Leahy who scored six of Kilkenny's fourteen points – his fifth a pressure free that equalised matters in the dying stages and his sixth as he wheeled away from Alan Lotty to send over the winner on the call of time.

It was a breathtaking game that ended 14 points to 2:7 in Kilkenny's favour. It was their 13th All-Ireland crown and their fifth by the margin of just one point.

It was Dan Kennedy's greatest hurling moment – his first and only All-Ireland triumph. Proudly he collected the MacCarthy Cup to return it to the Noreside after a lapse of eight years.

Dan made his début in the Kilkenny jersey at the age of 19 in 1945. That year in the All-Ireland final against Tipperary Dan and his partner Jimmy Murphy were supreme at midfield, particularly in the second half. Unfortunately for Kilkenny their brilliance wasn't sufficient to halt a Tipperary team that led at half time by 4:3 to 3 points and thanks to the brilliance of their goalkeeper, little Jimmy Maher, were a little fortunate to win in the end by 5:6 to 3:6.

At half time in the All-Ireland final of 1946 against Cork, Dan was switched from midfield, where he was partnering Terry Leahy, to centre halfback in an effort to curb the genius of Christy Ring.

The following year against the same opposition Kilkenny historian Tom Ryall recorded that 'Dan Kennedy captained the side from midfield where he dominated.'

In 1950 Kilkenny looked to be in trouble midway through the second half of the Leinster final against Wexford at Nowlan Park when they trailed by 2:10 to 3:4. Then their mentors made a switch that turned out to be inspirational. They shifted Dan Kennedy from full forward to midfield where he proceeded to put the shackles on, an until then rampant, Jim Morrissey – a move that turned the tide in Kilkenny's favour and saw them win by 3:11 to 2:11.

Three years later in 1953 Kilkenny again faced the Model County in the Leinster final – this time at Croke Park. In a nailbiting encounter Nicky Rackard goaled for Wexford in lost time to cut the Kilkenny lead to just two points. The score then stood 1:13 to 3:5. There followed a 21 yards free to Wexford. Nicky Rackard stepped up to deliver one of his pile driver specials as Kilkenny followers closed their eyes and held their breath. But the Noresiders' defence was equal to the occasion and saved the 'Rackard Special' at the expense of a seventy. There was more agony for Kilkenny supporters until the seventy, which was taken by Jim Morrissey, was cleared and the final whistle sounded. However, amid all the drama and excitement of the occasion the Man of the Match accolade went to Dan Kennedy who gave a masterful display of vintage hurling.

For a closer insight into Dan I spoke with Johnny McGovern – a hurling gentleman and a Kilkenny stalwart who gave outstanding service to his county and province in a career that lasted a dozen years and during which time he won All-Ireland medals in 1957 and 1963 and Railway Cup honours in 1954. Johnny was a clubmate of Dan's and six years his junior. Dan's county career was drawing to a close as Johnny's began. This is how Johnny remembers Dan.

> He was an inspiration at all times; a driving force – full of determination; he oozed determination – before a match, at half time, on the field during a game; with Dan there were no half measures; everything he did was given total commitment – his hurling, his golf and his work as a salesman with Mosses. He never stopped going – he was full of energy. Colleagues, particularly in the club, looked up to him. He was a leader and a forceful one. He was one of the most determined people I ever knew. His enthusiasm was infectious.

Dan was at all times a wholehearted hurler. His performances were sterling and stout. He played the game with verve and enthusiasm. I always thought that the type of game he played reflected Tipperary steel rather than Kilkenny style. He was rarely outplayed.

He died young. Ní raibh sé ach breis is caoga bliain. Beidh ainm an iománaí seo ceangailte le Craobh na hÉireann 1947 go lá an Luain.

The men Dan captained in the memorable year of 1947 lined out as follows:

Jim Donegan

Paddy Grace   Paddy Hayden   Mark Marnell

Jimmy Kelly   Peter Prendergast   Jack Mulcahy

Jimmy Heffernan   Dan Kennedy

Tom Walton   Terry Leahy   Jim Langton

Shem Downey   Willie Cahill   Liam Reidy

Ned Kavanagh replaced the injured Peter Prendergast.

Jimmy Walsh
ANTRIM
1943

The year 1943 represented a new milestone in the history of hurling. 'Green Flag' writing in the *Irish Press* described the 1943 championship as 'a crazy affair' with results that would never again be repeated.

Not since 1925 had an Ulster team participated in the senior hurling championship. However, in 1943 the Ulster champions were brought back into the senior championship because due to emergencies associated with World War Two the junior and minor championships were suspended – 1942–1945 inclusive and 1942–1944 inclusive, respectively. This would have left Ulster with no hurling competition.

Galway, unopposed in the West since 1923, were the Connaught standard bearers.

Kilkenny defeated Dublin in the Leinster final (3:9 to 2:6) and won back the crown they last held in 1940.

In Munster, Cork had an easy first round win over Kerry. They were, however, fortunate to emerge as Munster champions following a two-point win – 2:13 to 3:8 – over a gallant Waterford fifteen in a very exciting Munster final – a victory that gave them a place in the All-Ireland final.

Up North, Antrim had a good win over Down, 6:8 to 2 goals, and were led by their 32-year-old captain Jimmy Walsh.

There now followed a succession of results that made the hurling world sit up and take notice.

In a quarter final game at Corrigan Park, Belfast, on 4 July Antrim defeated Galway by 7 goals to 6:2. It was a surprise result. Danny McAllister from Glenariffe scored four of those Antrim goals.

The semi-final against Kilkenny was played on 1 August – again at Corrigan Park, Belfast. The final score was a cause of disbelief. Another historic win for Antrim – 3:3 to 1:6. In the hurling world it was a major shock. Antrim captain, Jimmy Walsh, attributed the victory to a hard training schedule and a determination to win.

Antrim now faced Cork in the All-Ireland final at Croke Park on 5 September. It was a unique occasion – the first time since the championships began in 1887 that an Ulster team would contest a senior hurling final.

The odds favoured Cork, reigning All-Ireland champions and title holders for the two previous years. They had a powerful team of seasoned and battle hardened hurlers who had been together since 1939. They were a well-oiled hurling machine, having defeated Dublin in the All-Ireland finals of 1941 and '42 by 5:11 to 0:6 and 2:14 to 3:4 respectively. The county had thirteen All-Ireland titles to its credit.

Antrim had now lost the surprise element which was a decided asset against Galway and Kilkenny. As well as that they no longer had home advantage at Corrigan Park – a pitch where they knew every blade of grass and where they played with added confidence. And then of course there was the question of Croke Park nerves. The Antrim men had never played there before. Cork on the other hand had contested the All-Ireland finals of 1939, '41 and '42. Many of the Cork men had the experience of playing in Railway Cup finals in Croke Park.

Unfortunately for Antrim it all went terribly wrong on final day before, what was for then, a huge attendance of 48,843 spectators. They travelled in hordes from Antrim and among the attendance was the future Cardinal Conway, himself an Antrim man. A fairytale campaign ended with a heavy defeat – 5:16 to 4 points.

Amid the gaze of the hurling world the pressure was really on Antrim. They had come into the senior championship cold from junior level. The gap proved too great to bridge at Croke Park on final day. And furthermore Antrim really only had about six hurlers equipped with the craft and cunning to match the Corkmen.

In retrospect, a well-intentioned decision by the Antrim County Board was probably partly the cause of the huge defeat. St. Malachy's College in Belfast, with its gym and various facilities, was offered to the team and the County Board accepted. Collective training followed and the players were put up in a city hotel away from their natural habitat and constantly surrounded by enthusiastic supporters each offering their own bit of advice. It all added to the pressures of final day. The training programme that brought about the fall of Galway and Kilkenny would almost certainly have produced a more relaxed outlook on final day and possibly a lesser defeat.

Jimmy Walsh was the Antrim captain. He played at centre halfback and hailed from the O'Connell's Club in Belfast – named after Daniel O'Connell, the Liberator. He distinguished himself in the game against Kilkenny with a fine display on the classy Jimmy Langton.

Christy Ring, who
captained Cork to
All-Ireland hurling
titles in 1946, '53
and '54. He
became the only
man in the history
of the game to life
the MacCarthy Cup
on three occasions.

Christy Ring poised for
the strike in the famous
Boston Red Sox uniform
during a United States
tour in the fifties.

Dan Kennedy (*right*), the Kilkenny captain, with Sean Condon, Cork winning captain in 1944, kissing Dr Kinane's ring with Phil Purcell (*referee*), prior to the All-Ireland final of 1947.

Jim Ware – in 1948 he was Waterford's first All-Ireland winning captain.

Sean Kenny,
Tipperary's
captain, 1950

Nick O'Donnell – Wexford captain
in 1955 and 1960.

Nick O'Donnell, with the MacCarthy Cup,
chatting with Eamon de Valera in 1960, in
the Hogan Stand.

Five captains of victorious Kilkenny teams, all from Bennettsbridge. N. Skehan (1972), M. Kelly (1957), S. Cleere (1963), J. Treacy (1967). (*inset*) the late Dan Kennedy (1947).

Frankie Walsh in 1959 leading the
Waterford team in the
All-Ireland pre-match parade.

Frankie Walsh

Frankie Walsh with the
MacCarthy Cup.

Matt Hassett (*right*) and Christy Ring race against each other for possession in the 1960 Oireachtas final.

Gerald McCarthy 1966

Jimmy Doyle, one of hurling's greatest artists, who led Tipperary to All-Ireland victory on two occasions, 1962 and 1965.

Eddie Keher, captain of the victorious Kilkenny team in 1969. (*Courtesy of INPHO*)

Eamonn Grimes, 1973, Limerick's All-Ireland winning captain.

Billy Fitzpatrick, who led the Kilkenny team to All-Ireland victory against Galway in 1975.

Ger Fennelly (Kilkenny).

Sean Stack (*left*) captained Clare to National League honours in 1978 with two hurling superstars, John Joe Doyle, Clare captain 1932, and Noel Drumgoole, Dublin captain 1961.

In the All-Ireland final he had to cope with the wiles of Christy Ring and did well to hold him to four points.

Jimmy was also a very successful athlete – both as an amateur and a professional. He travelled the world. He won the Irish Senior Cross Country in Thurles in 1936 following which the O'Connell's Club marked the occasion by making him a presentation. After that he went to England and then to Australia where he won a three-mile world championship race. In 1939 he was runner up in the Irish ten-mile championship.

The victory over Kilkenny always remained his proudest hurling moment. Special too was the tremendous cheer that echoed around Croke Park as he led the Glens men in their saffron and white colours onto the pitch for the All-Ireland final against Cork. Prior to the game Jimmy and the Cork captain made a token exchange of gifts – tea to Mick Kenefick of Cork – butter from the south for Jimmy. It was of course an era of rationing due to World War Two.

In early June 2000 prior to Antrim's championship game with London Jimmy Walsh and Danny McAllister, octogenarians of 89 and 81 respectively, came together in Belfast to reminisce, discuss old times and recall 'battles long ago'. These were two of five surviving members of the 1943 team – the other three being fullback Kevin Murphy who had some hectic exchanges with Ted Sullivan of Cork, left halfback Paddy McKeown and left half forward Joe Mullan.

Let's now recall the Antrim lineout of 1943.

John Hurl
(Kickham's, Creggan)

J. Currie	Kevin Murphy	W. Graham
(Loughgiel Shamrocks)	*(O'Connells, Belfast)*	*(Oisians, Glenariffe)*
John Butler	Jimmy Walsh	Pat McKeown
(McQuillans, Ballycastle)	*(O'Connells, Belfast)*	*(Creggan)*

Jackie Bateson	Noel Campbell
(Mitchel's, Belfast)	*(Mitchel's, Belfast)*

P. McGarry	D. McKillop	Joe Mullan
(Loughgiel)	*(Glenariffe)*	*(Rosses, Belfast)*
Kevin Armstrong.	Danny McAllister	Sammy Mulholland
(O'Connells, Belfast)	*(Glenariffe)*	*(Loughgiel)*

The game was refereed by Dr. J.J. Stuart of Dublin who in 1958 was honoured with the Presidency of the GAA.

Jack Lynch
CORK
1942

> I think that hurling typifies the Irish character and tradition more than anything else, with the exception of our language. It has a combination of skill, courage, speed of thought and action, and calls for a spirit of give and take more than most games . . . Can anything be more racy of the soil – the game itself, the camán, the men who play it.
>
> (Jack Lynch in *Giants of the Ash* (1991).

Jack Lynch once told me that there were times in the thirties when he thought he would never win an All-Ireland medal. But that fear was laid to rest when Connie Buckley captained Cork to All-Ireland glory in 1941. On the 14 October of that year Glen Rovers took their eighth county title with a good win over Ballincollig. Accordingly, the mantle of captain for 1942 fell on the shoulders of Jack Lynch. He was by then a player of great experience, having played at inter-county level since 1935.

Born on 15 August 1917, he was christened John Mary, the youngest son of Dan and Nora (micheál O'Donoghue). He grew to manhood 'neath the bells of Shandon. He learned his hurling at North Monastery, Cork, where he captained the successful Harty Cup team. In due course he followed his older brothers, Theo, Charlie and Finbarr into the Glen Rovers Club.

This great exponent of the game of hurling was destined to become Taoiseach of his country. In that field, too, he left a lasting impression. Liam Cosgrave, a political opponent, who also held the prestigious office of Taoiseach, described Jack as 'the most popular politician in the country since O'Connell'.

Historian John A. Murphy once said: 'He had the common touch incomparably.' On social occasions, in the company of hurling friends and colleagues, it wasn't unusual for Jack to render a verse or two of 'The Banks'.

The day after Jack's death on 20 October 1999 T.P. O'Mahony writing in *The Examiner* said: 'Whether as a talented sportsman or, as some would have it, a reluctant politician, Jack Lynch possessed that most enviable of qualities. He was entirely likeable.

'Lynch was the perfect athlete, who aged with distinction to become a Taoiseach for whom power sometimes seemed a burden but was never a barrier to his relations with ordinary people.'

Little wonder then that the people of his native city honoured him by calling the tunnel under the River Lee The Jack Lynch Tunnel.

Back now to the world of hurling. The opening game of the 1942 All-Ireland championship presented Jack with the greatest challenge of that year's campaign. It was against Limerick and took place at Limerick Gaelic Grounds. The game was full of thrills and spills and first time hurling. Cork's left halfback, the late Jim Young, always claimed it was the greatest game of hurling he ever played in. If the first half was exciting, the second was breathtaking. Within the space of eight minutes in the second half spectators were treated to four cracking goals, as the pace of the game grew in intensity – two each to either side – via Dick Stokes for Limerick and Derry Beckett and Johnny Quirke for Cork. And so the excitement continued. Entering the closing moments Limerick notched an equalising point. And when it looked as if it would end in a draw, Charlie Tobin with a one-handed effort from well outfield sent over a point that left Corkmen with a lasting memory of a spectacular effort. Almost at the final whistle Sean Condon gave Cork a two-point winning margin.

It ended Cork 4:8 Limerick 5:3. It was a close call for Jack and his team in a game where the teams were level twice, Limerick led twice, but Cork led three times and most importantly of all were ahead when Mick Hennessy of Clare sounded the final whistle.

Tom Morrison, writing in the *Southern Star* following an interview with the late Jim Young who played with Cork that day, wrote in the course of his article as follows:

It was one of the most exciting finishes in the history of Cork/ Limerick championship tussles and the absorbing contest left the crowd speechless as the game was packed with incidents and thrills. Beyond a shadow of doubt and there can definitely be no argument about it, this was the greatest game of hurling I ever played in and 'The Match I'll never forget,' said Jim Young from

Dunmanway who played at left halfback on that occasion . . . 'I was on three different players that day – John Mackey, the late Ned Chawke, God rest him, and Dr. Dick Stokes. Everyone played it hard and skilful and there were very few stoppages.' The day was perfect for hurling and the Gaelic Grounds exploded into a torrent of cheers and acclamation as Mackey's Shannonsiders made a dramatic exit from the Munster championship.

A few weeks later Jack faced Tipperary in the Munster final, acutely conscious that even though Cork were All-Ireland champions they had been rather surprisingly beaten by Tipperary in the delayed Munster final of 1941. The game was level pegging at half time (1:7 to 3:1). However, in the second half Cork took command and a final score of 4:15 to 4:1 confirmed their superiority, with Tipperary registering just one score – a goal.

In the All-Ireland semi-final against Galway at Limerick on 26 July, Cork had an easy win in a game that ended Cork 6:8 Galway 2:4. Now for a final showdown for the second year running against Dublin on 6 September.

Came the day. As Jack led his team in the pre-match parade around Croke Park, his mind, no doubt, went back to the final of 1939. He was captain that day too when they lost to Kilkenny by a point, scored with the last puck of the game by Jimmy Kelly of Carrickshock; an epic contest played throughout the second half in thunder and lightning and torrential rain; a game that Jack remembered more facets of than any other game in his long and illustrious career. He had a Munster medal from 1939 and an All-Ireland medal from 1941. No doubt, he hoped that by the final whistle he would have two of each.

Cork defended the railway goal in the first half. Jack operated at midfield with Paddy O'Donovan. For three quarters of the game Dublin did surprisingly well; three points behind at half time; one point adrift with a quarter of an hour to go. But then Cork's all round ability and class, coupled with the accumulated experience of recent years, began to tell. Their composure, allied to fast controlled hurling, led to several scores and they ran out winners on the convincing scoreline of 2:14 to 3:4. Jack, at midfield, contributed three of those points. It was Cork's thirteenth title. It was one of Jack's proudest days. He had captained a great team that was destined for greater heights.

When I was writing *Off the Field and On* which contained an article entitled 'The Day Jack Lynch Won his Football Medal', I decided to write to his wife, Maureen, to ask what memories she had of football final day 1945. In a lovely reply she wrote 'I do not know very much about Jack's early years. I am really sorry that I cannot help you.' She went on to say that Jack had been unwell.

I then decided to send Mrs Lynch a copy of the article I had written. In due course she responded and I noted for the second time that she possessed that rare gift of writing a delightful letter. I quote in part from her response to my article:

'I was very interested in the article you wrote about Jack . . . It was a lovely piece . . . You tugged my heart strings and made me feel sad – but very happy. When Jack is a little better I will read your article again and again to him – his memory is very short – as I know it will give him great pleasure.'

The 1942 Cork team captained by Jack Lynch lined out as follows:

Ned Porter

Willie Murphy   Batt Thornhill   Con Murphy

Alan Lotty   Din Joe Buckley   Jim Young
(0:1)

Jack Lynch   Paddy O'Donovan
(0:3)

Christy Ring   Sean Condon   Mick Kennefick
(0:3)   (0:2)   (0:2)

Charlie Tobin   Johnny Quirke   Derry Beckett
(0:1)   (1:2)   (1:0)

Connie Buckley
CORK
1941

'Where we sported and played, 'neath each green leafy glade,
On the banks of my own lovely Lee.'

On Sunday 9 September 1940, Glen Rovers captured their seventh Cork county senior hurling title by defeating Sarsfields on the score 10:6 to 7:5. It was a seventh in a row.

Connie Buckley, who as a schoolboy starred with 'North Mon' and captained a Munster Dr. Harty Cup team, was a key figure in all of those remarkable successes. Mighty teams fell before the hurling power of 'The Glen' – St. Finbarr's, Sarsfields, Carrigtwohill, Midleton and Blackrock.

Connie's brother Jack was part of the success story from 1935 onwards. And in 1938 a third brother, Din Joe, joined them to share in the glory of The Glen.

The 1939 defeat of history-laden Blackrock in the county final was probably their most celebrated success. An attendance of over 20,000 was treated to a superb contest – one of the greatest in Cork hurling. The final score was Glen Rovers 5:4 Blackrock 2:5. Connie and Jack were magnificent at midfield.

Club success was one thing but within the county, in hurling circles, there was an element of disquiet. It was being said that 'The Glen' triumphs in Cork were not being converted into All-Ireland titles for the county. During those years of glory in The Glen, Cork only contested two Munster finals.

The first was in 1939. It was a clash of Titans – Cork v Limerick. The game was an epic from start to finish. Level at 2:2 each at half time, Limerick held a one-point lead entering the final moments. Then a Cork movement saw Ted O'Sullivan finish the ball to the net. Cork supporters went wild. Soon the final whistle sounded. It heralded victory for Cork on the score 4:3 to 3:4.

They fell to Kilkenny at the last hurdle in Croke Park on 3 September. In a classic game Kilkenny stole it by one point with the last puck of the game. Cork's hour had not yet come.

The second Munster final was 1940. Again it was Cork and Limerick. Another clash of Titans. For drama and excitement it surpassed the 1939 encounter. It lasted longer too; a draw and a replay. Cork's cup of woe continued. Limerick edged them out on the score 3:3 to 2:4. 'The Glen' may have been in the ascendancy in Cork but they had yet to bring home the Liam MacCarthy Cup.

That was the challenge facing Connie Buckley when he was chosen as Cork's captain in 1941. He had under his command experienced and battle-hardened campaigners. Twelve of them were there when Kilkenny pipped them at the post in the thunder and lightning final of 1939. Fourteen had done battle in the Munster championship of 1940. They knew what it was to play in teak tough tests.

The key games of 1939 and 1940 are worth recalling briefly.

1939

v Waterford (7:4 to 3:2) at Fermoy

After being two points ahead at half time Cork pulled away in the second half to register a convincing, if somewhat unexpected, win over the reigning Munster champions and All-Ireland finalists before an attendance of 22,000.

v Limerick (4:3 to 3:4) at Thurles

Cork fielded the same team that beat Waterford. Connie Buckley was at midfield with Jack Barrett from Kinsale. Jack Lynch at right half forward was captain. A crowd of 40,000 was held spellbound for the entire hour. This was hurling that beggared description.

v Kilkenny (3:3 to 2:7) lost

Apart from the injured Paddy O'Donovan, who replaced Willie Tabb, Cork again fielded the same team. The attendance at just over 39,000 matched the year. Cork were blending together well. But it was still a case of so near and yet so far.

1940

v Tipperary (8:9 to 6:4) in the National League final

v Tipperary (6:3 to 2:6)
v Clare (7:6 to 3:5)
v Limerick (3:6 to 4:3) draw
v Limerick (2:4 to 3:3) lost

Cork were edging closer and closer to that coveted All-Ireland crown. However, they had yet to travel that extra mile. For Connie Buckley it was now a case of whither 1941.

Cork in 1941 were seasoned, well established and growing in confidence. And they knew where their greatest threat lay. It lay with Limerick and Kilkenny, the two outstanding teams of the decade of the thirties; the two teams that had thwarted them in the previous two years.

Then two things happened that changed the nature of the 1941 All-Ireland championship. The first occurred on 19 February when Paddy Mackey, younger brother of Mick and John of Limerick fame, died unexpectedly. In keeping with the custom of those days Mick and John played for neither club, county nor province for twelve months. Paddy Clohossey, star Limerick and Munster centre halfback, retired prematurely at 31 from the game.

The second event followed shortly afterwards. It was an outbreak of the virulent Foot-and-Mouth disease. Carlow in football, and Kilkenny and Tipperary in hurling were hardest hit. In Leinster, as recorded by that great Kilkenny GAA historian, the late Tom Ryall, in his book *Kilkenny, the GAA Story 1884–1984*: 'Kilkenny were drawn against Laois in the first round, but because of the Foot-and-Mouth outbreak they could not play and were given a bye into the Leinster final. The Department of Agriculture brought out an order that Kilkenny could not play in the Leinster final, until the county was three weeks clear of Foot and Mouth. The result was that Dublin were nominated to represent Leinster in the All-Ireland Hurling semi-final.' They played Galway at Roscrea on 14 September and disposed of the western challenge by 2:4 to 2:2. (A delayed Leinster final was played in November with Dublin defeating Kilkenny by 2:8 to 1:8.)

In Munster a postponed Tipperary v Waterford game, fixed originally for 1 June, was eventually played on 27 July. Tipperary won. They were now scheduled to play Cork in the Munster semi-final at Limerick on 17 August. However, six days before the game the Department of Agriculture issued instructions that the game be called off.

Limerick had earlier beaten Clare. The Munster Council decided that Cork and Limerick should now meet to decide who would advance from Munster to play in the All-Ireland final. The winners, it was decided, would play Tipperary later on in the year to determine the Munster titleholders.

Cork, National League champions since the spring for the second year in a row, and Limerick met on 14 September at Cork Athletic Grounds. Unfortunately, the epics of 1939 and 1940 were not repeated. Limerick, down three goals after ten minutes and minus Mick and John Mackey and Paddy Clohossey, fell to the might of Cork on the score 8:10 to 3:2.

The All-Ireland final between Cork and Dublin took place at Croke Park on 28 September. It was the sixth meeting of the counties in an All-Ireland final. The score to date stood at three to two in Cork's favour.

Travel restrictions, due to 'The Emergency' brought about by World War Two, kept the attendance down to 26,150; half the figure for the Limerick v Kilkenny final of 1936. Coal was very scarce. Train schedules were unpredictable. Petrol was rationed. And yet there were enthusiasts who cycled and walked huge distances to witness the game.

I met Connie Buckley when I talked with his brother Din Joe (featured in *Hurling Giants*) in September1993. He remembered the championship of 1941 as being 'a strange one. We had only to play two games to win the All-Ireland. We were very fit. Dublin couldn't match our speed and combination. I remember they won the toss and played against the wind. The game wasn't long on when Willie Murphy – you remember him, long puck Willie we used call him – pucked the ball out to the Dublin 21 yard line. Johnny Quirke met it – 'twas in the net – just two strokes. We never looked back. We won very easily; one of the easiest ever.' The final score was 5:11 to six points.

'The Cup was presented to me by Fr. McGouran, a President of Belcamp College. I was proud for 'The Glen' and for Cork.'

It was Cork's first All-Ireland title since 1931. Connie Buckley had led his county out of the hurling wilderness. He had, without realising it at the time, opened the door to a great run of four in a row All-Ireland successes – a record that still stands unequalled.

On 14 October 1941 Glen Rovers, led by Connie Buckley, won their eighth in a row county title. Connie was the only player to figure in all eight successes.

Two weeks later, 28 October, at Limerick Gaelic Grounds, Tipperary sprung a surprise by defeating All-Ireland champions Cork in a delayed Munster final by 5:4 to 2:5. But it mattered not – 'the prize we sought is won'.

Earlier in the year at the St. Patrick's weekend, the honour of leading his province to Railway Cup victory eluded Connie when Munster minus Mick and John Mackey lost to Leinster on the score 2:5 to 2:4.

Connie Buckley retired from the game of hurling, after a distinguished career, following defeat by Ballincollig in the Cork county championship of 1942.

These are the men Connie captained to victory in 1941.

Jim Buttimer

Willie Murphy   Batt Thornhill   Alan Lotty

Willie Campbell   Con Cottrill   Din Joe Buckley

Sean Barrett   Jack Lynch

Christy Ring   Connie Buckley   Jim Young

Johnny Quirke   Ted O'Sullivan   Micka Brennan

Subs: Paddy O'Donovan replaced Jack Lynch. James Ryng replaced Micka Brennan.

Mick Mackey
LIMERICK
1936 & 1940

In our part of Kerry we had a special love for Mick Mackey because we looked on Limerick as our hurling county. And we loved him for another reason – because he played with such obvious enjoyment. He took his craft seriously but not solemnly. He could laugh and joke on the field . . .

He gave the world far more that ever it gave him but he didn't worry too much about that . . .

He was a modest broadminded man who liked honest praise but was embarrassed by adulation.

I met him last about a year ago and it was obvious that he wasn't very well and I was loath to speak to him. But his splendid wife insisted that we come together. I will cherish the memory.

Con Houlihan – *Evening Press*

Mick Mackey, son of John 'Tyler' and May (née Carroll), was born on 12 July 1912.

Thanks to his ancestry, hurling skills, physical strength, courage and daring coursed through his veins. He had a temperament that was suited to the game and was the hurling phenomenon of his time. Ned Maher of Tubberadora, a Tipperary goalkeeper in the 1890s, declared 'Mick Mackey was the greatest hurler ever and I saw them all.'

His grandfather, Michael, captained the Castleconnell team in the infancy days of the GAA. In the open draw championship of 1887 he travelled to Dublin with the Castleconnell team to play Kilkenny. Due to a dispute within the county at the time – there were two county boards – a team from Murroe also travelled. A number of suggestions were made to resolve the matter. Unfortunately, none proved successful. Both teams returned home. Kilkenny were given a walkover.

His father, John, known as 'Tyler' since the day he purchased a new pair of stylish shoes in Tyler's shop in Limerick city, was among the leading hurling personalities of the first two decades of the twentieth century. His career lasted from 1901 to 1917. He captained Limerick in the All-Ireland final of 1910 when they failed to Wexford by one point on the unique and unusual score of 7 goals to 6:2. The following year he was again captain. Controversy regarding the venue led to Limerick refusing to play at Thurles rather than Cork with the result that Kilkenny were conceded a walkover in the All-Ireland final. After a long and illustrious career during which he failed to win an All-Ireland medal it was rather ironic that the year after he retired, Limerick had a resounding 9:5 to 1:3 win over Wexford in the 1918 All-Ireland final.

Mick's day of captaincy glory came in 1936. He was magical. It was a year in which he displayed all the power, speed, imagination, vision, composure, flamboyancy and daring that made him such an inspirational leader.

Reporting on Limerick's 8:5 to 4:6 victory over Tipperary in the Munster final the *Irish Independent* had this to say: 'If one man more than another is deserving of credit for bringing victory to Limerick, it was Mick Mackey, who was here, there and everywhere, and contributed no less than five goals and three points to the winners' total score . . . His initial essay as skipper of the side was marked by a marvellous display of hurling in which he rampaged from end to end of the field, opening up an attack or stemming a raid as necessity arose . . . while some of the scores that came as a result of his solo efforts were gems of constructive work.'

As Mick led his Limerick team – trained to the ounce – in the pre-match All-Ireland parade, one can only speculate as to what thoughts occupied his mind. Perhaps he thought of his grandfather Michael and his father John and vowed to succeed where they had failed. He may have glanced at Paddy Larkin as he led great Kilkenny names in the famed black and amber. And no doubt he was thinking of the previous year 1935 when in atrocious weather conditions Kilkenny and Limerick served up a classic and Limerick failed by one point. The story is told that Mick was asked what would have happened if it had been a draw in '35. In reply, with an impish smile and a ring of devilment in his voice, he said 'We'd have murdered them the second day.'

Jim O'Regan of Cork was in charge of the whistle and got the game underway. After a highly entertaining first half, Limerick held a narrow two-point lead 2:3 to 1:4. At this stage many foresaw the game developing into a titanic struggle that would rival the 1935 encounter. None could have foreseen what was about to unfold. With Mick continuing his star role and directing operations from the centre forward position, Limerick went into overdrive in the second half. They were rampant throughout the field. Kilkenny could only score one point. Limerick added 3:3.

The final score was Limerick 5:6 Kilkenny 1:5. It was a glorious occasion for Mick. He had led a superb team to a great victory.

Writing in *An Gaedheal*, 'Vigilant' had this to say. 'The men from the Shannonside fielded a combination of players that beyond all shadow of doubt proved itself to be one of the greatest hurling teams that Ireland has ever seen. It is a great all-round team with a back division that was almost literally unbeatable. I have seen and written about all the leading camán contests over a stretch of thirty years, and I can honestly say that I never saw a team better that this year's All-Ireland champions.'

Limerick, under Mick Mackey, lined out as follows:

Paddy Scanlon

Paddy O'Carroll	Tom McCarthy	Mick Kennedy

Mickey Cross	Paddy Clohessy (0–1)	Garrett Howard

Timmy Ryan   Mick Ryan

John Mackey (0–1)	Mick Mackey (0–4)	Jim Roche

Dave Clohessy (2–0)	Paddy McMahon (2–0)	Jackie Power (1–0)

Four years later, Mick was leading Limerick around Croke Park again. Kilkenny, reigning All-Ireland champions, led by Jimmy Langton, provided the opposition. Nine of the Limerick team of '36 were still in action. In the curtain raiser the Limerick minors took the title with a victory over Antrim. Mick Mackey was now in search of a Limerick double.

John Joe Callanan, a former Tipperary hurling star, set the game in motion. Limerick defended the canal end in the first half. Kilkenny set a blistering pace and had 1:1 on the scoreboard before Limerick settled and responded. It was close hard hip to hip stuff. By half time Kilkenny held a 1:4 to 1:2 lead and faced the second half with their backs to a brilliant sun. Mick Mackey moved from centre forward to midfield. He roamed the pitch and was the hero of the hour. Gradually Limerick took control. Paddy Scanlon in goal was brilliant and got great protection from his fullback Mick Hickey. Paddy Clohessy at centre back gave one of his greatest ever displays. Timmy Ryan at midfield added to his stature. In the forward line there were class displays from Dick Stokes, Jackie Power and John Mackey. The game ended 3:7 to 1:7 in Limerick's favour. Mick became the seventh captain to lead his county to more than one All-Ireland success.

It was a hard-won title as the campaign hereunder shows:

v Waterford (4:2 to 3:5)
replay (3:5 to 3:3)
v Cork (4:3 to 3:6)
replay (3:3 to 2:4)
v Galway (3:6 to 0:5)
v Kilkenny (3:7 to 1:7)

The Limerick lineout –

Paddy Scanlon

Jim McCarthy   Mick Hickey   Mick Kennedy

Tommy Cooke   Paddy Clohessy   Peter Cregan
                              (0:1)

          Timmy Ryan   Jim Roche
              (0:1)

John Mackey   Mick Mackey   Dick Stokes
    (1:0)   (0:3)   (1:0)

Ned Chawke   Paddy McMahon   Jackie Power
                                                  (1:2)

'I went back in 1940 to the final once again.
This time our brave Kilkenny met Mick Mackey and his men.
With the mighty Paddy Clohessy and midfield Timmie Ryan.
But Kilkenny couldn't match them and wound up two goals behind.
Jack Mulcahy and Jim Langton were the Black & Amber's best.
But the Mackeys, Stokes and Power were the men who stood the test.'
The old man reached to lift his glass and he made this proud remark.
'I'm glad that I was there to see Mick Mackey in Croke Park.'

(John Duggan)

The late Micheál O'Hehir of broadcasting fame held a special
affection and warmth for Mick Mackey. In a newspaper article he is
quoted as saying 'when I was growing up, Mick was my hero . . . He
was a great leader of the Limerick team, a very strong hurler and a
great character – there was a charisma about him. The word "great"

128

is thrown about like snuff at a wake, but the Limerick team of the 1930s and the 1940s – they deserved it.'

In the fifties P.D. Mehigan (Carbery) picked 'The Best Men of My Time'. Of Mick he had this to say: 'And the 40 yards mark on my hurling team, surely and without question, belongs to that "Playboy of the Southern World" – Munster's pride and Limerick's glory – the one and only Mick Mackey! For a combination of skill and power, of brains and brawn, the Castleconnell man, son of the great 'Tyler' Mackey, brought joy and thrills galore to thousands.'

My abiding personal memory of Mick centres around my visit to him when I was writing *Giants of the Ash*. At the time he was recovering from an illness. After he had autographed his page in the leather-bound journal in which I was assembling the handwritten recollections of players, I suggested to Mick that he record a special memory. He remained silent. Pensively he gazed for some seconds on the page in which he was about to write. Then, without lifting his eyes, he said in a quiet voice, tinged with melancholy, 'It's all memories now.'

> *'Oh God, please grant when this life I'll yield;*
> *That in Heaven you'll have a hurling field.*
> *With goalposts white and a green field grand –*
> *And sunny days and a good pipe band.'*
>
> (J. Ryan)

Lory Meagher
KILKENNY
1935

'Over the bar, said Lory Meagher'

Dan Hogan, nephew of Lory, showed me the passport that was issued to Lory prior to the Kilkenny team's departure to the United States in 1934.

This excerpt from it reflects the historical and political position of Ireland in those days.

We Patrick McGilligan Esquire, Minister for External Affairs of the Irish Free State, request and require in the name of his majesty George V King of Great Britain, Ireland, and the British Dominions beyond the seas, Emperor of India, all those whom it may concern to allow the bearer to pass without let or hindrance and to afford him every assistance and protection of which he may stand in need.

Other details were as follows:

Profession	farmer
Domicile	Irish Free State
Height	5'11"
Eyes	blue
Hair	black
Face	thin

Lory Meagher was born in 1899 and christened Lorenzo Ignatius. The name Lorenzo had been in the Meagher family for generations. A grand uncle named Lorenzo was a naval doctor.

Lory's father, Henry, was born in Tullaroan, the second smallest parish in the diocese of Ossory, in 1865. He is believed to have attended the inaugural GAA meeting in Thurles in 1884.

Lory had three brothers, Henry, Frank and Willie, all of whom played with Kilkenny in the 20s. Henry emigrated to America and figured on the U.S. Tailteann team of 1928. Father Frank, after ordination to the priesthood, went to Australia where he became the dean of a diocese. In the 1926 All-Ireland final against Cork, Lory, Henry and Willie all played for Kilkenny. Victory, however, went to Cork.

Of the four brothers Lory was the one destined for hurling immortality. He was a legend in his playing days and his fame echoed throughout the land. The hurley was an extension of himself and he gave expression to all that was delightful in hurling with his displays at midfield where, so often, he reigned supreme.

Tall, slim and hawk-like in appearance, he was equally adept at overhead and ground play. His delightful performances reflected a wide range of hurling artistry. He belonged to a small band of outstanding hurling men who possessed an almost flawless relationship with the sliotar. He could steal a score from far out in days when scores were hard to come by and a point from midfield could be worth a king's ransom and an inspiration to team mates. Little wonder that Limerick's star mid-fielder Timmy Ryan used to say of Lory 'you couldn't give him an inch or it was over the bar'. For there were many occasions when the hurley in Lory's grasp seemed to have an intelligence of its own.

In private life Lory was shy and retiring. He never married. He avoided the limelight and was known to give journalists the slip from time to time. Fame, when linked to publicity, weighed heavily upon him.

In 1935, eleven years after his county senior début against Dublin at Portlaoise, Lory, with the big wide shoulders and very long back and arms, was thirty-six years of age – an age when most inter-county hurlers would have retired from inter-county fare. On Sunday 1 September he led Kilkenny onto the pitch at Croke Park and gave a display in the All-Ireland final that came to be regarded as his greatest hour in the black and amber.

On the way to the final Kilkenny defeated:

Offaly (7:7 to 2:6) at Portlaoise
Laois (3:8 to 0:6) at Portlaoise
Galway (6:10 to 1:8) at Birr

Kilkenny were a seasoned and battle-hardened combination. They had entered the 1935 campaign with Leinster titles in 1931, '32 and '33 and All-Ireland titles in 1932 and '33 to their credit. Great names adorned their ranks. Hurling was second nature to them.

Their hot-favourite opponents were Limerick, undefeated in 35 games over two years, reigning All-Ireland and National League champions whose path to Croke Park was as follows:

v Cork (3:12 to 2:3)
v Tipperary (5:5 to 1:4)

Limerick were on a roll as they set forth into the 1935 championship. They had under their belt two Munster titles from 1933 and '34 and one All-Ireland crown from 1934. They were playing a delightful brand of hurling. They were drawing the crowds. A Kilkenny enthusiast returned from the games in Munster and proclaimed

131

'there's no stopping these Limerick chaps'. Their names were now legendary.

Paddy Scanlon, Ned Cregan, Tom McCarthy, Mick Kennedy, Mickey Cross, Paddy Clohessy, Garrett Howard, Timmy Ryan, Mick Ryan, John Mackey, Mick Mackey, Jim Roche, Jackie O'Connell, Paddy McMahon and Jimmy Close.

A hurling classic was in prospect. A record crowd of 46,591, for any GAA match up to then, thronged Croke Park. The rain came down in torrents. It fell during the entire game. Despite the awful conditions the teams served up an epic contest.

Lory, wily old warrior that he was, had done his homework well. Prior to going onto the pitch he said to his men, with reference to the sliotar, 'keep it on the ground, pull first time, keep it moving'.

He was a hurling strategist. He knew that those tactics coupled with the wretched weather conditions, would benefit Kilkenny.

He brought to bear on his display that day at midfield all the cunning and craft and artistry of a lifetime devoted to hurling. His matchless ball control and myriad of skills were invaluable to Kilkenny as he directed operations from midfield and like a magician did the ground work for vital scores as he guided the sodden sliotar over the rain-drenched pitch, sending intelligent and beautifully placed passes to his forwards.

After a thrill-a-minute first half the score stood at Kilkenny 1:3 Limerick 1:2.

Early in the second half Limerick equalised. There followed ten minutes of hectic exchanges without a score. Then Lory, from midfield, sent over a magnificent point for the lead – a lead Kilkenny never lost. Martin White added a point. Then Lory took a sideline cut and landed it in Martin White's hand. He turned and drove to the net 'and even the great Scanlon could not save that goal of goals' – Kilkenny five points up, ten minutes to go.

Croke Park was now no place for weak hearts as Limerick added a goal via Paddy McMahon and a point via Mickey Cross to cut the deficit to one point. They battered the Kilkenny defence in search of an equaliser, or a winner. Mick Mackey led the charge. A rock-like Kilkenny citadel stood firm. Tommy Daly sounded the final whistle. The scoreline read Kilkenny 2:5 Limerick 2:4. Great men won and great men lost.

'And they'll oft retell the story
Of the glory that was Lory's
When Meagher graced the black and amber
Of Kilkenny by the Nore.'

Lory's team of 1935 read as follows:

Jimmy O'Connell

Paddy Larkin   Peter O'Reilly   Peter Blanchfield

Ned Byrne   Padge Byrne   Paddy Phelan

Lory Meagher   Tommy Leahy
(0–1)

Jimmy Walsh   Jack Duggan   Martin White
(0–2)   (1–0)   (1–0)

Johnny Dunne   Locky Byrne   Mattie Power
                                                              (0–2)

Timmy Ryan
LIMERICK
1934

'Then Timmy Ryan at centre-field,
You heard his name before,
His prowess at the ancient game
Is known from shore to shore.'

I still have fond memories of my visit to Timmy Ryan in the autumn of
1980. He was then seventy years of age. To distinguish the Ryan clan,
which densely populated many parishes in Limerick and Tipperary,
each family had a nickname. Timmy was known as 'Timmy Good-Boy'.

Timmy radiated warmth, friendliness and gentlemanliness. His
abiding memories of his hurling years centred in the main around
the sheer enjoyment he got from playing the game, the people he
met, the friends he made, the friendships that endured and the
countless hours spent in the evenings in the local pitch, until dusk
called a halt to proceedings.

Those were the days when many a hurler 'spied that bend of growing ash', cut it down and 'shouldered home the 'soople' tree'. Then began the shaping of the hurley to suit the wielder, the paring and planing and finally the test as the finished product was held in the hands, swung left and right to ensure that the grip, weight and balance were in tune with the owner's requirements. And satisfied that all was well under those headings the 'spring' was tested. Sometimes there followed a coating of linseed oil. When the hurley broke it was spliced and hooped and mended. For a hurley was an extension of the wielder, each in tune and harmony so as to demonstrate the variety of skills associated with the ancient game of the Celt. In the making of hurleys Timmy was no exception. He made and repaired his own and always had a few spare ones.

> 'Oh! Cut me a hurl from the mountain ash
> That weathered many a gale,
> And my stroke will be lithe as the lightning flash
> That leaps from the thunder's flail;'

It was in the Munster championship of 1930 against Tipperary that Timmy made his début in the green and white jersey of Limerick. A colleague on the team that day was Tom Slattery of Pallas, father of Fergus of international rugby fame.

Timmy was one of the greatest midfielders the game has known. He was a master of the delightful art of overhead striking and in this facet of the game he was without peer. He was known to have doubled on puck-outs and sent the sliotar over the bar. He was a master of every stroke. He played the sliotar first time as it came to him – overhead, shoulder high, or on the ground. He always felt that too much lifting and handling the ball took away from the game of hurling as a spectacle.

Timmy spent his entire career in the midfield position and turned in consistently brilliant performances. He had the reputation of being scrupulously clean and sporting and was known to delay or halt his pull on the sliotar to avoid hurting an opponent.

In build he had a strong, rangy, sinewy frame. Within it there was strength and stamina and staying power. He had a great engine too – powered by a dynamo that generated massive levels of energy. Little wonder, as Garrett Howard told me, that his colleagues used to call him 'the horse'.

Timmy's hurling skills were honed, initially, in the Ahane colours. Ahane won their second county senior hurling title in 1933 with a 1:7 to 1:1 win over Croom. That victory paved the way for Timmy to captain Limerick in 1934, the Jubilee Year of the GAA. A special set of All-Ireland medals was struck for the occasion. Every hurling county wanted to win them.

Timmy told me that 'my special memory of matches was to captain the Limerick team in the Jubilee Year of the GAA' to All-Ireland success.

In assuming the captaincy he was acutely conscious of the events of 1933. Limerick had made the breakthrough in Munster that year after a lapse of ten years and faced Kilkenny in the All-Ireland final. It was the year of Johnny Dunne's famous goal for Kilkenny – the only one of the game. Kilkenny won by 1:7 to 6 points. One commentator wrote, 'they (Limerick) won the day in practically every section of the field save the one that mattered most . . . the scoreboard'. Timmy Ryan always maintained that 'inexperience cost us dearly in 1933'. He was determined to go one better in 1934.

So let's look now at the background to a championship campaign that consisted of six very testing games before Limerick emerged as All-Ireland champions. Before the championship began Timmy had the following positive results to reflect on:

- 17 March, Railway Cup final, Munster 6:3 Leinster 3:2. Timmy was captain of the Munster team and six more Limerickmen helped Munster to victory – Paddy Scanlon, Ned Cregan, Tom McCarthy, Mickey Cross, Paddy Clohessy and Mick Mackey. Paddy Scanlon was superb in goal. Paddy Clohessy was the outstanding man on the field. Timmy Ryan himself had a slight edge over the great Lory Meagher. Mickey Cross, now a veteran, added to his great reputation.
- 25 March, National League final at the Gaelic Grounds before an attendance of 10,000 people who paid gate receipts of £435. Limerick 3:6 Dublin 3:3. John Mackey stood on a plane apart in this game.
- 21 May, Whit Monday. Monaghan Cup Final at Woolwich Stadium, London – Limerick 5:4 Kilkenny 4:5.
- 3 June at Croke Park, Áras na nGaedheal Tournament final for a set of medals presented by Hospitals Trust Ltd. Limerick defeated Dublin.
- 7 June, Thomond Feis Final – Limerick 3:6 Cork 3:4.

135

When the 1934 Championship began Timmy Ryan knew he was leading a team that was on a winning roll. They were winning in tight finishes and extricating themselves from tight corners. They were being moulded into a cohesive unit and were gaining in confidence. The games ahead would be a test of steel and resolve and hurling craft.

Now to the Jubilee championship. Clare presented the opposition in the opening game at the Gaelic Grounds on 24 June. The brilliance of Paddy Scanlan in the Limerick goal kept Clare at bay in the first half when it seemed as if the Dalcassians might spring a surprise. But when Limerick settled and took a grip on the game they finished with a convincing win on the score 6:4 to 3:2.

Limerick then faced Cork in the Munster semi-final at Thurles. Timmy Ryan knew this would be a tough one. In the Thomond Feis final Cork, playing excellent hurling, had led by five points at half time and in the end only lost by two points.

Two goals in the opening quarter, via Jackie O'Connell, gave Limerick a cushion for what lay ahead. And they needed it. For this was eye-ball to eye-ball stuff – no flinching on either side in what was a test of steel. Five minutes into the second half Micka Brennan sent Cork supporters wild with delight when he netted the equalising goal. The score stood at 2:2 apiece. It remained that way for twenty minutes more as the tide of battle ebbed and flowed. Every effort, Herculean at times, brought no reward on the scoreboard to either side. Now five minutes remain. The sides are still deadlocked at 2:2 each. Supporters of both sides are tense with excitement.

Then the break came. It favoured Limerick. Mick Mackey in possession sent to Dave Clohessy and the green flag waved. Cork had wilted and in the minutes remaining the Mackey brothers, Mick and John, whipped over points and Limerick with a five-point victory were on the way to a Munster final meeting with Waterford.

In the game with Waterford at Cork it took until the third quarter for Limerick to assert their authority and win in the end by 4:8 to 2:5. The team was then led in triumph to the Victoria Hotel, by the Boherbuoy band, where celebrations ensued.

The All-Ireland semi-final against Galway at Roscrea proved to be a very tough assignment. Limerick's growing capacity to survive in tight finishes came to the rescue and in the final ten minutes they clinched the issue with scores that gave them a winning scoreline of 4:4 to 2:4.

Dublin presented the final barrier to the Jubilee medals. Their credentials were very good. After a Leinster final draw they defeated reigning All-Ireland champions Kilkenny in the replay by 3.5 to 2.2. They were regarded as one of the finest and fittest teams ever to come out of Leinster.

Timmy Ryan was aware of this and while confident that he could lead his team to victory he was conscious that but for John Mackey they would have lost the league title to Dublin.

Notable absentees on league final day, Tom McCarthy, Paddy Clohessy and Dave Clohessy were now back in the lineout and therein lay a decided plus.

An attendance of almost 35,000 had gathered for the All-Ireland final by the time Stephen Jordan of Galway set the game in motion. Limerick led by a point at half time. Despite having a goal disallowed in the second half, Limerick appeared to have the game won when entering the last minute they led by a goal. It was then that Dinny O'Neill struck for his second goal of the day and the 1934 All-Ireland hurling final was taken to a replay.

The replay was fixed for Sunday 30 September. In preparation for the game the Limerick mentors secured the services of Cork trainer Jim Barry. He concentrated on first-time ground hurling. When all was in readiness for the big day a bombshell hit the Limerick camp. Star goalkeeper Paddy Scanlan went down with a poisoned finger. Into the team was drafted former Limerick and Munster goalkeeper, Tommy Shinny of Fedamore. He gave a superb performance.

At half time the teams were level – low scoring – Dublin 3 points, Limerick 1 goal. With five minutes remaining it took a third goal by Dave Clohessy, following a high delivery into the Dublin square by Timmy Ryan, to level matters again for Limerick. It began to look like 1931 all over again – a second draw and a third game.

But it wasn't to be. Two minutes remained – the teams still level. Mick Mackey struck and sent over the lead point. Fortune favoured Limerick in the final seconds. Jackie O'Connell – tormentor in chief of Cork in the Munster semi-final – sent over another point to be followed by Dave Clohessy's fourth goal of the day. At the final whistle the score was Limerick 5:2 Dublin 2:6 in a game where there was no place for either handymen or players with flaws of the spirit.

Great men won and great men lost. One reporter summed it up well – 'The game was one sweep of clinched courage.'

And Carbery wrote, 'In the 35 hurling finals I have seen, never a one approached last Sunday's in uniform thrill, in speed, in magnificent ground play . . . What struck me most about this game, as compared with the great finals of the past, was the power and quality of the ground hurling . . . It was a finish for the gods.'

Now came Timmy Ryan's greatest hurling moment as Archbishop Harty, Patron of the Association, presented him with the MacCarthy Cup in the Jubilee Year of the GAA. And when the train carrying the team drew up at Limerick railway station, they were met by an enthusiastic gathering of 20,000 people who joined with the Boherbuoy Band in a rousing rendering of 'Garryowen'.

The Limerick team lined out as follows:

Tommy Shinny
(Fedamore)

Ned Cregan
(Newcastlewest)

Tom McCarthy
(Fedamore)

Mick Kennedy
(Young Irelands)

Mickey Cross
(Claughaun)

Paddy Clohessy
(Fedamore)

Garrett Howard
(Portroe)

Timmy Ryan
(Ahane)

Mick Ryan
(Murroe)

John Mackey
(Ahane)

Mick Mackey
(Ahane)

Jim Roche
(Croom)

Jackie O'Connell
(Croom)

Dave Clohessy
(Fedamore)

Jimmy Close
(Ahane)

Paddy Scanlan and Bob McConkey played in the drawn game.

For Timmy there was an epilogue to 1934.

He was captain again in 1935. He believed Limerick could make it two in a row that year. In May, at Nowlan Park, in one of the classic games of hurling history, Limerick retained their league title with a narrow 1:6 to 1:4 win over Kilkenny.

They retained their Munster title – a third in a row – with convincing and decisive victories over Cork and Tipperary – 3:12 to 2:3 and 5:5 to 1:4 respectively.

Now to the final against old rivals Kilkenny. They too looked formidable. In the Leinster final they beat Laois 3:8 to six points and in the All-Ireland semi-final Galway fell heavily at Birr 6:10 to 1:8.

Hurling fans expected a classic final. And they got it, all 46,591 of them – the largest attendance up to then that Croke Park had ever seen. The rain came down in torrents. Yet, these hurling gladiators from Nore and Shannonside served up a breathtaking epic.

With time running out Kilkenny, under the glorious leadership of Lory Meagher, held a one-point lead. Limerick were awarded a twenty one yard free. What followed left a memory Timmy could never erase.

In a talk with Con Healy published in the *Limerick Association Yearbook* of 1991, Timmy had this to say about those dying seconds. 'Dr. Tommy Daly of Clare was referee and as he placed the ball he said to me, as he was entitled to do, that time was up and that I had to score directly. As captain I decided to take responsibility myself, although Mick Mackey mostly took the close-in frees. Mick came up and claimed it. I left it to him. He failed to rise the wet ball sufficiently to strike it over to level the match. Time was up then and our chance had gone. The rest is history often indeed bent in the telling.'

This is how the moment was recalled by Tom O'Riordan in an article in the *Sunday Independent* of 29 December 1985, following an interview with Timmy.

> At the time Mick Mackey and Ryan would alternate between taking frees and as Timmy Ryan ran towards the ball to line it up for the free the referee, the late Tommy Daly of Clare, gave his jersey a little tug and said 'Timmy, you know what to do with this.' However, as Ryan was about to bend over the ball, Mick Mackey came up from behind, pushed him away and said 'It's ok, Timmy, I'll take it.' The outcome is enough to make it the one disappointing memory in Ryan's hurling career. Mackey failed to lift the ball and Kilkenny survived by one point. 'What really annoyed me was that I knew we would beat them in the replay,' reckons Timmy, who was captain on that occasion. 'It still rankles with me.'

Is it any wonder then that when I met Timmy he should have said to me, 'My regret was that we should have won in 1935.' It was the thought still uppermost in his mind.

Eudi Coughlan
CORK
1931

'I always wanted to be a Blackrock hurler.'

Blackrock, a fishing village in bygone decades, is located about two miles down the river Lee from Cork city. The parish has given many outstanding names to hurling lore. Among them are Jim Hurley, Johnny Quirke, 'Balti' and 'Gah' Aherne, Gerry and Mossie O'Riordan, Ray and Brendan Cummins, John Horgan, Sean Óg Murphy, Pat Moylan, Dermot McCurtain, Mick Cashman and his sons Tom and Jim, Paddy Delea and Jimmy Brohan.

However, in many ways, perhaps the greatest name is Coughlan (in Cork it is pronounced 'Cawlan'). One member of that clan is Eugene, known to all hurling followers as Eudi. He hurled with Cork from 1919 when he was a sub in the All-Ireland winning team until 1931 when he led his county to a memorable and historic win over Kilkenny following which he collected his fifth All-Ireland medal.

He won National League titles in 1926 and 1930; was chosen on the Tailteann games team of 1928; represented Munster in the Railway Cup competition from inception in 1927 to 1932 inclusive, missing out only in 1930 (was victorious in 1928, '29 and 1931); was selected by popular opinion in 1961 on a Gael-Linn Best Ever Team as wing forward.

What made this tall, spare, athletic figure of a man such a wonderful exponent of the ancient game of hurling? A glance at his forbears is most revealing.

His grandfather had five sons – Pat, Denis, Dan, Jerh and Tom.

Pat was Eudi's father. At 5'11" he was a fine build of a man. As a hurler he was one of the outstanding backs of his era and was a master of strategy, strong and fearless. He won All-Ireland medals in 1893 and 1894. He was known as 'Parson'.

Denis, known as Lyonsie, was a six footer plus – a splendid figure of manhood who won an All-Ireland title in 1894. He was a gentle, kindly and sensitive person. He accidentally injured a colleague and friend, as both pulled on a dropping ball. The injury proved to be fatal. So much to heart did Denis take the death of his friend that he slowly pined away and died.

140

Dan, better known as Big Dan, was a great wingback and highly skilled with the camán. He stood over 6' and was immensely strong with a massive chest and shoulders. In a Cork county championship game he was seen to lift the ball and with the fall of the ground and wind in his favour he drove it 140 yards. He won All-Ireland hurling titles in 1892 and 1902. He later emigrated and was lost to hurling.

Jerh, known as Big Jerh, was a quiet, shy, unassuming man of 6' plus. He didn't play much hurling in his young days but when he did take it up seriously he was good enough to be a very effective centre forward and won All-Ireland honours in 1903.

The youngest of the brothers was Tom — known to all as Honest Man. He measured five feet ten and a half and turned the scales at thirteen stone. Centreback was his position and masterly he was in that demanding berth. He won All-Ireland titles in 1902 and 1903.

All five were hardworking men and set the highest standards in sportsmanship and good behaviour.

Carbery summed them up as follows: 'All favoured the back positions, where their strength and accuracy were of full purpose. Parson was, perhaps, the toughest man; Dan was the longest hitter; Denis was a neat, sweet striker and nimble too; Tom, the youngest, perhaps combined the art of all. The Coughlans were born leaders of men.'

Eudi's mother was a Dorney. Her brothers, William known as 'Bill Bill' and Michael known as 'Down Down', were both prominent in Blackrock and Cork hurling.

Little wonder then that Eudi was the hurler that he was. The game was in the genes and in the blood. An rud a bheirtear sa chnámh is deacair scarúint leis sa bhfuil.

I had the pleasure of meeting Eudi at his home in Blackrock in 1981. He was eighty-one years of age. 'Hurling was my life,' he said to me. I wondered if he would select a team from the great men of his era. His wife gently interjected to say he wouldn't do that. Too many good men, I thought to myself, and to name fifteen would devalue the others. Nor would Eudi mention one hurler above another. He gave parity to all hurling men.

He didn't hide his dissatisfaction with aspects of the present day game. 'The game was faster in my day. You didn't play around with the ball. If you didn't get rid of it quickly you got a flake off a man and the ball was flaked away from you. You had a man to mark and that was your job. It was hard honest hurling – you took it and gave it and that was it – and you got on with the game.'

Eudi could cope with hardship. His father had a fishing business. As a youngster Eudi rowed a boat on the River Lee. He toiled picking mussels and then prepared them for despatch to Liverpool – 'hard work'. Later he was employed by Fords – 'hard work too' – before getting a job with the Cork Harbour Board.

Eudi's county senior hurling career began in 1919. He was a sub on the team that beat Dublin in the All-Ireland final of that year. In the twenties he had further All-Ireland successes in 1926, '28 and '29. His array of hurling talents and speed on the wing made him stand apart. He was captain in 1930 but Cork fell to Clare in the Munster championship.

Then came 1931. Eudi was captain again. It was the year that the name 'Cumann Lúthchleas Gael' was first used and that a score effected directly from a sideline puck was allowed. Cork were destined to meet Kilkenny in the final. It would take three games to decide the issue. Since the championships began the counties had met in six finals. The score stood at four to two in Kilkenny's favour. And three of those Cork losses were by just one point.

Kilkenny's path to the 1931 final was as follows:

v Wexford (8:8 to 1:1)
v Meath (5:9 to 1:2)
v Laois (4:7 to 4:2)
v Galway (7:2 to 3:1)

The news of the victory over Galway reached Kilkenny Post Office around 5 p.m. and a large gathering greeted the news with enthusiasm. Cork had to play four games to reach the final. They were, however, far tougher and more demanding encounters.

v Clare (3:4 to 1:6)
v Tipperary (3:5 to 2:3)

This clash attracted a capacity crowd of 30,000 spectators. It was a typical Tipperary-Cork confrontation – tense, tough and torrid. In the early minutes Tipperary goaled. Paddy Delea equalised for Cork. Eudi Coughlan followed with two great goals that sent Cork supporters wild. It was three goals to two goals at half time. The second half was hectic. Eudi contributed two points.

142

v Waterford (1:9 to 4:0)

Waterford supporters were agog as their hurling men found gaps in the Cork defence to lead at half time by 3 goals to 5 points. In a close-marking second half Cork gradually narrowed the gap. Eudi scored their only goal of the hour and towards the end he pointed a seventy to leave Cork just one point behind. Deep into time added on Jim Hurley equalised for Cork. It was due in the main to Eudi's artistry – he cut close-in frees over the bar off the ground – that Cork survived to fight a second day.

v Waterford (5:4 to 1:2) replay

Cork learned from the drawn game. Their defence was tight. They spread the ball wide and opened up play. It paid dividends.

The All-Ireland final took place on 6 September. A magnificent contest, as it turned out. In the replay against Waterford Eudi received a nose injury that made him a doubtful starter for the final. But when the day arrived he was there to do duty for Cork. He excelled. A point from an acute angle while on his knees in the second half is still recalled in hurling lore. His display saved the day for Cork.

Eudi was brilliant in the replay. However, it was in the second replay on 1 November that he played the game of his life – considered by many to be the greatest of his career – and he played many great ones.

Details of the three games are as follows –

6 September (Cork 1:6 Kilkenny 1:6) Attendance 26,460
11 October (Cork 2:5 Kilkenny 2:5) Attendance 33,124
1 November (Cork 5:8 Kilkenny 3:4) Attendance 31,935

After the first replay officials pressed for extra time. But Eudi, canny and experienced old veteran that he was, wasn't having any of it. He knew Kilkenny were a younger team and were likely to have more in the reserve tank.

It was suggested at a meeting of Central Council that both counties be declared joint champions. On a vote it was defeated by 10 to 5. If the proposal had been successful a suggestion made in some quarters that a half medal be given to each player would have come up for consideration.

In appreciation of the outstanding contribution made by the players of both teams Central Council presented them with a watch each.

On the occasion of my visit to Eudi he took from the top of the glass case the three sliotars used in the 1931 finals. He handed them to me. There was a certain sensation in handling the sliotars used fifty years earlier in a unique GAA occasion. Inscribed on each was the relevant scoreline. For Eudi the sliotars were a cherished possession. Having replaced them he produced a miniature gold hurley which was presented to each member of the Cork team.

Eudi was a religious man. He knew the limits of human endeavour. After Cork's great All-Ireland triumph of 1931 he offered thanksgiving to the Sacred Heart in the Messenger.

He was also a stubborn man. He took umbrage at the action of the Cork County Board in taking from his club, Blackrock, the selection of the county team in 1932. 'That finished my time for Cork. I never put on a red jersey for them again.'

This is the team Eudi captained in the historic final of 1931.

John Coughlan
(Blackrock)

Morgan Madden   E. 'Marie' O'Connell.   Paddy 'Fox' Collins
(Redmonds)   *(Blackrock)*   *(Glen Rovers)*

Dinny Barry Murphy   Jim O'Regan   Tom Barry
(Eire Óg)   *(Eire Óg)*   *(Carrigtwohill)*

Mick O'Connell   Jim Hurley
(St. Finbarr's)   *(Blackrock)*

Eudi Coughlan   Paddy 'Balty' Aherne   Peter 'Hawker'
(Blackrock)   *(Blackrock)*   O'Grady
                                                      (Blackrock)

Paddy Delea   Willie Clancy   Michael 'Gah' Aherne
(Blackrock)   *(Mallow)*   *(Blackrock)*

George Garrett of Blackrock came on as a substitute in both replays, for Morgan Madden and Peter O'Grady respectively.

'If you wanted a hurler you'd find him for sure,
Ballinlough, Ballintemple, and around Ballinure,
I don't care what you say but give me the old stock,
And stand up and hurl with the boys of Blackrock.

Can you equal the Coughlans, the Ahernes, the Sheas,
Scannell, Cremin, Curtis, and match Stephen Hayes,
I can mention their names from the round of the clock,
The men that won credit for Cork and Blackrock.'

Dinny Barry Murphy
CORK
1929

'Grant me, O Lord, a hurler's skill,
With strength of arm and speed of limb.
Unerring eye for the flying ball
And courage to match what 'er befall.'

(Seamus Redmond)

In boxing parlance, Dinny Barry Murphy, physically speaking, was a lightweight. But in the ancient art of hurling he was a super heavyweight – all-time great material. He was a wonderful sportsman and a gentleman on and off the field.

No wonder then that some admirer felt prompted to express this little piece of doggerel about him:

'Dinny Barry Murphy, boy
Great hurler, boy
He'd take the ball out of your eye, boy
And he wouldn't hurt a fly, boy.'

John Maher, the great Tipperary centre halfback of the 1930–'45 era, described him as 'the complete hurler'. He was equally at home on the wing in either the halfback line or the half forward line. When John Maher selected his team for me, his halfback line read: Dinny Barry Murphy, Jim O'Regan, Garrett Howard.

Dinny Barry Murphy had two absorbing passions in the sporting world. These were hurling and greyhounds. And where greyhounds were concerned his deep interest extended to both track and coursing.

He played in the historic three games of the 1931 All-Ireland final against Kilkenny. The second game produced super hurling, played at great speed. Referring to the early stages of that game, he is reputed to have said that the pace was so hectic that for a while he didn't quite know what was happening and added that it was no place for handymen.

147

Dinny Barry Murphy was born of farming stock in 1904 and in his hurling days turned the scales at 10st. 6lbs. and measured 5' 8". In the professional world he was an employee and director of Cork Farmers Union Ltd – a meat processing company. He received his secondary education at St. Finbarr's, Farranferris, and played on all the top college teams. He played club hurling from 1922 to 1942, beginning with his home club Cloughduv. His county senior career stretched from 1926 to 1935 inclusive. It was a productive innings. It coincided with a golden era in Cork hurling, the county's second in the history of the Association and the first in the twentieth century. Provincial honours, All-Ireland titles, National League triumphs and Railway Cup successes all flowed in abundance during those years. And the name Dinny Barry Murphy adorned the hurling scene.

The following is a brief history of his playing career.

- Won an All-Ireland junior hurling title with Cork in 1925
- Won four All-Ireland senior titles (1926, '28, '29 (Capt) 1931)
- Won two National League titles (1926 and 1930)
- Had six Railway Cup successes, out of eight successive appearances with Munster and was captain in 1930
- Played in the Tailteann games of 1932
- Played with Cloughduv (1922–1926), junior hurling
- Played senior with Blackrock in 1927 and won the county title
- Played senior with Eire Óg in 1928 and won the county title
- Played senior with St. Finbarr's (1932–1936)
- Resumed with Cloughduv (1937)
- Won mid-Cork junior titles (1938 and 1939)
- Won county Cork junior title 1940
- Won county Cork intermediate title (1941)
- Played senior in 1942 championship – he was 38 – his last playing season

When Eire Óg beat Mallow in the Cork county senior final of 1928, it opened the door for Dinny Barry Murphy to captain Cork the following year. He was succeeding a great captain in Sean Óg Murphy, who according to Martin Kennedy of Tipperary full forward fame was, 'the best fullback who played the game'.

Dinny Barry Murphy led great men in 1929. Cork had won the Munster titles of the three previous years and had converted 1926 and 1928 into All-Ireland crowns. Prior to that they had experienced famine times. Having won a sixth All-Ireland title in 1903 they didn't win again until 1919.

The road to victory in 1929 read as follows:

v Tipperary (3:4 to 2:1) at Cork
v Waterford (4:6 to 2:3) at Dungarvan
v Galway (4:9 to 1:3) at Croke Park

It was a campaign in which Cork were never really threatened. Experience and a rock-like defence were key factors in the 1929 success that brought Cork a third title in four years.

After the Munster semi-final against Tipperary Carbery commented as follows:

> The hurling was fierce but not foul – a struggle without poisoned gas. Men crashed into one another. One, two, three, four men went down in sequence. Virile manhood was manifested in all its power and glory. Willie Gleeson – the referee – knew his men well and let them flake away. It was great to see Cork and Tipperary hurlers engage in friendly conversation as they walked to their dressing-rooms when the fray was over.

A gallant Waterford effort, led by Charlie Ware at fullback who fronted his brother Jim in goal, failed to halt a rampant Cork who made it four Munster titles in a row.

Galway, whose hurling fortunes in recent times had been on a downward curve, fell to the Munster champions in the All-Ireland final at Croke Park on 1 September before an attendance of 18,000. Cork defended the railway goal in the first half and for a time withstood fierce Galway pressure. They had on occasions to give way in some stirring exchanges. However, Cork's class, combination and experience gradually began to tell. They led at the break by 3:3 to 1:2 and only conceded one point in the second half to the Tribesmen. The final whistle heralded a tenth All-Ireland crown for Cork. The MacCarthy Cup, via Dinny Barry Murphy, was on its way to the Leeside for the third time.

I owe a debt of gratitude to Con Murphy, a former Cork hurling great of the forties, for much of the information in this article. Dinny

Barry Murphy was an uncle of Con's wife, Tess. Tess's mother died when she was very young and she was reared in Dinny Barry Murphy's home where her aunts and uncles resided. In Con's words 'she was reared on hurling stories'.

Dinny Barry Murphy died in 1973 aged 69.

This is the team he led to victory in 1929, in likely lineout format.

J. Burke

Morgan Madden   E. 'Marie' O'Connell   Paddy 'Fox' Collins

Dinny Barry Murphy   Jim O'Regan   Tom Barry

Mick O'Connell   Jim Hurley
(0:3)

Eudi Coughlan   Peter 'Hawker'   Paddy 'Balty'
(0:2)   O'Grady   Aherne

Michael 'Gah' Aherne   John Kenneally   Paddy Delea
(0:3)   (2:1)   (2:0)

Mick Gill
DUBLIN
1927

'Fada siar mo smaointe,
Páirc fhada réidh leathan!
Na hiománuithe ag rith is ag iomarscáil,
Ag tabhairt fé an liathróid bheag bheodhach.'

(Cairbre)

Mick Gill was a vastly experienced hurler when he led his adopted Dublin team around Croke Park on the 4 September 1927, prior to the All-Ireland final against Cork. He had leadership qualities and the mantle of captain rested lightly on his shoulders.

So let's now trace Mick's career up to that point. He was born in Ballinderreen in south Galway in 1899 – a parish that had a hurling tradition prior to the founding of the GAA in 1884.

In his youth he displayed natural talent. At the age of eighteen he played with the local junior club. He progressed from there to the senior team. He began as a defender before eventually making his name as a brilliant midfielder. In his playing days he measured about 5'10' and turned the scales at 13st. 4lbs. He had a powerful physique and that allied to a fine turn of speed and great stamina made him an ideal midfielder. He also had a reputation as a good accurate free-taker.

Mick played his first All-Ireland championship game with his native Galway on 26 August 1923 in Galway. It was the occasion of the 1922 All-Ireland semi-final against Tipperary. He played at right halfback that day and despite his polished and highly impressive performance Galway had to yield to the Munster champions on the score 3:2 to 1:3. It is of interest to note that due to a heavy downpour the referee took the unusual step of stopping the game for a period of fifteen minutes.

Mick grew in stature in subsequent games. He was very much to the fore in Galway's defeat of Kilkenny in the All-Ireland semi-final of 1923, played at Croke Park on 18 May 1924. Kilkenny were reigning All-Ireland champions and Galway's victory of 5:4 to 2:0 was an indicator of the quality of the western team. Indeed, Galway held Kilkenny scoreless until the last quarter of the game when Mattie Power and John Roberts took the bare look off the scoreboard with a goal each.

There was an air of confidence in the Galway camp when, following a vigorous training schedule, they faced a very fancied Limerick fifteen in the All-Ireland final of 1923. It was played at Croke Park on 14 September 1924. Mick at midfield was Galway's outstanding performer. He made a major contribution to Galway's surprise victory of 7:3 to 4:5 over a Limerick team that was at the time a major force in Munster hurling and had captured All-Ireland honours in 1918 and 1921.

Prior to the 1923 All-Ireland semi-final against Kilkenny Mick had joined the Garda Síochána and was based in Dublin. He was, however, eligible to play with his native Galway in the 1923 championship. No declaration rule existed at that time, so a player could only play with the county in which he was resident.

It was this combination of circumstances that led to Mick being eligible to play for Dublin, and only Dublin, following the

All-Ireland final of 1923 which was played on 14 September 1924. The Metropolitan selectors were, of course, only too delighted to have a man of Mick's calibre available to them.

Dublin victories over Offaly in the Leinster final and Antrim in the All-Ireland semi-final on 9 November booked them a place in the All-Ireland decider. In the second semi-final on 23 November at Croke Park, Galway accounted for a strong and talented Tipperary fifteen. It was close – just one point in it – on the score 3:1 to 2:3. These semi-final results led to a first ever final pairing of Dublin and Galway. Mick Gill now found himself playing against his native Galway and former 1923 colleagues in the All-Ireland final of 1924. The game was played at Croke Park on 14 December 1924. Dublin won a closely contested game by 5:3 to 2:6, after being in arrears at the interval 2:6 to 3:0. Galway's scoreless second half was due in the main to a dazzling performance by Tommy Daly in the Dublin goal, while Mick Gill, now in the Dublin jersey, gave a quality performance for his adopted county.

The victory brought Mick his second All-Ireland medal within the space of three months and in the same calendar year. It established a record, unique to Mick. He was now, for the time being at any rate, a Dublin hurler.

In 1925 his adopted Dublin fell victims to the 'punctuality rule' when, after defeating Kilkenny in the Leinster final by 6:4 to 4:7, they were stripped of their provincial crown following a Kilkenny objection.

In 1926 Dublin made an early exit from the championship but they returned with a bang in 1927. Kilkenny fell in the Leinster final by 7:7 to 4:6. This victory earned Dublin a place in the All-Ireland final against firm favourites and reigning All-Ireland title-holders Cork who had legendary names in their ranks – among them, Sean Óg Murphy, Dinny Barry Murphy, Jim Hurley, Jim O'Regan, Paddy Delea, Eudi Coughlan, Mick Leahy, 'Marie' O'Connell, 'Balty' and 'Gah' Aherne.

As Mick Gill proudly led his team of non-native Dublinmen around Croke Park on a lovely sunny autumn afternoon, it is unlikely that he would have harboured any fears of the opposition. He was captaining very fit athletic men – nine from the Garda club and three from Army Metro.

He would very likely have reflected on the fact that on the previous St. Patrick's Day, Leinster, with nine of the Dublin team (he

152

himself at midfield with the Kilkenny maestro Lory Meagher), had defeated Munster with eight of the Cork team, in a classic game of hurling, in the Railway Cup final on the score 1:11 to 2:6.

With Dublin defending the railway goal, Dinny Lanigan of Limerick got the All-Ireland final of 1927 under way. Dublin set the pace from the throw-in and with Tommy Daly in goal giving an inspired performance, the men from the capital city led at the interval by 2:3 to one point. Dublin continued to dominate in the second half and at the final whistle, were worthy and convincing winners on the surprise scoreline of 4:8 to 1:3.

Mick had been an outstanding captain and contributed four points to the Dublin tally. Victory gave him his third All-Ireland medal. He became the second Galway man to lift the MacCarthy Cup and the first to win three hurling medals.

In the mid-twenties Wills Cigarettes issued a series of what we used call 'Fag Pictures'. The series honoured fifty hurlers of that time. Mick Gill was one of them. The commentary on the back read as follows: 'At present captain of the civic guards, whom he led to victory in the county championship, Mick first came to prominence while assisting his native Galway to win the All-Ireland final in 1924. Of powerful physique and with youth and speed on his side, he is ideally equipped for the strenuous duties of centre field. He places his vanguard with strategic passes and on frees and seventies is a deadly marksman. Always a favourite with the Dublin Selection Committee. Won All-Ireland with Galway 1923 and again with Dublin in 1924. Height 5'10". Weight 13st. 4lbs.'

Mick was regarded as one of the greatest and most consistent midfielders of his era. This view was confirmed in 1961, following a Gael-Linn poll, when he was chosen at midfield with Lory Meagher on 'The Greatest Hurling Team Ever'.

Honours, subsequent to 1927, that came Mick's way included:

- Being selected every year until 1931 for Leinster, losing on each occasion to Munster.
- Chosen on the Tailteann Games team of 1928.
- National League title with Dublin in 1929 when Cork were defeated.
- National League title with his native Galway in 1931 when Tipperary went under. The Declaration rule was then in vogue and Mick had just declared for his native Galway.

153

D'imigh Mick ar shlí na Fírinne i 1980 in aois bliain is ceithre scór. Ach tamaillín sular éag sé, is mór an gliondar croí agus an t-aoibhneas a bhain sé as an mbua a bhí ag a Ghaillimh dhúchais, ar Luimneach, i gcluiche Chraobh na hÉireann ar an gcéad Domhnach de Mheán Fómhair na bliana sin.

The team Mick led in 1927 lined out as follows:

Tommy Daly
(Clare)

Joe Bannon *(Tipperary)*	Pa 'Fowler' McInerney *(Clare)*	Bill Phelan *(Laois)*

Ned Tobin *(Laois)*	Martin Hayes *(Limerick)*	Jim 'Builder' Walsh *(Kilkenny)*

Mick Gill   Jack Gleeson
(Galway)   *(Clare)*

Tom O'Rourke *(Clare)*	Dinny O'Neill *(Laois)*	Garrett Howard *(Limerick)*

Tom Barry *(Tipperary*	Ned Fahy *(Clare)*	Mattie Power *(Kilkenny)*

Interestingly, men from six counties and three provinces.

In dealing with 1927 it is, indeed, fitting that we should record the death of Maurice Davin, one of the founders of the GAA, that took place on 26 January of that year.

Sliabh Ruadh, in his book *Twenty Years of the GAA from 1910–1930*, wrote as follows:

> The death is now recorded (January 26) of Mr. Maurice Davin of Carrick-on-Suir, one of the founders of the GAA and its first President. He was a member of the Fenian brotherhood, and as an athlete held the world's hammer-throw from 1875 to 1880, and also held the world's record for the 56 lbs. weight.

Sliabh Ruadh then went on to quote the following without giving the source. 'A man of giant strength and ability in the athletic arena,

154

Maurice Davin possessed equally high qualities of mind and heart, and his name will go down to countless generations as a model of the highest type of Irishman.'

'Beannacht Dé le hanam an Bhile!'

Johnny Leahy
TIPPERARY
1916–1925

'They hold the hopes of bygone years,
They love the past – its smiles and tears –
But quavering doubts and shrinking fears
Are far from Ireland's Hurling men.'

(Brian O'Higgins)

I remember my father telling me one day, when I was very young, the two great hurling clubs of Tipperary – Toomevara and Boherlahan.

The parish of Boherlahan lies in the heart of the Golden Vale between Holycross and Cashel. One of the men that helped to make Boherlahan famous was Johnny Leahy – a hurler in the sporting world, a farmer by profession, a bachelor all his life.

Johnny came from a great hurling family and grew up on tales of heroes of the past from places such as Tubberadora, Thurles and Moycarkey.

His brothers Mick, Tommy and Paddy all played inter-county hurling. Paddy won All-Ireland honours with Tipperary in 1916 and 1925. Tommy was a member of the successful Tipperary team of 1930. Mick was a sub when Tipperary won in 1916. Later he moved to Cork where he ran a very successful business. He hurled with Blackrock, then at the height of their power and glory; won an All-Ireland medal with his adopted county in 1928 and was a sub in the memorable victory of 1931.

Johnny, who was born on 1 January 1890, was one of the most beloved captains of all time. His diplomatic way of handling matters made him a born leader. Genial and gregarious, he endeared himself to all with his easy-going manner and a boyish exuberance that he carried with him throughout his whole life. He was big hearted and generous and there was nothing he loved more than relating anecdotes and recalling incidents from the playing field.

For twenty years Johnny graced the hurling fields of Ireland and left a lasting impression. His first and last love was hurling – a game that was blood and oxygen to his very being.

Johnny took part in the War of Independence and deeply regretted a civil war that saw former comrades involved in a bitter campaign. When it ended Johnny held no grudges, for it wasn't in his nature to bear malice. His brother Jimmy was Vice-Comdt. of Tipperary No. 2 Brigade of the IRA.

Johnny's GAA activities were not confined to the hurling field. In his time he was a member of the Munster Council, chairman of Tipperary County Board and secretary of Tipperary County Board.

He is believed to have played his first game with Tipperary in a tournament at Fethard in 1909 but didn't establish himself on the county team until around 1915. He played his last game at the age of 40 when Boherlahan had to give best to Toomevara in the county final of 1930.

In between those years Tipperary appeared in four All-Ireland finals:

1916 v Kilkenny
1917 v Dublin
1922 v Kilkenny
1925 v Galway

On each occasion Tipperary were captained by Johnny Leahy. He was victorious in 1916 and 1925 and the first one like all firsts was special.

The 1916 final was played on 21 January 1917. It was a time of political unrest. Special trains for the game were prohibited by order of the British Government. The crowd was small – estimated at about 5000. Willie Walsh of Waterford got the game under way at 12.15 p.m. It turned out to be the best final for many years between two teams well matched in terms of fitness and skills. All-Ireland successes stood at eight to seven in Tipperary's favour.

The game was scoreless for the first quarter. By half time Tipperary had forged ahead and led by 1:2 to 1 point. On resumption Kilkenny turned on the style and the best hurling of the hour was witnessed

156

in the third quarter. It prompted a bookie to shout '2 to 1 against Tipp.' 'Little did he know Tipperary and he lived to regret his rashness,' wrote Carbery. With ten minutes to go Kilkenny led by two points. It was then that Johnny Leahy roused his men. They rallied and drew level. The momentum continued. Both teams were reduced to fourteen men when Tom Shanahan of Tipperary and Dick Grace of Kilkenny were sidelined. In an incredible finish Johnny Leahy's men unleashed a final flurry that brought a rash of scores and produced a final scoreline of 5:4 to 3:2 that belied the possibility fifteen minutes earlier.

The 1916 campaign was as follows:

v Kerry (4:2 to 1 point) at Fermoy
'Unequal to the task, Kerry hurlers walked off the grounds in a shower of rain.' (*The Tipperary GAA Story* by Canon Philip Fogarty. Published by *Tipperary Star* (1960).

v Limerick (4:4 to 2:4) at Dungarvan
In a great game of hurling – fiery, brilliant and classical – Johnny Leahy's men pierced the famous Limerick halfback line – the Hindenburg Line, comprised of Keane, Hough and Lanigan – on sufficient occasions to give Tipperary victory over their Shannonside neighbours.

v Cork (5:0 to 1:2) at Dungarvan
A great gathering looked forward to a thriller. Tipperary were quietly confident following their victory over Limerick, but hadn't anticipated that they would overcome Cork with a resounding win following a display of fearless, aggressive hurling.

v Galway (8:1 to nil) at Athlone
It was one-way traffic. So much so that Galway did not resume for the second half.

After the final with Kilkenny, as Johnny Leahy shook hands with Kilkenny's captain Sim Walton, Sim said 'we were the better hurlers' to which Johnny Leahy replied 'we were the better men' and moved on to collect the national trophy which was a new Railway Cup.

Johnny's second success as captain came in 1925. It was an easy All-Ireland title. Only Cork tested the Tipperary metal. In the first round Kerry fell. At half time in the Munster semi-final with Cork, played in Limerick, Tipperary, who dominated the first half, led by 4:2 to one goal. Cork put in a rousing second half rally and almost snatched a winning goal in the final moments. The game ended Tipperary 5:3 Cork 5:1. Carbery commented 'Tipp. got roused and resurrected the unquenchable fire of the past. They need stout opposition to call forth their best effort.'

The remaining games were a mere formality:

v Waterford – Munster final (6:6 to 1:2)
v Antrim – All-Ireland semi-final (12:9 to 2:3)
v Galway – All-Ireland final (5:6 to 1:5)

In 1926 the Tipperary team toured America, captained by Johnny Leahy. They were the first team to go to America since the 'Invasion' of 1888. It was a coast to coast tour – the trip of a lifetime – organised by Patrick Cahill, President of the Chicago GAA, who hailed from Holycross and practised in Chicago as an attorney. The team departed on 11 May and arrived back on 24 July. While in the States they played seven games – winning all – one each at Boston, San Francisco, Buffalo, and two at New York and Chicago. It was this trip that earned Johnny the title 'Captain Johnny'.

When Johnny died in November 1949 'Semper Fidelis' wrote the following in 'An Appreciation'.

He had the tenderness of a woman and the anger of a hero and he overcame violence with a smile, obstinacy by perseverance, and ignorance by truth. Whatever his just anger it passed off. This brave and tender man in every storm of life was oak and rock, but in the sunshine he was wine and flower . . . Were everyone to whom he did some loving service to bring a blossom to his grave he would sleep tonight 'neath a garden of flowers . . . He was a raconteur of the highest order. Yes, indeed, it was a veritable delight to feast on the language that fell from his lips with the invincible charm of sincerity.

Mick Kenny
GALWAY
1923

'Ar dhroim an domhain níl radharc is áille
Ná tríocha fear ag bualadh báire,
Ar pháirc mhór ghlas faoi taitneamh gréine,
Is na gártha molta ag dul cun spéire.'

(Seán Ó Finnéadha)

Galway (Meelick) contested the first All-Ireland final – the final of 1887 – played at Birr on 1 April 1888. They lost to Tipperary (Thurles) by 1 goal 1 point and 1 forfeit point to no score. Galway wouldn't contest another All-Ireland final until 1923.

The first significant sign that Galway were putting together a team capable of competing with the best came in the All-Ireland semi-final of 1922. The game was played on 26 August 1923 at Galway and the home team gave a right good account of themselves. They lost in the end to a fine Tipperary outfit by 3:2 to 1:3. They looked with hope to the future.

Galway emerged unopposed in Connaught in 1923.

The All-Ireland semi-final of that year between Galway and Kilkenny was played at Croke Park on 18 May 1924. Kilkenny were reigning All-Ireland champions. However, Galway showed that they had arrived in the big time with a convincing 5:4 to 2 goals victory.

Captained by Mick Kenny of Tynagh – the leading hurling club in Galway in the twenties – they now faced Limerick (who had earlier accounted for Donegal in the other semi-final), in the All-Ireland final.

The final of 1923 was originally fixed for June 1924. It was a time of political unrest in Ireland. On a matter relating to prisoner detention, Limerick declined to travel. There followed an emergency meeting of the Central Council. The match was awarded to Galway. They refused, emphatically, to accept a bloodless victory.

Fortunately the political position improved and with the prisoner issue resolved the final was refixed for 14 September 1924.

Mick Kenny had some great men under his command. There was Mick Gill, one of the great midfielders not only of his era, but of all time. In the Gael-Linn poll of 1961 to select 'The Greatest Hurling

159

Team Ever' he was chosen at midfield. You had Ignatius Harney who played a style of hurling that made the game look easy. Then there was Jim Power at fullback and Mick Derivan in the left corner, both excellent last line defenders. According to Carbery 'Mick Derivan at left fullback was one of the finest natural hurlers I ever saw. His grand drives off either hand and his accuracy overhead were models of supreme camán artistry.' In attack Galway had goal-scoring forwards in Andy Kelly and Bernie Gibbs. Bernie Gibbs and Mick Derivan were on the Tailteann games team of 1924. In 1928 Mick Gill and Mick Derivan were chosen on the Tailteann games selection.

Limerick, All-Ireland champions in 1918 and 1921, were favourites. Playing with the breeze they went 1:1 up inside ten minutes. Then Mick Kenny, playing at midfield, settled his team who up to then were showing signs of Croke Park nerves. He gathered a long puck out and went through for a goal. In the last three minutes of the first half, Galway struck for two crucial goals via Leonard McGrath and Dick Morrissey. They retired at the interval on level terms.

Galway resumed the second half just as they had finished the first. In less than ten minutes they had found the net on three occasions from the hurleys of Andy Kelly, Bernie Gibbs and Leonard McGrath. Those five goals on either side of half time set Galway on the road to a wonderful, if unexpected, victory on the score 7:3 to 4:5.

Their preparations stood to them. They had gone through a collective training programme. Speed in the forward line proved to be their trump card where they had the stylish Ignatius Harney of the elusive swerve, Dick Morrissey the vigorous 14st. centre forward and the swift, stylish and hard-tackling Leonard McGrath.

It was a great occasion for Galway hurling when Mick Kenny became the third hurling captain to receive the MacCarthy Cup. Galway confirmed their 1923 All-Ireland campaign form when, under the captaincy of Mick Kenny, they defeated Tipperary in the All-Ireland semi-final of 1924 at Croke Park on 23 November of that year. The score was 3:1 to 2:3.

With the grateful assistance of Michael Harney of Tynagh, son of Ignatius, I got the following information on Mick Kenny. Mick was born in 1893 in Feogh, Duniry — a neighbouring parish of Tynagh. As he grew to manhood he developed into a fine physical specimen — 6'2", 14st. 7lbs., a head of black hair. He was one of a family of ten consisting of six boys and four girls. The harsh economic conditions of the Ireland of their day forced some of the family to emigrate to America where they made a new life for themselves.

Mick worked initially at Larkins Shop in Lisheen. However, with a view to making him eligible to hurl with Tynagh, Ignatius Harney gave him a job in his business. Mick's brother Jack, who played with Galway in 1911, took a rather dim view of Mick's decision to move from Duniry to Tynagh. It, therefore, gave Jack great personal satisfaction when Duniry met Tynagh in a tournament final and victory went to Duniry.

In due course Jack inherited the home place. Mick got a Land Commission farm in Boula, Portumna. He married a girl from Co. Westmeath. Sadly, she died leaving Mick with three daughters. He remarried and had two more daughters during his second marriage.

His brother died Tom on 25 June 1954. By a strange coincidence Mick died five years later to the date on 25 June 1959. He is buried in Portumna.

These are the men Mick captained to a famous All-Ireland victory in 1923.

Junior Mahony
(Ardrahan)

Tom Fleming
(Galway City)

Jim Power.
(Tynagh)

Mick Derivan
(Tynagh)

Mick Gill
(Ballinderreen)

Ed Gilmartin
(Gort)

J. Garvey
(Cappataggle)

Mick Kenny
(Tynagh)

Jimmy Morris
(Gort)

Ignatius Harney
(Tynagh)

Dick Morrissey
(Craughwell)

Martin King
(Galway City)

Leonard McGrath
(Cappataggle)

Andy Kelly
(Tynagh)

Bernie Gibbs
(Gort)

Wattie Dunphy
KILKENNY
1922

> There is something wild and pagan about hurling. It speaks of an Ireland before the taming influence of Christianity. If myth and legend are anything to go by, the game had its devoted followers more than a thousand years before the birth of Christ. To think of people long turned to dust who played, watched and discussed the game in the mists from Cú Chulainn on down the ages gives it a status which dwarfs most other popular sports.
>
> (Sheila Leahy – daughter of Terry)

The year 1922 represented for Kilkenny an oasis in a hurling desert. Let's see why.

A golden era in Kilkenny hurling existed between 1904 and 1913 inclusive. In that ten-year period the county won seven All-Ireland titles – a record that still stands.

A second golden era began in 1932 and continued throughout the thirties. But for 1922 a barren stretch of 19 years would have been recorded. Even then it was a very close call – a late late rally snatched victory from the clutches of Tipperary in 1922.

Indeed, so imminent was the Tipperary triumph that many of their supporters had departed before the final whistle and some of them – to their dismay – only learned of defeat when the last train pulled in at Thurles.

I must express my thanks to Dick Dunphy, a nephew of Wattie, for his kind assistance with information about his uncle. Dick and his brother Joe inherited the hurling genes – Dick being the understudy goalie to the great Ollie Walsh for a time during the sixties and Joe in captaining Kilkenny to two successive All-Ireland minor wins over Tipperary in 1961 and 1962, setting a record that has yet to be equalled.

Wattie Dunphy of Mooncoin – a parish famed in hurling lore – captained his county in a dramatic 4:2 to 2:6 win over Tipperary in 1922 and became the first Kilkenny man to take the MacCarthy Cup to the Noreside. He played in the All-Ireland final of 1926 when

Kilkenny had to give way to a superior Cork outfit. On St. Patrick's Day 1927 Wattie captained Leinster to a 1:11 to 2:6 victory over Munster in the inaugural final of the Railway Cup competition. Stalwart hurling men filled every position on the pitch and the game is remembered as one of the finest contests in the history of hurling.

Wattie, who was born circa 1895 and died in 1972, was a farmer by profession — a big, strong, broad-shouldered man turning the scales at around 13 stone plus. He played at centre back for club and county and excelled in that position in an era of close marking and first time ground hurling. He had four brothers: Joe, who before entering the priesthood gave a classical performance at full forward on Pa 'Fowler' McInerney in the Leinster final of 1929 against Dublin; Eddie, who played in the All-Ireland finals of 1922 and 1926; William, who was a sub on the defeated All-Ireland team of 1935 and Richard, whose hurling was confined to his club Mooncoin.

The All-Ireland final of 1922 was played on 9 September 1923 and attracted a crowd of over 26,000. Hurling fans were conveyed to our capital city in over thirty special trains.

Kilkenny with victories over Laois, Dublin and Galway went into collective training for the final. Tipperary with two epic Munster final games against Limerick were equally fit.

The All-Ireland final was one of the greatest games up to that time in the history of the GAA. John Roberts was the Kilkenny full forward. Here's how he described the game when I met him in 1982. 'It was a very sporting encounter — great ground hurling. There wasn't a scratch on any player — it was fast and free-flowing and most enjoyable.' This is how he described one of those late three Kilkenny goals. 'I had the ball in front of me and tried to move goalwards but Johnny Leahy blocked my way; the forwards were like a swarm of bees in the square. I tipped the ball to Dick Tobin on the right. He sent it back to me; I moved it to the left, where Mattie Power was on hand to send the ball to the net.'

At half time the scores were level at Kilkenny 1:1 Tipperary 0:4; low scoring, a product of close tackling, ground hurling and man-to-man marking.

A goal ten minutes into the second half put Tipperary in the lead and on the road to seeming victory until Kilkenny's late late rally turned the tide.

It was the sixth meeting of these counties in an All-Ireland final and the Kilkenny victory made it three wins each – Tipperary in 1895, 1898 and 1916; Kilkenny in 1909, 1913 and 1922.

Following their victory the Kilkenny team spent Sunday night in a Dublin hotel and on Monday Wattie Dunphy and his victorious team returned to a wonderful welcome in Kilkenny city.

Bob McConkey
LIMERICK
1921

'Where the Gaels are greeting
There's a cleaner fight;
And the camáns meeting
Makes a goodly sight;
Well may Ireland boast them –
Hers they are alone –
And her lovers toast them:
"Ireland's Cornerstone".'

(Maeve Cavanagh)

The Young Irelands Club won the Limerick county senior hurling title of 1920 when they defeated Newcastle West by 5:4 to 1 point. That victory paved the way for Bob McConkey to captain Limerick in the All-Ireland championship campaign of 1921.

It was an era of political upheaval and unrest. The championship of 1921 wound its way through those difficult days and wasn't completed until 1923.

It is interesting to recall, very briefly, the key political events of those times:

- War of Independence, truce called 11 July 1921.
- Anglo-Irish Treaty signed 6 December 1921.
- Following the signing of the Treaty Michael Collins, one of the signatories, wrote to a friend and said 'Will anyone be satisfied . . . I tell you this – early this morning I signed my death warrant.'
- Treaty approved by the Dáil 7 January 1922 by 64 votes to 57

- Civil War followed 28 June 1922.
- Arthur Griffith (a signatory to the Treaty) died suddenly 12 August 1922.
- Michael Collins, killed in Civil War 22 August 1922.
- Civil War ended officially 24 May 1923 but some issues lingered on.

Limerick's 1921 All-Ireland campaign was as follows:

The Munster final took place at Thurles on 28 May 1922 between Limerick and Cork. Cork were All-Ireland champions in 1919 and All-Ireland finalists in 1920. Limerick had a facile victory, as the score of 5:2 to 1:2 would suggest. It was the only game of the 1921 championship played in the province.

The All-Ireland semi-final took place against Galway — then a rising force — at the Markets Field, Limerick, on 25 June 1922. The game was a personal triumph for Bob McConkey who scored four goals for Limerick in their 6 goals to 2:2 win.

Because of the Civil War the final against Dublin at Croke Park didn't take place until 4 March 1923. Dublin, reigning All-Ireland champions, came through in Leinster after a great provincial final with Kilkenny. Present at that game was Michael Collins who, having spoken to the players, threw in the ball to start the game.

In the All-Ireland final, Dublin fielded a dozen of the victorious team of 1920. They were favourites to retain the title. They had brilliant hurlers in their lineout — men from the country residing in Dublin, talented, fit and experienced. Let's name them. Bob Mockler, John Joe Callinan, Mick Darcy, Joe Bannon, Jim Cleary (Tipperary), Martin Hayes, Tom Hayes, Mick Neville (Limerick), Tommy Daly, Bob Doherty, Jim Clune (Clare), Frank Burke (Kildare), Jim Walsh, Tommy Moore (Kilkenny), Ned Tobin (Laois).

A keen, close contest was in prospect for the attendance of over 18,000 — who paid gate receipts of £1080 — when the teams lined out for the throw-in on a cold, dry spring day with Willie Walsh of Waterford in charge of the whistle. The game opened at a hectic pace — play swung from end to end as players first timed the sliotar on the ground and stood hip to hip in the physical exchanges.

Gradually, however, Limerick asserted themselves. The defence was rock-solid. The mid-fielders were on top. The attack had the measure of their men. Bob McConkey, in particular, was causing all kinds of problems for the Dublin rear guard and his three goals in the first half gave Limerick an 11 point lead at the break on the score 4:1 to 2 points.

The pattern of the second half was the same. Bob McConkey added his fourth goal and endeared himself to the Limerick fans – 'The little fellow with the grey cap – the skipper who knows more about finding the net than most.' Limerick's superiority stripped the game of the tension and excitement associated with a close encounter. At the call of time the score stood at Limerick 8:5 Dublin 3:2.

For the first time in the hurling championship the Liam MacCarthy Cup was presented to the winning captain. It was a very proud moment for Bob McConkey who, in the unavoidable absence of the donor, was presented with the cup by Dan McCarthy of Dublin, President of the GAA. It gave Bob a special place in GAA history.

The Cup – described by the *Irish Independent* as 'of racy and costly design' – was donated by Liam MacCarthy, born in England in 1853 of Irish emigrant parents. His father, Eoghan, hailed from Ballygarvan, Co. Cork. His mother, Bridget Dineen, from whom Liam became imbued with his love of Irish games, customs and traditions, was born in Bruff, Co. Limerick. The new trophy replaced the Great Southern Cup which was last won by Dublin in 1920 and as such they now became the outright owners of it.

In the 1921 All-Ireland triumph, Bob McConkey had many out-standing and skilful hurling men under his command. Ten of them had played on the victorious 1918 team.

- Paddy McInerney of Young Irelands at cornerback, had few equals. He emigrated to America and cherished his hurling days to the day he died in New Mexico in 1983, aged 88.
- The halfback line of Jack Keane, Willie Hough and Dinny Lanigan was famous for its defensive brilliance and was known as 'The Hindenburg Line'.
- Five of the 1921 team were chosen on the Tailteann games team of 1924.
- Midfielder, Willie Gleeson, of Fedamore.
- Midfielder, Jimmy Humphreys of Murroe, who was captain. Following victory over the U.S. team, on the score 4:3 to 1:3, he had the honour of receiving the New Ireland Assurance Company Cup from patriot and Fenian, John Devoy (1842–1928), who

following the abortive rising of 1867 spent much of his life in the U.S.

- Dave Murnane, a fullback of the first order.
- Garrett Howard of Croom, who would win five All-Ireland medals — three with his native Limerick (1921, 1934 and 1936); and two with his adopted Dublin (1924 and 1927); and also Railway Cup honours with Leinster and Munster.
- Willie Ryan of Cappamore, whose sons Seamus and Liam would play with Limerick in the 50s until ordination to the priesthood lost them both to the game of hurling.

This was an era when Limerick hurling flourished. They contested eight Munster finals in a row (1917 to 1924 inclusive); won three (1918, 1921 and 1923); lost two others following a replay (1917 and 1922); played in three All-Ireland finals (1918, 1921 and 1923) and took victory on two occasions (1918 and 1921).

Bob made his début in the Limerick jersey in 1918 and won an All-Ireland medal. In his time he was one of the best forwards in the game. His performances at full forward enabled him to stake a claim to rank with the great ones who adorned the position. Bob was fast, elusive and clever. He would whip on a ground ball from any angle and find the net. He would double overhead with equal effectiveness.

Bob was still going strong in 1934 when Limerick and Dublin again came face to face in the final of that year. Earlier on Whit Monday, at Woolwich Stadium, London, Limerick played Kilkenny in the annual Monaghan Cup game. In that game Bob was facing staunch Kilkenny fullback Peter O'Reilly. Over the hour, in a game Limerick won by 5:4 to 4:5, the veteran full forward displayed all the craft, cunning, dash and opportunism for which he had become renowned.

In the All-Ireland semi-final against Galway, Bob was called into action when Jackie O'Connell tore a cartilage and ligament as he turned to whip on a fast ball close to half time. Bob rose to the occasion in admirable fashion, drawing on all his experience and giving a display of flair and élan in what was a tough and, at times, over-robust encounter.

Bob played in the drawn All-Ireland final of 1934 and was replaced by Jackie O'Connell in the last quarter. In the replay he was among the substitutes. Limerick won an epic contest by five points. Bob McConkey collected a third All-Ireland medal.

However, his association with Limerick success didn't end there. In 1947 he trained the Limerick team that defeated Kilkenny in a replayed National League final.

When Jim Young, a Cork hurling star of the forties, picked his best fifteen for one of the national newspapers, he placed Bob McConkey at full forward. Paddy 'Fox' Collins, a Cork star of the thirties, suggested to Jim that he had never seen Bob play and wondered about his choice. Jim's reply to 'Fox' Collins was a classic – 'You don't have to see a man to know he was the best – did you ever see Jesus Christ?'

The Limerick team of 1921 lined out as follows:

Mick Murphy

Tom Mangan   Dave Murnane   Paddy McInerney

Jack Keane   Willie Hough   Dinny Lanigan
                          (0:1)

        Willie Gleeson   Jimmy Humphreys
            (2:2)

Willie Ryan   Garrett Howard   Mick Mullane
                          (0:1)

Christy Ryan   Bob McConkey   Tom McGrath
                          (4:0)   (2:1)

Bob Mockler
DUBLIN
1920

'God bless you Horse and Jockey,
May your courage never fail,
In your many hard-fought contests
You were never known to quail.'

We first hear of Bob Mockler of Horse and Jockey, at county level, away back in 1908. He played with his native Tipperary against Dublin in the drawn All-Ireland final of that year. He didn't take part in the replay which was won by Tipperary.

The following year, after a 2:10 to 2:6 win over Cork in the Munster final, Bob saw victory snatched from the Premier County by Leinster champions Kilkenny, on the score 4:6 to 12 points. That was a 17-a-side encounter. Bob Mockler, now a muscular youth, was starring at handball and hurling and showing tremendous potential.

Four years later in 1913, with teams now reduced to 15-a-side for the first time, Tipperary again faced Kilkenny in the All-Ireland final; this time with high hopes. Their path to the All-Ireland final which was played at Croke Park on 2 November was as follows:

v Waterford at Waterford (6:0 to 2:2)
v Clare at Limerick (3:2 to 2:0)
v Cork at Dungarvan (8:2 to 4:3)

This Munster final was played before an attendance of 13,000. Congress had decided that counties should choose distinctive colours and register them with GAA Headquarters. Cork lined out in blue and saffron. Tipperary donned crimson and gold with crossed keys of kings of Cashel on centre of jersey.

v Roscommon at Croke Park (10:0 to 1 point)

A crowd of 25,000 turned up for the All-Ireland final. As in 1909 victory went to Kilkenny, this time on the scoreline of 2:4 to 1:2. Bob was learning that All-Ireland medals were an elusive commodity. However, he was able to take some consolation from Tipperary's victory over Kilkenny in the final of the Croke Memorial on the score 5:4 to 1:1 at Dungarvan in May of that year.

Sometime later Bob moved from his native Horse and Jockey to Dublin and joined the Faughs club. Then things began to happen for him. In 1917, Dublin with a Collegians selection, faced Tipperary with a Boherlahan selection, in the All-Ireland final. Bob, then in his glorious prime, was at midfield where he gave a heroic display of masterful hurling for the county of his adoption against his fellow countymen from Horse and Jockey, Moycarkey and Boherlahan. Two other Tipperary men on the Dublin team that day were Jim Cleary and Martin Hackett whose brother Stephen lined out with Tipperary.

Bob opened the scoring for Dublin with a wonderful point from eighty yards and followed up with a second point from a seventy.

Over the hour he contributed 1:2. Dublin won by 5:4 to 4:2. Bob collected his first All-Ireland medal. The winning team consisted of twelve Munster men with Laois, Kilkenny and Kildare supplying one each. Writing on the game Carbery said 'Tipperary suffered a sensational defeat after a sensational game.'

In 1920 Bob was appointed captain of the Metropolitan team. It was a year when the War of Independence intensified. Politically things were in a state of flux. GAA games were severely disrupted. Many postponements took place. The Munster final of 1920 wasn't played until April 1922. Cork defeated Limerick and qualified for the All-Ireland final. This game was played on 14 May 1922. It was a repeat of the 1919 All-Ireland final when Cork and Dublin did battle for supremacy. This time, however, the result was reversed. Bob Mockler and his men had a decisive 4:9 to 4:3 win over the Munster champions. Bob collected a second All-Ireland medal and in so doing displayed wonderful anticipation and overhead skills.

He had captained a team of non-Dublin men.

Tommy Daly
(Clare)

Ned Tobin Martin Hayes John Ryan
(Laois) (Limerick) (Limerick)

Bob Doherty Jim Clune Jim 'Builder' Walsh
(Clare) (Clare) (Kilkenny)

Tom Hayes Bob Mockler
(Limerick) (Tipperary)

Tommy Moore John Joe Callinan Jim Cleary
(Kilkenny) (Tipperary) (Tipperary)

Frank Burke Mick Neville Joe Phelan
(Kildare) (Limerick) (Laois)

For the third year in a row Dublin reached the 1921 All-Ireland final. It was played on 4 March 1923. Their opponents were Limerick. Bob was again captain. As usual he was to the fore and was Dublin's scorer in chief with a contribution of 1:1. However, his best efforts, supported by many able and talented lieutenants, were not enough to stem a Shannon tide that swept Limerick to victory on the score 8:5 to 3:2.

More hurling honours and glory awaited Bob in 1924. Dublin defeated Galway in the final of that year on 14 December at Croke Park. The final score was 5:3 to 2:6. For Bob it was a case of a third All-Ireland medal in the space of eight years – without a doubt a good return.

In 1934, writing in the Jubilee GAA supplement of the *Irish Independent*, Carbery had this to say about Bob Mockler. 'Midfield was Bob's natural place. His superb physique, his speed, his unerring judgement, and his fine control of ash made him the most spoken of centre field man of his day. It was the irony of things that he should have taken a big share in the defeat of his native county in the 1917 final.

'Ever since he has been the pillar of the game in the metropolis. A hurler from his infancy, Bob played with head and hand in unison. His command of falling balls and his mighty length of puck often sent crowds into ecstasies.

'Bob was an expert at 70s and frees at all distances. At Croke Park (156 yards) I have seen Mockler score from far behind the half way. For curiosity I measured a ball of his one day after a match in which he pointed a free. It was 98 yards clear.'

In summary, Bob played in eight All-Ireland finals that spanned a period of 17 years. 1908, having played in the drawn game with Tipperary against Dublin, he didn't take part in the replay which was won by his native Tipperary.

1909 Tipperary failed to Kilkenny.
1913 Tipperary again defeated by Kilkenny.
1917 Bob wins a first All-Ireland medal with his adopted Dublin.
1919 Dublin defeated by Cork.
1920 Dublin reversed the 1919 result – a second All-Ireland medal for Bob who was now team captain.
1921 Dublin defeated by Limerick.
1924 Dublin overcome Galway – Bob wins his third All-Ireland medal.

Willie Hough
LIMERICK
1918

'Then see that surging, swaying pack,
As they parry and poise and hurl and hack;
Multi-colours blend together,
Clashing ash and flying leather,
Mind and muscle, might and brawn,
Behind each stroke of the stout camán.'

(Sliabh Ruadh)

William (Willie) Hough came of a well-known Gaelic and hurling family of west Limerick. Hough was a regular Hercules of a man. He carried great speed with his strength and was one of the smoothest and most commanding hurlers I have ever seen in action. A schoolteacher by profession, he loved hurling from his youth and took good care that every one of his boys had the camán and used it with skill.

Willie Hough at centre back was a master of every stroke, and every movement known to first-class hurling. He used his powerful wrists and shoulders with fine skill and many of his strokes, whether on the turf or overhead, were half a field's length. I often travelled 100 miles to see Willie Hough in action at centre back and 'twas worth every mile. He was nature's gentleman. (Carbery)

Willie Hough was born in 1892 in Monagea, a parish in west Limerick, located a few miles from Newcastle West. As he grew to manhood he saw plenty of GAA activity in his native parish and was influenced, among others, by his father who excelled at hurling and football and who was chairman of the West Limerick Board from 1902 to 1910.

Willie's performances on the hurling field with De La Salle College, Waterford, brought him to the attention of the Waterford county senior selectors and in 1913 he played with Waterford and starred as their captain in their game against Tipperary in the Munster championship. Victory went to Tipperary. The *Waterford Star* reported as follows on the game.

172

Never was a team better captained and never did a commander infuse more hope and spirit by sheer example than Hough. He was here, there and everywhere . . . always on the ball . . . now playing tig with his opponents and slapping shots into the forwards with a frequency and accuracy that charmed those who could appreciate hurling at its best.

Having qualified as a national teacher at De La Salle College he got a job in Baltimore in west Cork and hurled with UCC. He was offered a place on the Cork team but wasn't prepared to forsake his native Limerick.

Willie Hough was a class hurler who would have got his place on any county team in any era. In his hurling days he weighed around 14 stone. He had that wonderful gift of being able to read a game perfectly and as a result be in the right place at the right time. He was renowned for his positional sense, clean striking and long ground clearances.

During his hurling days with Limerick he operated, once he established himself, at centre halfback. With his wingmen, Jack Keane and Dinny Lanigan, he formed a halfback line so effective that it was known as the Hindenburg Line. Carbery described it as one of the greatest halfback lines in the history of the game.

His career with Limerick lasted from 1915 to 1926. He made a comeback in 1929 for the championship match against Waterford but defeat was Limerick's lot. Willie lived in an era when, for many, no effort or sacrifice was too great when it came to playing and promoting our national games.

In retirement he took up refereeing and distinguished himself in National League games and Munster championship clashes. His greatest honour came when he had charge of an All-Ireland semi-final between Galway and Kilkenny.

He also excelled in administration. From 1924 to 1928 he was vice-chairman of the West Limerick Board. In 1936 he was elected treasurer of the Munster Council and remained in that post, unopposed, for a period of twenty-six years. It was an indication of the commitment and dedication of a man who once cycled twenty-nine miles to Limerick to play a game against Tipperary at the Markets Field and after the match cycled home.

Now to 1918 and hurling glory. Willie Hough captained Newcastle West when they won the Limerick senior hurling title in 1917. Up to

173

then the county selection rested with the county titleholders. However, Newcastle West decided to forego this honour and leave the matter to a selection committee.

Politically, it was a difficult time in Ireland. In July 1918 British authorities issued an order banning all GAA games except under permit from the RIC. The Central Council of the GAA directed that the order be ignored and proclaimed the 4 August as Gaelic Sunday and arranged for games to be played all over Ireland. No move was made by the authorities. Their order had failed. But other issues were fresh in the minds of the people too: the noble aspirations of the idealistic men of 1916 and the ruthless retribution exacted; the conscription attempt during World War 1; the land question now finally resolved; the release of prisoners in 1917; the failed Home Rule efforts.

That was the background against which a strong Limerick selection embarked on the 1918 All-Ireland campaign. After a 5:3 each draw with Tipperary, in a hectic encounter at the Markets Field, Limerick, the team under the guidance of trainer Jim Dalton went into special training at Foynes. The replay, at Cork Athletic Grounds, was won by Limerick on the score 3:0 to 2:2. Clare were easily overcome in the Munster final.

The scene was now set for a meeting with Wexford who had defeated Dublin, the reigning All-Ireland champions, in the Leinster final by 2:3 to 1:2. In an earlier Leinster championship tie with Offaly the game finished on the remarkable scoreline of Wexford 10 goals Offaly 6 goals. Due to the great 'flu epidemic Wexford were unable to field a team. Limerick were offered a walkover but declined a bloodless victory. The final was then refixed for 26 January 1919. Limerick were favourites and were appearing in their fourth All-Ireland final. In 1897 they defeated Kilkenny; 1910 saw them lose by one point to Wexford; they conceded a walkover to Kilkenny following a venue dispute in 1911.

Wexford, if you include the 1901 home final against Cork, were appearing in their sixth final. They lost to Cork, Kerry and Tipperary respectively in 1890, '91 and '99. Like Limerick, they had one success to date – 1910, when they defeated Limerick.

Referee Willie Walsh of Waterford threw in the ball at 3:10 p.m. Unfortunately, for the attendance of 12,000, the game turned out to be very one-sided. Limerick, superior in all sectors of the field, were

174

victorious on the score 9:5 to 1:3. Their superiority lay in their preparation which had them trained to the ounce; their overall strength as a unit; and their first time hurling on the ground and in the air.

Wexford's hopes of completing the first leg of a senior double were dashed. Willie Hough was presented with the All-Ireland cup by Kilkennyman and President of the GAA, Jim Nowlan. The team returned that night to Limerick by train. There were no enthusiastic supporters there to greet them. It is said that a passer-by asked 'Where was the match today lads?'

D'éag Willie i 1976. Bhí clú agus cáil agus iomrá air le linn a shaoil, ní amháin mar iománaí ach mar ambasadóir, mar riarthóir agus mar theachta freisin do Chumann Lúthchleas Gael.

Jack Finlay
LAOIS
1915

'Is maith an t-iománaí an té a bhíonn ar an gclaí.'

A special word of thanks to Paddy Lalor – former Laois hurler, former Fianna Fáil Dáil deputy and former M.E.P. – for his very kind assistance with some of the detail in this article.

Ballygeehan, a small rural parish in County Laois, won the county junior hurling title in 1913. The following year they had to go senior and surprised many by capturing the senior crown – a feat they repeated, under Jack Finlay's captaincy, for five years in a row (1914–'18 incl.).

After winning the 1914 county senior title they had a major input to the selection of the county senior team. Heads rolled from the 1914 county selection that had failed to Clare in the All-Ireland final. Several new faces appeared on the county team.

Jack Finlay was honoured with the captaincy. He was an ideal man for the job. He had a strong personality. On the pitch he always set about rallying the weaker players and encouraging the good ones. He was born in 1890 at Ballycuddy in the parish of Aghaline, of farming stock. He, too, farmed and in later life became a politician and represented Laois/Offaly as a Fine Gael T.D. in the forties.

On the 1915 team with Jack was his eighteen-year-old brother Tom who played at right halfback. Tom was an outstanding sportsman. He won an All-Ireland title with Dublin in 1924 and was chosen at right fullback on the Laois Millennium team. He was also a first class horseman. As Comdt. Tom Finlay, he won fame for Ireland with the Army Equestrian Jumping Team in Europe and the U.S.A. Among their greatest triumphs was victory in the first Nations Cup at Lucerne in Switzerland.

In the 1915 hurling championship, Laois advanced in Leinster with a first round win over Offaly. In the next game they faced Kilkenny whom they had beaten the previous year by one point in the Leinster final on the score 3:2 to 2:4.

A goal from a close-in free in the closing stages of the 1915 game gave Laois another one point victory over the Kilkenny men. The free resulted from an incident between Jack Rochford of Kilkenny and J. Hiney of Laois. The free was taken by Jack Daly and tapped to Tom Finlay who finished the sliotar to the net for a sensational winner. Final score 4:1 to 2:6 in a game where Laois led at half time by 3:1 to nil.

An ever-improving and confident Laois met Dublin in the Leinster final and became provincial holders on the score 3:2 to five points. It was Laois's second Leinster title – a two in a row in fact.

With no opposition from Ulster, Laois were now in the All-Ireland final for the second year in a row. Clare, as reigning Munster and All-Ireland champions, were nominated to represent Munster against Galway in the All-Ireland semi-final. They won by 2:1 to 1:1 at Gort on 8 August but failed subsequently in the Munster final to Cork who then advanced to the All-Ireland final which was played at Croke Park on 24 October. Earlier Cork had defeated Tipperary in the first round and were awarded an unfinished Munster semi-final against Limerick at Thurles.

In preparation for the All-Ireland showdown with Cork, Jack Finlay's men had the benefit of the guidance and counsel of 'Drug' Walsh, one of Kilkenny's greatest hurling sons. He prepared them well, physically and mentally. It was Bob O'Keeffe, a Kilkenny man on the Laois team – later to become President of the GAA in 1935 – who made arrangements for the services of 'Drug' Walsh.

Cork entered the final as favourites and would have felt very confident. In their ranks were several of an excellent 1912 team that were beaten, rather unluckily, by Kilkenny by one point in the All-Ireland final of that year. Among the newcomers was Sean Óg Murphy of Blackrock who was destined to make a lasting impression in the hurling arena. The Cork C.V. was also very impressive and from the bookies' point of view it would have tipped the scales in favour of the Leesiders. Cork had built for themselves a strong hurling tradition, supported by six All-Ireland titles. Laois on the other hand had no great tradition, never won an All-Ireland title, and had failed badly on the scoreboard in the final of the previous year against Clare. Not a huge crowd travelled. Pre-match comment said it all – 'the game was over'.

When Cork jumped into an early three goal lead the outlook for Jack Finlay and his O'Moore County colleagues looked bleak. However, Laois rallied and by half time had closed the gap to one point on the score 3:0 to 2:2.

The late Liam O'Neill of Laois (he was a brilliant minor and gave an outstanding display for his county at left fullback in the All-Ireland

(*left to right*) Sean, Kevin, Liam, Kevin (father), Brendan, Michael and Ger Fennelly. The late Kevin Fennelly with six of his sons. His youngest son, Dermot, whose hurling days still lay ahead of him, is absent from the photograph. (*Courtesy of Tom Brett.*)

Pat Fleury (*right*) Offaly's cornerback, with Michael
Connolly, the Galway captain, and George Ryan, the
referee, before the 1985 All-Ireland final.

Joe Connolly, who captained Galway
their second All-Ireland title in 198
after a lapse of fifty-seven year

Brian Cody, a Kilkenny hurling star and captain of the victorious 1982 team with
his wife Elsie Cody (née Walsh), a great Wexford camogie star, who captained
Leinster in 1988 and 1991.

Bobby Ryan, from Borrisoleigh, led his native Tipperary to All-Ireland victory in 1989 after a lapse of eighteen years.

Tom Cashman, son of the great Mick Cashman, led Cork to All-Ireland victory in 1986.

Tomás Mulcahy, outstanding Cork forward.

Anthony Daly formed part of a great half-back line from Clare in their historic victory over Offaly in 1995 after a lapse of eighty-one years and repeated their success in 1997 against Tipperary.

Declan Carr, 1991.

Willie O'Connor (*left*) with friends celebrating the 2000 All-Ireland victory for Kilkenny.

Tommy Dunne, captained Tipperary to
All-Ireland victory in 2001.

Mark Landers, 1999.

September 8th, 2002, Kilkenny captain Andy Comerford celebrating victory
against Clare in the 2002 All-Ireland Hurling final.
(© Brendan Moran/SPORTSFILE)

Kathleen Mills – fifteen All-Ireland titles make her camogie's first superstar.

Bridget Doyle with her son Paul.
(*Courtesy Ger Carty, Enniscorthy.*)

Angela Downey, the Lory Meagher of Kilkenny camogie and daughter of the great Shem Downey.

Jovita Delaney kept goal for Tipperary in their three-in-a-row run of successes from 1999 to 2001.

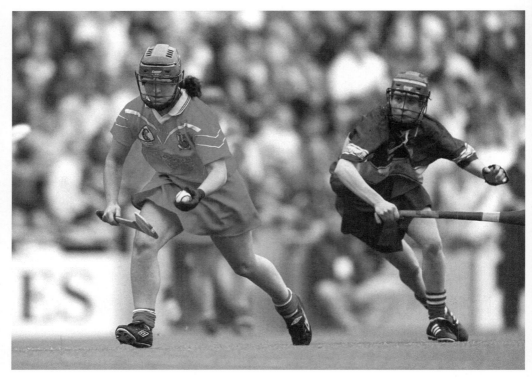

September 15th, 2002 Caoimhe Harrington, Cork, against Paula Bulfin Tipperary in the 2002 All-Ireland Camogie Final. (© Aoife Rice/SPORTSFILE).

Wexford, All-Ireland senior camogie champions 1969: At rere (*left to right*) – Margaret O'Leary, Joan Murphy, Annie Kent (sub), Bernie Murphy, Peggie Doyle (sub), Bridget O'Connor, Teresa Shannon (sub goalie), Ellen Shannon (sub), Ann Foley. In front – Mary Doyle, Carmel Fortune (sub), Mary Walsh, Brigid Doyle (captain), Cathy Power, Annie Kehoe, Peg Moore, Mary Shannon, (Not in picture – sub Eileen Allen).

final of 1934 against Tipperary – a game lost by 4:3 to 3:5 when in the eighth minute of injury time Tipperary got the winning goal) told me that rain marred the 1915 final. He remembered being told that the Laois team came out for the second half wearing raincoats and only took them off as referee Willie Walsh of Waterford was about to restart the game.

With Jack Finlay – a tall wiry man, strong and hardy, wearing a black velour hat – playing fine hurling at midfield, leading by example and exhorting his men to greater effort, Laois kept a firm grip on the second half. Cork were outplayed and outscored. The Laois men added four goals. Cork could only manage 1:1. A great day for Laois ended with the score reading Laois 6:2 Cork 4:1. They had beaten the choicest hurlers in Munster.

When the victorious heroes arrived back at Abbeyleix they were met by bands and a huge gathering of well-wishers. A parade through the town followed. Later in Ballygeehan, Jack Finlay and the local players were greeted with bonfires and jubilant celebrations.

For a county that was destined to produce great hurling men in future decades it would have been impossible in 1915 to believe that the success of Jack Finlay and his men was the only All-Ireland hurling crown of any description that Laois would win in the twentieth century.

Jack is buried in the family burial ground at Clough, near Aghaboe. The Laois Millennium team is worth recording here:

Timmy Fitzpatrick
(*Kilcotton*)

Tom Finlay	Jackie Bergin	Mick Mahon
(*Ballygeehan*)	(*Abbeyleix*)	(*Rathdowney*)

Olly Fennell	Tom Byrne	John Taylor
(*Clonad*)	(*The Rovers & Clonad*)	(*Portlaoise*)

Pat Critchley   Billy Bohane
(*Portlaoise*)   (*Clonad*)

Michael Walsh	Harry Gray	Christy O'Brien
(*Ballinakill*)	(*Rathdowney & Faughs*)	(*Borris-in-Ossory*)

Frank Keenan	P.J. Cuddy	Paddy Lalor
(*Camross*)	(*Camross*)	(*Abbeyleix*)

Amby Power
CLARE
1914

'And fierce Cú Chulainn comes, his Godlike face,
With yearning wild to grip in hand once more
The lithe camán and drive the hurtling ball.'
(Rev. James B. Dollard D.L.)

Amby Power, a native of Quin in Co. Clare, was born in 1887 and christened Ambrose. However, from an early age he became known to all as Amby.

I am indebted to Seamus Reddan of Quin for the following information which he sent me about this great exponent of the ancient art, who hurled in the early decades of the twentieth century.

Amby was born in Brooklodge, Quin, of farming stock. He had two brothers, Joe and Fred, and one sister. Amby married Katie Reddan of Killorglin, Co. Kerry, who inherited a public house in Quin known as 'Marie Reddans'. Katie was a niece of the old lady. He farmed a small farm with the business and in later life was elected Fine Gael county councillor for Clare. He was 6'1", or 6'2" in height, not the giant you claim of 6'4", and was playing hurling around 13 stone. He died at the age of 73 years on 26 February 1960.

Hurling Champions of Ireland – such was the boast after they had beaten Laois before 15,000 spectators in Croke Memorial Park, Dublin, in October1914 with a victory margin of 5:1 to 1:0 for Laois. The Clare team trained in Quin, and they were accommodated in Quin before the game. So the slogan goes –
'Amby Power led them
And Marie Reddan fed them.'

Clare, playing in white jerseys with a green sash, were captained by their centreback, Amby Power. Joe Power, brother of Amby, was cornerback on the team, together with Mick Flanagan, also a member of Quin H.C.

180

It was not until 1932 that a Clare team again shaped like an All-Ireland winning side – going down to Kilkenny in the All-Ireland final by a score of 3:3 to 2:3. That team trained in Quin and was managed by Amby Power.

Thirteen special trains ferried fans to the capital city for the All-Ireland final. There, a special tram service was provided to the pitch. Gate receipts totalled £475. The team colours contrasted – Laois in black and amber jerseys with horizontal stripes, Clare in white jerseys with a green sash.

The game got under way in ideal weather conditions with Clare defending the railway goal. Laois never played with the fluency that characterised their displays against Dublin and Kilkenny.

Clare, on the other hand, who had done special training under the watchful eye of Jim O'Hehir – father of Micheál of broadcasting fame – gave an accomplished performance of dash and verve reminiscent of their displays against Limerick and Cork. A rock-solid defence, superbly marshalled by their captain Amby, kept the shackles on the Laois men throughout the field. Amby Power's men excelled in the finer points of the game. They finished the hour with fourteen men, convincing winners on the score 5:1 to 1 goal.

Present to see Amby Power receive the Great Southern Challenge Cup was Clare M.P. William Redmond. After the presentation the Clare team travelled in motor cars – a real treat of luxury in those days – to Wynn's Hotel to further celebrate a historic first All-Ireland crown.

The following morning *The Freeman's Journal* carried the following comments: 'Clare Defeats Leix in Decisive Manner; Splendid Contest at Croke Park, Witnessed by Huge Crowds'.

It was a great year for Clare hurling. They also won the junior title – defeating Cork by 6:2 to 5:2 in the Munster final and Laois by 6:5 to 1:1 in the All-Ireland final.

These are the men who brought honour to Clare in 1914 by winning the senior hurling title.

Pa 'Fowler' McInerney (goal), John Fox, Jack Shaloo, Ned Grace, Martin Moloney, Amby Power (Capt), Mick Flanagan, Joe Power, Jim Spellissey, Bob Doherty, Willie Considine, Jim Guerin (1:0), Brendan Considine (0:1), Tom McGrath (2:0), Jim Clancy (2:0).

181

In subsequent years Pa 'Fowler' McInerney, Bob Doherty and Brendan Considine won All-Ireland medals with Dublin.

Brendan Considine was a student at St. Flannan's College, Ennis, and seventeen years of age when he played with Clare in 1914. Years later, as he reflected on the great All-Ireland occasion and the men who fashioned victory, here is how he recalled some of them.

They were a fine body of men. Most of them were six foot or over. Many of them were highly skilled in the art of doubling on the flying ball. The captain of the team was Amby Power – he was the team's giant. The 'Dodger' – that was my brother Willie – played a wonderful game in the final. He had strength above the ordinary. Martin Moloney, who was better known as 'Handsome', was a beautiful player and a lovely striker of the ball. Tom McGrath from O'Callaghan's Mills was a fine full forward. He had great drive and speed. Bob Doherty from Newmarket-on-Fergus always played with determination and distinction and he later hurled with Dublin. The Clare forward line of that era was known as 'The Forward Machine'.

Dick 'Drug' Walsh
KILKENNY
1907, '09 & 1913

Through the kind assistance of Tom Dunphy the following detail on 'Drug' Walsh of Mooncoin was obtained from a local enthusiast. Born Rathkieran, Mooncoin, 1878; died Mooncoin 1958; buried in Carrigeen Cemetery.

By the turn of the century 'Drug' Walsh had acquired the necessary skills on the land, the river (as a fisherman) and the hurling field. He normally played fullback on the Mooncoin team, whereas his usual position on the county team was centre halfback.

Wiry, medium-sized, sure and positive in his play, with exceptional speed of delivery, right or left on the ground or overhead. His extreme fitness, ever present, enabled him to outpace, outstay and outplay his opponent. An astute tactician he marshalled and directed his men to good purpose on the field of play. A legend while yet playing, he won seven Leinster and All-Ireland medals, captained three All-Ireland winning hurling teams, captained Leinster to win the Railway Shield outright in 1908. Won one Munster Feis Medal. Won three county senior hurling championship medals with Mooncoin, two of them as captain.

During his lifetime Dick Walsh came to abhor the use of the word 'Drug' as a nickname. A more acceptable form of the name, accepted by himself, was 'Dhroog', a corrupt south Kilkenny form of the first part of the word 'dragoon'.

Following in the footsteps of Mikey Maher of Tipperary, Dick 'Drug' Walsh became the second hurler in the history of the GAA to lead his county to three All-Ireland hurling successes. Those wins were achieved in 1907, '09 and '13. Subsequently, only Christy Ring of Cork in 1946, '53 and '54 joined the elite group.

Dick made his county senior début in the successful All-Ireland campaign of 1904. The following year 1905 in the absence of 'Fox' Maher, 'Drug' lined out in goal – his first between the posts – in the All-Ireland final at Tipperary against Cork. Having let in three goals early in the first half he was replaced at half time by Joe Glennon and he then reverted to his normal defensive role. The game was lost by 5:10 to 3:13. However, following an objection by Kilkenny and a counter objection by Cork, a replay was ordered. Kilkenny reversed the result of the first meeting on the score 7:7 to 2:9 at Dungarvan.

When I was growing up I heard hurling men talk about Mooncoin and they spoke of it with the same reverence that they attached to Tullaroan. And well they might. For Mooncoin produced some stalwart hurling men.

Many people wonder how Dick got the nickname 'Drug'. The story goes that he acquired it at school. Apparently, he was very fond of the song 'Clare's Dragoons'. In singing it he appeared to pronounce dragoons as 'drugoons'. And so his schoolmates christened him 'Drug'. It stuck.

Dick was a man of medium build – fit, athletic and sinewy. He played hurling in an era when the game got little if any publicity in the national newspapers. Compared to today, hype was non-existent. Dick returned by train from one All-Ireland he played in and as he headed for home people asked him who had won and what was the score.

His hurling days preceded, by several score years, the concept of sponsorship, marketing, promotions, ticket hunting, foreign holidays and foreign trips. Hurling for the men of those days was for many a way of life. Glory won, was very much for the 'honour of the little village'.

When the trips to America started in the early fifties for the National League winners, Dick was intrigued by the publicity surrounding them. If he lived today the glamour and publicity associated with the game would mesmerise him.

In the ten years from 1904 to 1913 inclusive, Kilkenny qualified for seven All-Ireland finals and were successful on each occasion. Dick Walsh participated in them all and collected seven Leinster medals and seven All-Ireland medals. Three other colleagues, Sim Walton (Tullaroan), Jack Rochford (Threecastles) and Dick Doyle (Mooncoin) shared the great honour. The record Dick and his three colleagues established stood until 1953 when Christy Ring of Cork equalled it after a rather tempestuous All-Ireland final against Galway. The following year he surpassed it when victory over Wexford gave him an eighth All-Ireland medal. In 1964 John Doyle of Tipperary matched the seven All-Ireland wins of the great Kilkenny men. And the following year victory over Wexford gave John an eighth All-Ireland medal and a place in the history books with Christy Ring.

When Dick Walsh led the Kilkenny team around Dungarvan pitch on 21 June 1908 to contest with Cork, captained by the renowned James Kelliher of Dungourney, the seventeen-a-side All-Ireland final of 1907, he already had two All-Ireland successes under his belt (1904 and 1905). The two teams produced the greatest exhibition of the ancient craft seen up to then. That game became the benchmark by which subsequent performances were measured. The attendance of about 15,000 was held spellbound for the entire hour by the splendour of the contest. Dick Walsh, doing sterling work in defence, led his men to a one point victory on the score 3:12 to 4:8. Just as the game looked like ending in a draw Kilkenny snatched as dramatic a winner as was ever seen on a hurling field. John Anthony of Piltown cleared his lines. Jimmy Kelly of Mooncoin raced to the falling sliotar. He met it on the drop – and in that instant the game was won and lost as his effort swept in for a point. Referee M.F. Crowe of Limerick blew the final whistle. It was glory for Kilkenny – and much more yet to come. On that great occasion the Kilkenny team played in Tullaroan jerseys because Mooncoin supplied the captain. This agreement was reached with a view to preserving unity within the county.

Describing the match in *Sport*, Fr. James B. Dollard, who spent most of his life in the sacred ministry 'in far foreign fields' in Canada, and who threw in the ball to start the game, had this to say:

> In such a tremendous struggle the almost entire absence of any exhibitions of ill-temper among the hurlers was truly marvellous. Hurling, as played by these premier teams, is truly a national game to be proud of, a national heritage, a national glory . . . If the young men of Ireland could only be made see the fact as it really is, namely, that one grand day like that at Dungarvan (no matter who wins) gives purer enjoyment and more genuine satisfaction than a thousand years of America or other foreign lands, they would know how privileged they are, and would choose the better part of staying in the old country working for her weal; living and dying within the four walls of her holy hills . . . Ireland will be a great country yet – and soon, Knock-na-gow is not gone, and the people of Banba – "Kindly Irish of the Irish" – will yet possess their shadowy vales in peace and prosperity.

As already mentioned, Fr. Dollard of Mooncoin threw in the ball. It may well be that faith or superstition – call it what you like – played a role in Kilkenny's one point win. It seems there was a belief among Kilkenny players that if one of their priests threw in the ball they would win. Well, win they did – proof perhaps that faith can move mountains.

In 1907 the GAA lost one of its first patrons when John O'Leary, the noted Fenian, died on 16 March of that year.

Dick Walsh was at the helm again in 1909. It is noteworthy to record that in the All-Ireland semi-final of that year at Jones's Road, on 14 November, Kilkenny defeated Derry by 3:17 to three points. At Cork on 12 December he captained his men to victory over Tipperary 4:6 to 0:12. He was brilliant throughout the hour, despite efforts to unnerve him through hard physical exchanges. It was another great day. Dick had won his fourth All-Ireland medal. The future held more. It was Tipperary's first defeat in nine All-Ireland finals.

In 1913 Dick made hurling history when he became the first man to captain a 15-a-side team to All-Ireland honours. He also became the first and only hurler to captain 17-a-side and 15-a-side teams to

All-Ireland glory. The 1913 victory created for Kilkenny their first, and to date only, three in a row success – albeit with a walkover from Limerick in 1911 over a venue controversy that did not involve Kilkenny.

The 1913 All-Ireland final was played at Croke Park. Tipperary, as in 1909, provided the opposition and had to give way on the score 2:4 to 1:2. Interestingly, each side got only one score each in the second half – Kilkenny a goal, Tipperary a point.

Kilkenny's path to that final is worth recalling.

v Glasgow 10:6 to 5:2 at Glasgow on 21 June

Tom Ryall in *Kilkenny, the GAA Story 1884–1984*, recorded as follows: 'The winners left by train on the Friday at 11 a.m., took the boat from the North Wall and arrived in Greenock at 8 a.m. on Saturday. They then travelled by train to Glasgow.'

v Laois 8:3 to 2:6 at Portlaoise
v Lancashire 4:4 to 1:4 at Liverpool on 4 August
v Dublin 0:3 to 1:0 at Wexford
Replay v Dublin 7:5 to 2:1 at Wexford

The Freeman's Journal reported as follows on the final against Tipperary. 'It was the fastest hurling final that we have ever witnessed. It was a long way ahead of last year's final between Cork and Kilkenny. The ball travelled with lightning rapidity, and every man on the field seemed to be a sprinter of the first order. It was a hard game, but it was a game of champions – and, more than that, it was between scientific Kilkenny and dashing Tipperary.'

The result ran contrary to expectations. Earlier in the year Kilkenny were well beaten by Tipperary in the Croke Cup final and they lost a gold medal tournament final to Limerick. However, Kilkenny did intensive preparation in a rigorous training programme for the final. It paid handsome dividends on final day. Following victory Dick Walsh accepted the Great Southern & Western Railway company trophy – the first All-Ireland trophy to be presented to a victorious team captain.

Ned Quinn, at present (April 2001) chairman of Kilkenny County Board, told me – 'I remember "Drug" at the age of 70 skipping through the tyre of a bicycle. And he had a chest full of an assortment of hurleys and sliotars – some of them twice the size of the present-day ball. The chest also had a few golf balls and a golf iron. "Drug" would go to the field at the back of the house and belt the golf balls. He'd have made a success of golf too. He was just a natural athlete.'

After 1913 Dick Walsh had one more All-Ireland success – this time as trainer. Laois in 1915 had the benefit of his vast repertoire of hurling knowledge. It is likely that Bob O'Keeffe, a Kilkenny man playing with Laois and destined to become President of the GAA in 1935, was influential in obtaining Dick's invaluable services. He prepared them well. Laois surprised a fancied Cork side and won by 6:2 to 4:1.

This is the Kilkenny team that made history in 1913.

John T. Power

Dan Kennedy Jack Rochford Jack Keoghan

Jack Lennon Dick 'Drug' Walsh Dick Grace

Matt Gargan Pierce Grace

James J. Brennan Sim Walton Dick Doherty

Dick Doyle Jimmy Kelly Mick Doyle

'Come all ye young fellows, to my story give ear,
I tell of a stalwart, 'mong hurlers a peer
Whose name is still cherished wherever they join
By sportsman and trueman – "Drug" Walsh from Mooncoin.

With eagle-eyed vision and speed of a deer,
No matter how hectic, in combat – no fear
His wristwork – an artist's, Kilkenny's own Doyen
Reigned that Prince among hurlers, "Drug" Walsh from
  Mooncoin.'

(Rev. Michael O'H.)

Sim Walton
KILKENNY
1912

'Oh look at Walton their posts assaulting,
At last he raises the final score;
Our shouts were heard on the Hills of Clara
When he beat O'Meara, the "Barn Door".'

Kilkenny, captained by Sim Walton, were led onto the field by their own pipe band prior to the All-Ireland final of 1912 against Cork at Croke Park on 17 November.

Since the championships began in 1887 Cork had contested ten All-Ireland finals and won six.

Kilkenny qualified for nine and were successful on five occasions.

On the face of it not much separated the counties. However, Kilkenny were now on a roll having won all their titles since 1904 whereas Cork's last success was in 1903.

On the way to the final Kilkenny were fortunate to overcome Wexford who were still a formidable hurling force. Wexford led by two points entering the dying seconds. It was then that Kilkenny produced one of their dramatic finishes and a goal by Tom McCormack gave them a 4:4 to 4:3 victory. Easy wins followed over Laois in the Leinster final and Galway in the All-Ireland semi-final.

Cork on the other hand had two tough games in Munster with Limerick and Tipperary. Here is how Sliabh Ruadh described the clash with Limerick, Munster champions and All-Ireland finalists of 1910 and 1911. 'One of the toughest and most terrible tussles ever waged for a Munster crown . . . stubbornly fought from start to finish with a slight advantage in favour of Limerick. Leading by a point coming on to time, Limerick fought like demons. Then Byrne of Sarsfields pulled at a wing ball, up to Kennefick, the latter crossed to Kennedy of Carrigtwohill and the Limerick citadel fell.' Final score Cork 2:2 Limerick 1:3.

Sim Walton would have been well aware of what he had to contend with in the final of 1912. Against Cork he would have felt a slight psychological advantage following one point All-Ireland final victories in 1904 (1:9 to 1:8) and 1907 (3:12 to 4:8). So let's now look at Sim's background prior to 1912.

Sim, affectionately known as 'Little Sim', was born at Reimeen, Tullaroan, in 1880. From his father, John, who won a county senior title with Tullaroan in 1887, he inherited a great love of hurling and from an early age became immersed in the game. Of medium height, he weighed around 11 stone in his playing days. Speed, sudden bursts and accuracy acquired from regular practice, moulded him into a potent forward. He excelled at centre forward and full forward. His performances set him apart, made him legendary and the name Sim Walton contributed in a large way to the magic associated with Tullaroan.

If a series of Millennium Teams were selected to cover all decades of the GAA, Sim Walton would be a certainty for a place on one of them.

He was one of the most experienced captains ever to lead a team around Croke Park. He had been playing with Kilkenny since 1903 and had won five All-Ireland titles. He was captain in 1911 when Kilkenny got a walkover from Limerick in the All-Ireland final. His sportsmanship, affable personality and calm temperament made him an ideal captain.

Seventeen trains brought hurling fans from different parts of the country. Patrons paid a total of £589. There were four different entry fee categories – 6d, 1/–, 2/– and half-crown. Translated into euro currency they read 3c, 6c, 13c and 16c. A crowd of about 20,000 saw referee M.F. Crowe get the game under way. It turned out to be a hectic encounter – the last of the 17-a-side contests. All the skills that thrill a gathering were in evidence – overhead play, long ground strokes, manly tackling, evenly matched sides and a close contest.

Cork had the better of the first half and registered 1:2. Kilkenny's only score, a point, came from the stick of Sim Walton.

Kilkenny's next score also came from Sim. He lashed on a flying ball that had been cleared by the Cork defence and watched with delight as it beat Andy Fitzgerald in the Cork goal. The score was now Cork 1:3 Kilkenny 1:1. The titanic struggle continued.

Close games are often won – and indeed lost – by the unexpected and the bizarre. And so it was with the 1912 final. From well outfield Matt Gargan hit a great ground ball that reduced in pace as it approached the Cork custodian. With plenty of time to gather the ball, Andy Fitzgerald chose instead to nonchalantly pull. He missed as the sliotar, having hit uneven ground, hopped over his hurley. To his consternation and that of the Cork following the ball dribbled over the goal-line.

From then to the final whistle Cork lay siege to the Kilkenny goal, bombarding it and storming in again and again. But to no avail. They couldn't change the score-line. At the call of time the score read Kilkenny 2:1 Cork 1:3.

Through the good offices of the *Kilkenny People* word of the great victory arrived in Kilkenny by telegram shortly after 5 p.m. Preparations immediately began so as to give their hurlers a hero's welcome home.

Sim collected his sixth All-Ireland medal. A year later he would make it seven.

This great sportsman of farming stock also had a very keen interest in greyhounds. He kept many a good one and the most famous of all called Captain Sim ran in the Waterloo Cup.

Sim died in 1966 at the age of 86. But the hurling skills of the bloodline lived on. Liam Doyle who excelled for Clare in their victorious All-Ireland campaigns of 1995 and 1997 was a grandnephew of Sim's. Briseann an dúchas.

The heroes of 1912 were:

Sim Walton, John T. Power, Jack Keoghan, Pierce Grace, Dick Grace, Dan Kennedy, Dick 'Drug' Walsh, Eddie Doyle, Mick Doyle, Dick Doyle, Jimmy Kelly, Dick Doherty, J.J. Brennan, Matt Gargan, Paddy Lanigan, Tom McCormack, Jack Rochford.

'Now Captain Sim is looking serious
And the Munster goalman gets a fright,
For Sim is coming both fast and furious
At last he raises the flag of white.'

Dick Doyle
WEXFORD
1910

'Thus for the hour the battle raged,
Hotter and fiercer they each engaged;
Those stalwarts bold, unknowing fear,
Their county's honour alone held dear,
Seeking no gain or paltry pelf,
Reckless of limb and life itself;
Each heart true and stout and brave,
No spirit there of serf or slave.'

(Sliabh Ruadh)

Prior to compiling this article I had the pleasure of talking with Pat
Doyle of Coole, Castlebridge, son of Dick who captained Wexford to
All-Ireland hurling honours in 1910. They had a convincing victory
over Offaly (5:12 to 1:7) in the first round of the Leinster championship. In the Leinster final they had a decisive and surprising win
over Dublin (3:3 to 1:1). A feature of this game was the long pucking
of the Wexford men. In the All-Ireland final they had a narrow and
heart-stopping triumph over Limerick (7:0 to 6:2).

Dick, a farmer by profession, was born in 1879 to Patrick and Hanna
(née Doran). In his hurling days he was a strong, sturdy athlete,
measuring about 5'10" and turning the scales at 13 stone.

Dick and the men he captained were in the main hardy sons of the
soil, used to physical work and well able to cope with the rigours of
an hour on the hurling field.

It isn't always realised nowadays how hard the men of those
distant decades trained and how seriously they took the training.
Pat detailed some of it to me.

> There was what was called the four mile block. It was a kind of
> triangle incorporating Castlebridge, Kilcorral and Mullinagore.
> Running that triangle was part of the training drill. The training
> schedule was, however, very much a community effort. Blessed
> candles were lit by the households and placed in the windows.
> It was a form of prayer, a symbol, a display of solidarity, an
> expression of support. It was, I suppose, a reflection of the faith

191

of those days. It was the community's way of saying to the players as they ran those miles – we are with you, we are supporting you, we are thinking of you.

The running stints built up stamina and endurance. Little wonder then that *The People* reporter writing on the final was able to record 'Sean Kennedy, Dick Fortune and Sim Donohoe can run two hours as well as one' – a fact that is believed to have saved the day for Wexford in the final of 1910.

The Wexford v Limerick All-Ireland final of 1910 was an extremely close affair, with Wexford, who led at half time by six goals to 3:1, grimly holding on to a one point lead and withstanding fierce Limerick pressure when referee Michael Crowe blew full time. The score then stood Wexford 7:0 Limerick 6:2. Gate receipts of £288 was a record at the time.

Wexford were worthy and deserving champions, for the first time, after four final appearances (five if you count the Home Final of 1901). A measure of Wexford's hurling prowess in 1910 can be gleaned from the fact that in 1908 they defeated Kilkenny – then going through a golden era – by 1:8 to 10 points in the Leinster championship, only to lose the game following an objection.

In the All-Ireland final against Limerick in 1910 Dick Doyle, at full forward, scored Wexford's first goal and over the hour was their scorer-in-chief. By half time he had netted three. In the second half he got his team's only score – a goal – and it proved to be the winner.

It may well be that Limerick hadn't been forewarned about the goal-scoring potential of Dick. In those days our games received very little national coverage in the newspapers. There was little hype about individual performances. If there had been, word might have spread to Limerick that in the Leinster final against Dublin Dick scored 3:1 of Wexford's total of 3:3.

Pat remembers that his father used often recall the train journey to Dublin for the 1910 final. For many of the players it was the first such trip. Those who are familiar with the Wexford/Dublin railway line are well aware that for much of the journey the train travels right along the seafront and in places is quite high above the sea. Many of the players were terrified as they gazed out the windows of the train at the vast expanse of sea far below, and beyond, and wondered if the train would stay on the tracks at all.

As the years rolled on after 1910 and the sliotar in use grew smaller in size, Dick would look back bemused, and reflect on what they had played with.

Pat takes up the story.

> The old ball used in 1910 used be on display in the 'Reading Rooms' in Castlebridge. I'm not sure whether it is still there or not. 'I interrupted Pat to ask what were the "Reading Rooms".' Thomas Davis (1814–1845), the Young Irelander, founded the 'Reading Rooms'. It was his way of dealing with the literacy problems of his day. Local people would come in, in the evening, and a reader would read from the newspapers to them. The place is now a kind of club. People pay a small fee for membership. But back to the ball. It had a leather cover and when it got wet it swelled. Of course, it also became heavier. It took some strength to drive it any distance then. The hurleys were made for the task. They were heavier than nowadays and had a rounded handle. And they were designed for ground hurling – more like a hockey stick really.

Pat recalls that his father used say that Davy Kavanagh and Bill McHugh were regarded as the stylish men of the team. He remembers too that his father was very proud of his 1910 medal and used often talk about the occasion. The victory, and indeed the 1910 campaign in general, gave Wexfordmen much raw material for fireside stories and discussion during the winter nights. Dick was, by all accounts, a fanatical lover of our games – especially hurling – and delighted in reminiscing about the past.

Pat, however, didn't display any great enthusiasm for our games and didn't pay much attention to his father's reminiscences. By contrast, his late brother, Thomas, showed greater interest and he, understandably, inherited the 1910 hurling medal.

No senior hurling championships took place in Wexford for the four years 1906–1909 inclusive. It would seem that Dick was chosen as captain for his undoubted leadership qualities – and a fine captain he proved to be. He was also captain of the Wexford team in 1909 when the Model County lost to Laois in a highly entertaining Leinster semi-final at Kilkenny on the score 4:6 to 2:11; the Laois winning point coming in the closing moments.

Dick died in July 1946 aged 67. Pat recalled how hard he worked and the difficult times he lived through. 'The year he was born, 1879, saw the establishment of the Land League. There followed the land war and the reforms it brought continued throughout his youth. He was 12 at the time of the "Parnell Split" in 1891. Then there was the First World War and the 1916 Rising. After that you had the War of Independence and the Civil War. Just when things looked like improving, the economic depression of the 30s came and that was followed by the Second World War. He saw harsh and difficult times.'

The following is an excerpt from a report on the game in *The Free Press*, 26 November 1910.

Wexford were by far the best team in the first half-hour. They were a little behind in the first quarter of the last half. The next ten minutes were Limerick's in toto. Then Wexford came along in the last couple of minutes and had the best of matters. Such is the sum total of the game and Wexford deserved their win on the day's play.

Now to the match itself. There was not a man who could conscientiously say before the match that Wexford would win. All were doubtful. Limerick had the reputation of beating the renowned Corks and playing close games with the gallant Tipps. . . . But we all knew that once Rich Doyle would lead them out, they would get there and stick there. They got there the first half, and by Jove, didn't they stick it and that in such determined fashion they brought forth the heartiest cheers from friend and foe ever given in Jones's Road. . . .

Limerick were on the field sharp on time and all Wexford eyes were focused on them. They were trained to a nicety and their lithe movements caused no surprise. A lusty cheer had us standing up to see what was happening. It was only the boys coming out. When they came into the arena there was unmistake-able appeal. It was a cheer that required answering and Rich Doyle looked around as much as to say 'Very well, you will have your request complied with.' Yes, the lads answered it nobly, and Wexford men aye, and the women too, be they at home or scattered in many distant parts of the earth, were shaking hands with you in spirit for your heroic deeds at Jones's Road on Sunday.

The closing moments were described as follows:

> Limerick, with a couple of skiers were again in possession, and the forwards securing close up rushed in and scored a goal amidst great excitement. Limerick were now only one point behind and matters were looking exceedingly dangerous. It seemed as if the vim and speed had departed from the Slaneymen and their marking was not so well . . . These last seven minutes were nerve-racking minutes, now was the time for the lads to respond and didn't they. The cheering was deafening and the efforts of the players mighty. The honour of All-Ireland champions hung in the balance, and a straw would have brought down the scales one way or the other. Every man, woman and child stood there breathless, and the strained countenances and staring eyes were studies . . . Again did Limerick return and drove wide. The delivery aided Wexford to invade, but again Limerick returned for Parker to effect a clearance . . . The long whistle sounded.
>
> Rich Doyle did all the damage to the Limerick net. I have never seen him in such form. He missed nothing. He rose to the occasion, and his endeavours were cheered to the echo: 'Bravo Rich'.
>
> The scene at Amiens Street Station and Harcourt Street Station as the trains set off for the return journey would be impossible to describe. 'The Boys of Wexford' was lustily rendered.

The 17-a-side team of 1910 was as follows:

> Dick Doyle, Dave Kavanagh, Mike Cummins, Andy Kehoe, Bill McHugh, Jim Shortle, Paddy Mackey, Sim Donohoe, Pat Corcoran, Mick Neville, Michael Parker, Jas Mythen, Dick Fortune, Sean O'Kennedy, William Devereux, Jas Fortune, Pat Roche (goal).

In 1910 the GAA made some radical changes that paved the way for the modern day games:

- The side posts (as in Australian football) and the soccer-style goal-scoring area were abolished.

- Two uprights, 21ft. apart and 16ft. high with a crossbar located 8ft. from the ground, formed the new scoring area.
- Nets were introduced behind the goal-scoring area.
- A parallelogram 45ft. x 15ft. was located in front of goal. Goals scored were only allowed provided attacking players were not therein before the arrival of the ball.

Tom Semple
TIPPERARY
1906–1908

"Twas an autumn day, and the sun shone down
With a cheerful ray o'er the seaside town,
And dense the crowds that thronged them there
And joyous the shouts that rent the air;
For there were gathered our country's pride
From Lee, Suir, Nore and Shannonside;
And came they too from Sarsfield's town
And forth from the shadow of Knockmealdown;
E'en from the West were gathered there
Young men comely and maidens fair;
And with anxious step and eager pace,
Hurried they on to the trysting place;
For here today, in contest fleet,
Tipperary's best and Cork will meet –
Here beneath the Comeragh's frown
They'll cross camáns for the Munster crown.'

(Sliabh Ruadh)

At the dawn of the twentieth century a towering figure of a man, standing 6'3", made his début in the colours of his native Tipperary and won his first All-Ireland hurling medal with a 2:5 to 0:6 win over London in the final of 1900 which was played at Jones's Road

196

on 21 September 1902. A county career that lasted a dozen years ended in 1912.

By 1906 he was captain, when his native Tipperary set forth in search of their seventh All-Ireland crown and their first since 1900. The men of Tipperary were in the hands of a born leader.

Tom Semple was more than a captain. He was a general who captained through discipline; but in a style and manner that generated enthusiasm, respect and incredible loyalty. He trained his men to the last — hurling practice for teamwork and combination, walking and skipping for endurance and stamina.

It took five games to win the 1906 title. However, Semple and his men were only really tested in the Munster final and to a lesser extent in the All-Ireland final.

Against Limerick (Caherline) in the first round at Cork, Tom Semple and his men proved too powerful as the game progressed and won in the end by 2:12 to 4 points.

The victory over Clare at the Markets Field, Limerick, in the Munster semi-final was even more decisive. For twenty minutes it was neck and neck but once Tipperary moved into top gear the result was never in doubt. It ended 5:10 to 7 points.

Tipperary prepared diligently for what they knew would be a major assignment against Cork in the Munster final at Tipperary. Cork had been undisputed champions in Munster with five titles in a row from 1901 to 1905. But these Cork hurlers held no fears for Tom Semple and his men. The pairing attracted a huge crowd that paid record gate receipts.

A great first half saw Tipperary lead narrowly at the break by 1:3 to 4 points. The second half continued like the first — no quarter anywhere on the field as fit hardy men displayed vim, vigour and boundless energy. Both sides had prepared well and were trained to the ounce. But it was Semple's men who prevailed and at the call of time Munster had new hurling champions. Tipperary 3:4 Cork 9 points. It was heroes all on the Tipperary side but none more so than their gallant captain, Tom Semple.

'What is your fear boys whilst Semple is with you,
That gallant old captain who leads in the fray?'

Galway fell heavily in the All-Ireland semi-final at Limerick (7:14 to 2 points).

In the final against Dublin, which was played in pouring rain at Kilkenny on 27 October 1907, Dublin captained by Tipperary-man Dan McCormack led at half time by 2:7 to 1:7. However, in the second half Semple and his men asserted themselves and surge after surge of attacking play brought their full-time score to 3:16 as against Dublin's 3:8, in what had been a splendidly contested final. The result was greeted with wild enthusiasm and one observer remarked that no matter who won it would have been a Tipperary triumph as something like eleven of the Dublin team were natives of Tipperary.

Tom Semple made it a personal double in 1906 by winning the Long Puck championship with a drive of 96 yards with the 9oz. sliotar.

The 1908 All-Ireland win was in many respects a replica of the 1906 success. Only Cork in the Munster semi-final tested the Tipperary metal. There was a huge gathering for the encounter at Fermoy. A splendid game was in prospect and it lived up to all expectations. Referee Willie Walsh of Waterford controlled the game well. The sides were level at half time (1:4 each). The second half turned into an epic struggle as Tom Semple exhorted his men and called for a supreme effort. He badly wanted to win this game. In the Munster final of the previous year before a crowd of 20,000 at Dungarvan Tom Semple stood over a close-in free in the closing moments. His team were a point in arrears. Tom put every ounce of his strength behind the shot but the redoubtable Jamsey Kelliher of Dungourney was equal to the task. He saved and cleared for Cork to add another point and win by 1:6 to 1:4.

The second half of the 1908 Munster semi-final ebbed and flowed. The match hung in the balance right through every puck of the game. Two points down entering the closing stages Tom Semple got his winning wish when Bill Harris got Tipperary's second goal that clinched a famous victory on the score 2:11 to 3:7.

Paddy Mehigan (Carbery) hurler and athlete – and in later life a renowned journalist and author – was a member of the Cork selection. Not for the first time his visions of an All-Ireland medal disappeared into dreamland.

Earlier in the championship Tipperary had a runaway victory over Waterford in the first round and subsequent to the game with Cork they got a Munster final walkover from Kerry followed by an easy All-Ireland semi-final win over Galway.

The campaign up to All-Ireland stage read as follows:

v Waterford (7:16 to 0:5)
v Cork (2:11 to 3:7)
v Kerry (walkover)
v Galway (5:15 to 1:0)

As in 1906 Dublin provided the opposition in the 1908 final. It was played at Jones's Road on 25 April 1909. Tipperary were fortunate to escape with a draw (2:5 to 1:8) for Dublin. But they learned and made no mistake in the replay at Athy on 27 June 1909. It was easy really (3:15 to 1:5).

That was a Home Final. Glasgow were in line for a final confrontation. They conceded a walkover — wisely maybe.

In the 1950s Carbery selected a team entitled 'The Best Men of my Time'. At left half forward he choose Tom Semple, guardsman of the G.S. & W. Railway, stating 'I can find no peer for the great Tom Semple of Thurles; a deer of a man and a glorious striker of the ball, captained great teams.' About twenty years earlier writing in a GAA Golden Jubilee Issue of the *Irish Independent* (Easter 1934), he had this to say about the Tom Semple he saw in 1902 at *Tír an Úir* (Terenure). 'How my young eyes feasted on that six-foot-three lath of a man, handsome as a Greek god; brown hair a clump of close curls; limbs like a thoroughbred; all life and nervous movement . . . Great long strides Semple had, and such a sweep of ash! Grounder of 90 yards off either hand; lightning lifts and soaring pucks goalwards; fierce and fearless at hurling; kind and gentle as a maid at festive board. Such was Tom Semple, prince of hurlers.'

D'imigh Tom ar shlí na Fírinne in Aibreán 1943. Fiche cúig bliana ina dhiaidh sin i 1968 baisteadh 'Semple Stadium' ar Pháirc an Imeartha i nDúrlas Éile le hurraim dó.

Jer Doheny
KILKENNY
1904

'See on the green and springy sward
The banded hurlers stand
(Glory and fame their sole reward),
With swift camán in hand!
Ho, knaves and foemen stand aside,
No carpet knights are they!
God save our matchless hurling men,
Our Irish Gaels. Hurrah!'

(Rev. James B. Dollard D.L.)

Jer Doheny, son of John and Annie, was born in Ballycallan in 1874. However, he spent most of his life in Tullaroan. He was a first cousin of Pat 'Fox' Maher, a contemporary and one of Kilkenny's greatest hurling sons.

I had the pleasure of spending a most enjoyable afternoon talking and reminiscing with Jer's eighty-one-year-old son – also named Jer – some weeks after Kilkenny's great All-Ireland victory of 2000 over Offaly. We looked at photographs and an assortment of medals of varied and beautiful design while talking of 'far-off things, and battles long ago'. This genial and affable octogenarian, whose gait and energy belie his years, was only ten years old when his father died.

Accordingly, his recollections of him were understandably sparse. He remembers him as 'a big athletic man, measuring over 6ft and weighing over 13 stone. He played cricket as well as hurling. A lot of the hurlers of those days played cricket. The cricket jerseys were white and when Tullaroan club came to decide on the club colours they just added a green sash to the white cricket jersey. He refereed matches, including a number of county finals. For five years he was County Chairman from 1908 to 1912. Ah, he was active in GAA affairs all his life.'

Did you inherit the hurling genes? I queried. 'Some. I played junior with Waterford in 1941. I won a Waterford county senior title with Erin's Own in 1942. When Vin Baston was injured in 1943 I was chosen at midfield with Mick Hickey on the Waterford team that played Cork in the Munster final. Paddy O'Donovan and Jack Lynch were our opponents that day. We lost by only two points. The same day Antrim beat Kilkenny in Belfast in the All-Ireland semi-final. The final was a farce. Cork walked away with Antrim.'

Let's now return to his father, a man of the soil who farmed for a living. When Jer Doheny, one of several players sporting a moustache, led the Kilkenny team, drawn from Tullaroan, Threecastles, Erin's Own, Mooncoin and Piltown, onto the field in Carrick-on-Suir on 24 June 1906 to face Cork (St. Finbarr's) in the All-Ireland final of 1904, he must have done so with considerable trepidation and in hope rather than confidence.

There were two main reasons for this. In the first place Kilkenny, up to then, had contested four All-Ireland finals — five if you include the Home Final of 1903 — and lost on each occasion. They fell to Cork in 1893 and 1903; to Tipperary in 1895 and 1898 and to Limerick in 1897.

Secondly, by 1904 Cork had six All-Ireland titles under their belt and had just annexed four Munster titles in a row. They were a mighty team with many superb hurlers. In many hurling quarters they were perceived as being well nigh invincible.

Jer arrived on the county scene in 1893 and tasted All-Ireland defeat on the five occasions referred to.

However it's a long road that has no turning. Seventeen years after the championships started Jer became the first man to captain Kilkenny to All-Ireland hurling glory.

On that June day in 1906 at Carrick-on-Suir, in a 17-a-side contest, Jer played in the right full forward position. He had under his captaincy a blend of youth and experience which in recent games had combined hurling skills with traits of verve and tenacity.

The team was sprinkled with names whose artistry with the camán would echo their fame throughout the land in the years ahead. And they would be remembered long after they retired; even long after they died. You had Dick Doyle, Sim Walton, Jack Rochford and 'Drug' Walsh, all of whom won seven All-Ireland medals each. You had the Doyle brothers, Dick and Eddie, who were joined by their brother Mick in 1907. Between them they amassed the remarkable total of 18 All-Ireland medals — Dick 7, Eddie 6 and Mick 5.

The path to the final was as follows:

201

v Laois at Mountrath (3:15 to 2:10) on 4 March 1906
v Offaly at Portlaoise (3:11 to 1:4) Leinster semi-final

Kilkenny were then nominated to represent Leinster in the All-Ireland semi-final

v Galway at Athlone (2:8 to 1:7) on 13 May 1906

This game attracted 10,000 spectators and the railway authorities provided seven special trains.

v Dublin at Enniscorthy (2:8 to 2:6) – Leinster final

A memorable All-Ireland final encounter – the start of which was delayed by half an hour due to a heavy shower – with Cork ended with a one point win for Kilkenny on the scoreline 1:9 to 1:8. This game set the scene for many more hurling classics down the years between these two counties – quite a few of them ending with a winning margin of one point.

Jer played a captain's part that day in Carrick-on-Suir, scoring the opening point, disrupting the Cork defence, inspiring his colleagues and leading by example in a game of never-say-die spirit that was marked by much brilliant play. Kilkenny excelled at speed and combination and their goalkeeper 'Fox' Maher had a superb hour between the posts. Kilkenny, facing the breeze in the first half, sent their large following wild with excitement when Dick Doyle goaled early on – a goal that gave the Noresiders a 1:5 to 5 points lead at half time. The victory marked the high point for Jer in a brilliant club and county career.

We can only speculate on the level of joy and elation the great win gave to Jer. He had beaten a great band of Cork hurlers heading for three-in-a-row All-Ireland titles. The Kilkenny victory proved to be the harbinger of a golden era in Noreside hurling that was to bring them six more titles by 1913 – seven titles in ten years – a record likely to stand for ever and a day.

Jer retired from the inter-county hurling scene in June 1906, immediately after the 1904 success. He was thirty. It was the year of the death of two great GAA men. On 1 June 1906 Michael Davitt died at the age of 60 – one of the first patrons of the GAA; an avowed opponent of landlordism; founder of the Land League; a visionary and one of Ireland's greatest political figures and reformers. On 27 November 1906 Michael Cusack died; founder of the GAA and the driving force behind the organisation in its infancy.

Jer still hurled at club level with Tullaroan and added county medals in 1907, 1910 and '11 to those he had already won with the Club in 1895, '97, '99, 1901, '02 and '04 and to his first ever with Threecastles in 1888.

He won Leinster titles in 1893 (a walkover from Dublin), 1895 v Dublin, 1897 (a walkover from Wexford), 1898 v Dublin, 1900 v Dublin, 1903 (it ended 1:5 each v Dublin, but the Dublin goal was disputed and the game awarded to Kilkenny), 1904 v Dublin. Leinster medals, however, were only presented since 1900 following the establishment of the Leinster Council on 4 November 1900.

Jer married Annie Keoghan in 1913. 'She was a sister of Jack Keoghan who won All-Ireland medals with Kilkenny in 1907, '09, 1911, '12 and '13. He went to America in 1914 and played on the U.S. Tailteann games team in 1928. And would you believe it, when Kilkenny toured America in 1934, he was still playing hurling at fullback. He was then 46.'

Sadly, Jer's life innings was a relatively short one. Ghlaoigh Dia air go luath. He died in 1929 at the age of 55. Imíonn na daoine ach fanann na cnuic. There was a huge gathering and a hurling Guard of Honour at Tullaroan Church to bid a last fond farewell to a beloved hurling son.

These are the men, captained by Jer, who brought a famous first to the Noreside.

Jer Doheny, Pat 'Fox' Maher, Sim Walton, Jack Hoyne, Martin Lawlor, Paddy Saunders, Jim Lawlor (Tullaroan), Dick Doyle, Eddie Doyle, Pat Fielding, Dick 'Drug' Walsh (Mooncoin), Jack Rochford, Dick Grace (Threecastles), Dick Brennan, Dan Stapleton, Paddy Lanigan (Erin's Own), John Anthony (Piltown).

Stephen (Steva) Riordan
CORK
1903

"Twas coming from the fair of Ross, I spied that bend of
  growing ash,
And swore I'd cut the making's true, before the night was done.'
                                                    (Carbery)

I had the help of Jimmy Brohan, prince of cornerbacks in his day, with this article. And while researching same he discovered to his surprise that Steva was born at Ballintemple in the parish of Blackrock where he himself first saw the light of day.

Steva, as he was affectionately known, won a Cork county title with Dungourney in 1902 and was a member of a great Blackrock team that captured a ninth Cork county title for the village by the Lee in the hurling championship of 1903.

In the 1903 county final, played in 1904, Blackrock led St. Finbarr's by 1:5 to 1 point at half time. They had to withstand a great second half rally by St. Finbarr's and were fortunate to escape with a one point victory (2:8 to 1:10).

Steva had the honour of captaining Cork – described by Carbery as a 'painstaking captain' – in the All-Ireland championship of 1903. He skippered a Blackrock selection supported by players from Dungourney, Sarsfield's, St. Finbarr's and Redmonds.

In Munster, Cork defeated Tipperary by 4:6 to 1:10 in the first round at the Markets Field, Limerick. It was Steva's sternest and indeed only real test in the All-Ireland campaign. Waterford who had defeated Kerry fell heavily in the Munster final to the men of Cork (5:16 to 1:1).

Galway conceded a walkover in the All-Ireland semi-final. The other semi-final was played at Jones's Road on 18 June 1905. Kilkenny (Threecastles) had a runaway victory over Antrim (6:29 to 3:2).

The way was now clear for a Home Final between Lee and Nore. For the 5,000 spectators who attended at Fraher Field, Dungarvan, on 16 July 1905 the contest was a disappointment. Cork were in a class apart and won by 8:9 to 8 points. The records have credited

Andy 'Dooric' Buckley with 7:4 of Cork's score. The game was refereed by Luke O'Toole, Secretary of the GAA.

The final against the exiles, London (Hibernians), took place at Jones's Road, on 12 November 1905, with John McCarthy of Kilkenny in charge of the whistle. Steva and Cork continued their all-conquering march. It was really no contest and ended on the score 3:16 to 1:1. Victory qualified Steve for a second successive All-Ireland medal. He had led Cork to their sixth All-Ireland title.

In terms of All-Ireland victories 1903 was the end of an era for Cork. Sixteen years would elapse before they would win their next title in 1919.

Six months after the 1903 All-Ireland victory on 12 November 1905, Steva added another gold medal to his collection. On 27 May 1906 Cork faced Wexford in the Croke Cup final at Dungarvan. The Croke Cup was a highly prestigious competition and the gold medals a coveted prize. Cork won on the score 5:9 to 5 points. Steva as captain took possession of the magnificent perpetual Croke Cup trophy.

Steva was one of the great players of his era and had a club career that lasted almost twenty years during which time he won several county titles. He was of sturdy build and measured about 5'10". He gave outstanding displays at left fullback – a position in which he knew all the skills of the game – a master at hook, pull, block and parry. A man of boundless energy, he would finish a game as fresh as he started.

Carbery described him as 'a loveable social character, he could sing a good song, tell a droll story and was a fine dancer – the heart of corn'. Carbery, who hurled with London Irish, Cork and Dublin attributed much of his hurling technique to the guidance and coaching he received from Steva.

Steva took part in the War of Independence and was captured and interned in Ballykinler Camp. There, his comrades disguised him by shaving off his moustache and hair – for he was a much wanted man. On learning of Steva's internment I couldn't help wondering if my late father, Jim, had known him. As a member of General Sean McKeon's Brigade in Longford he too was captured and following imprisonment in a number of gaols was transferred by ship from Dublin to Ballykinler in Co. Down. Perhaps their paths did cross.

Steva played in four All-Ireland finals and lost in 1904 and 1907 to Kilkenny by just one point on each occasion.

All the honours of his era came his way – All-Ireland titles, Munster titles, county titles, Croke Cup successes and on a personal level the captaincy of his club and county.

Jim Kelliher
CORK
1902

'I'm eighty years come Michaelmas, and shaking is this hand of mine,
Your shape recalls the happy days when I was young and gay;
Last week at dusk when stripping thatch, I found you on the rafter-line –
My old camán, that served me well, from Cork to Ballyhay.

You made your name in championships when Gaelic men ranged side by side,
St. Finbarr's Reds, Dungourney men with Blackrock in the van;
Tip'rary fame, Kilkenny's pride, the fearless men from Shannon's tide –
But by my word, my honest ash, you never maimed a man!'

(Carbery)

The village of Dungourney is located about five miles north east of Midleton in east Cork.

It owes its place on the map of fame to Jim Kelliher. Jim was a hurler and a horseman. He excelled at both – a horseman supreme, a hurler par excellence.

He has been described as a dapper man, 5'9" in height, wide-shouldered and neatly built from head to ankle. His early life was spent between the plough and the hunt. On Sundays he patronised his favourite camán game. He was always match-fit and throughout his life remained a non-drinker and non-smoker. He had the ideal temperament for competitive sport and his calm disposition and equanimity enabled him to handle victory or defeat with graciousness.

He bred and trained many first class hunters and won several cross-country trophies. His victory, on a mare called Home Chat, in a point-to-point race (a steeplechase) against many of the leading gentry of the day was widely acclaimed.

In *A Story of Champions* written by John P. Power the following is recorded. 'The story of his victory in the open steeplechase at Ceim, near Rathcormac, in the early days of the century, when it was an unheard of thing for a farmer to ride against the "gentlemen" of the country – let alone beat them – sang like a ballad into the hearts of Corkmen. For that gruelling six-mile not only did Jamesy Kelliher win a horse race but he also won a kind of freedom for the people.'

In the GAA world he is remembered for his matchless hurling skills. He was one of the outstanding men of his time. Carbery described him as 'perhaps the greatest Roman of them all' and added 'Kelliher had brains, skill, stamina and ash-craft in abundance. I saw him play in twenty-six major matches and he never left the field without being the outstanding hurler of the hour.' It used be said that a Cork team without him would have been like Hamlet without the prince.

He usually played at fullback or centre halfback but he was no stranger either to the forward division. He could dribble the sliotar and course it with the hurley – a great skill that died some decades ago – before sending a rasping grounder to test the alertness of the opposing goalie.

He led his native Cork with a Dungourney selection to All-Ireland victory in 1902 – the year the country mourned, on 22 July, the death of Dr. Croke, Archbishop and Patron of the GAA. In the 1901 final he was on the losing side when Cork (Redmonds) rather surprisingly lost to London – albeit narrowly 1:5 to 4 points – at Jones's Road on 2 October 1903.

The 1902 campaign was as follows:

Munster final v Limerick (2:9 to 1:5).
All-Ireland semi-final v Galway (10:13 to nil) at Tipperary 20 March 1904.
(In the second semi-final Dublin beat Derry 6:19 to 0:6 at Drogheda 5 June 1904.)
All-Ireland Home Final v Dublin (1:7 each) at Tipperary 3 July 1904.
Replay v Dublin (2:6 to 0:1) at Tipperary 17 July 1904.
All-Ireland final v London (3:13 to nil) at Cork 11 September 1904.

The Home Final games were refereed by Patrick McGrath.

The final, which was attended by several thousand people, was refereed by Luke O'Toole, Secretary of the GAA.

The following year, 1903, Jim won his second All-Ireland medal when Cork under the captaincy of Steva Riordan of Blackrock defeated Kilkenny in the Home Final and London in the final.

In 1904 Jim was on the losing side when Kilkenny (Tullaroan) pipped Cork (St. Finbarr's) by one point – 1:9 to 1:8.

The Fates dealt unkindly with Cork in 1905. Jim Kelliher was captain and led his men to victory over Kilkenny at Tipperary on 14 April 1907. Kilkenny lodged an objection and Cork lodged a counter objection. Central Council ordered a replay for 30 June 1907. Cork lost on this occasion under the captaincy of C. Young at Dungarvan.

At this juncture it is worth noting, too, that the gods were not smiling on Paddy Mehigan (Carbery). He was with London in 1902 when losing to his native Cork.

He was back with Cork in 1905 when Kilkenny's objection robbed him of what would have been a coveted All-Ireland medal.

Cork and Kilkenny met in the All-Ireland final of 1907 at Dungarvan on 21 June 1908. Jim Kelliher captained the team that contained the vast bulk of the 1902 successful lineout.

A game that turned out to be a classic was got under way by referee M.F. Crowe of Limerick. The attendance was held in suspense for the entire hour. Just when it seemed like ending in a draw Jimmy Kelly doubled on a dropping ball as it hit the ground and sent over the winning point for Kilkenny on the score 3:12 to 4:8. The game became the benchmark against which all future games were measured.

Cork didn't reach another final until 1912 when they faced their now arch-rivals Kilkenny at Jones's Road on 17 November. As Jim Kelliher and his Cork team-mates took the field under the leadership of Barry Murphy of Blackrock he must have been wondering what sort of a hand the gods would deal him. He was hoping for a third All-Ireland medal. Kilkenny had denied him in 1904, '05, and '07 – by a point, through an objection and by a point respectively.

Seventeen trains converged on Dublin and an attendance of 20,000 was treated to an enthralling contest. But the gods were in capricious mood. Cork led by 1:2 to 1 point at the break and now, after a tough Munster campaign with gruelling victories over Limerick and Tipperary, they looked the stuff of potential champions. They were still leading by 1:3 to 1:1 in the second half when the gods pounced. Cork's brilliant goalkeeper, Andy Fitzgerald, instead of stopping a slow incoming ball, decided to pull first time. The ball hit a rough spot and hopped over his hurley to barely cross the goal-line. Cork a point down. From then to the end Cork tore in on the Kilkenny goal in battering attacks. But to no avail.

It was the great Jim Kelliher's last hoorah. However, defeat failed to dent or diminish the image and reputation of one of hurling's greatest exponents of whom it used be said 'he could call the ball and tell it where to go'.

Carbery held James Kelliher in the highest regard and placed him at centre back in his team entitled 'The Best Men of My Time', chosen in the fifties.

John J (Jack) Coughlan
LONDON
1901

'Whilst love and praise we e'er accord
The men of might and brawn,
Who foot the leather o'er the sward,
And wield the stout camán!
We'll not forget the exiled ones,
Our brothers stout and brave,
Who plod and toil on foreign soil —
The Gaels beyond the wave!'
Phil O'Neill (Sliabh Ruadh)

The borders of the nineteenth and twentieth centuries represented a special era in Irish affairs. It should be remembered that at that time we were part of the British Empire and ruled from Westminster. A deep sense of renewal and identity prevailed. The national spirit and the ideals associated with it were reflected in many fields.

In 1893 the Gaelic League (*Conradh na Gaeilge*) was established in Dublin. Its chief objective was to foster and revive the Irish language. This ideal transcended religious and political divides. One of the founders of the Gaelic League was Douglas Hyde, a member of the Protestant community and destined to become Ireland's first President.

The purchase of the land of Ireland for Irish tenant farmers was ongoing. It began with the foundation of the Land League in 1879. The Ashbourne Act of 1885 made available a loan of £5m. at 4% interest, repayable over a forty-nine year term, to assist tenants with the purchase. The Balfour Act of 1891 provided a further loan of £50m. The Wyndham Act of 1903 surpassed all previous ones and provided a loan of £100m.

On the political front Home Rule was the key issue. Those pursuing it were endeavouring to bring to fruition the aspirations of Thomas Davis, John Mitchell, Daniel O'Connell, O'Donovan Rossa and many others.

The Gaelic Athletic Association (GAA) was founded in 1884 'for the preservation and cultivation of our National Pastimes'. It began a renaissance and 'swept the country like a prairie fire'.

It was against the foregoing background that, for the purposes of GAA competitions, England was granted the status of a fifth Irish province in 1900. As a consequence, the winners of the championship in England would meet the winners of the Home Final (i.e. the championship winners in Ireland) to decide the All-Ireland title holders.

Extensive street-paving and building contracts attracted Irish men of strong physique to London. Wrote Carbery, 'friendly Irish contractors brought a few Irish hurlers across; the few brought many'. Thus was assembled a mighty hurling force captained by Dan Horgan of Cork and with a great defence built around Sean Óg Hanley of Limerick, the greatest hurling fullback of that time. In the final of 1900 played 26 October 1902, London, in an absorbing contest at Jones's Road came within a whisker of dethroning the fearless men of Tubberadora, the pride and cream of Tipperary hurling.

And so to 1901.

The death took place of the noted Fenian James Stephens, on 29 March at the age of 77. John O'Leary, patron of the GAA, gave the graveside oration.

The Association also lost two of its devoted servants. Michael Deering of Cork who was elected President in 1898 died on 25 March. P.P. Sutton of Dublin, official Handicapper of the Association, sports journalist, athlete and hurler, died on 15 June.

Luke O'Toole of Co. Wicklow was elected Secretary of the Association – a position he held until his death in 1929.

Alderman James Nowlan of Kilkenny was elected President of the Association. He remained in the position for twenty years and having indicated his desire not to seek re-election was succeeded in 1921 by Dan McCarthy of Dublin.

In the All-Ireland final of 1901 (played 2 August 1903) a London selection faced Cork (Redmonds) at Jones's Road. Many of the men of 1900 were in the line-out. Among them was the current captain Jack Coughlan who had made his mark across the Irish sea, not only as a hurler but also in the field of athletics, from which he amassed a large collection of trophies. Jack hailed from Tulla in Co. Clare – a parish that was passionate about the game of hurling. A branch of the GAA was established in Tulla in November 1885 and a club was formed on 1 January 1887.

Jack made his name in the Tulla jersey in the Clare county championships. He was prominent in the Tulla victory of 1:6 to 3 points over O'Callaghan's Mills in the county final of 1896.

'And the people came in thousands
From the moorlands and the hills,
To see the final championship
Between Tulla and the Mills.'

Jack was on the Clare team that won the Croke Cup competition of 1896 with victories over Tipperary (2:3 to 1:3), Limerick (2:3 to nil), Galway (7:10 to nil), and Wexford (5:16 to 2 points). In that 17-a-side victory he played at left fullback. In those days the Croke Cup competition vied for status with the All-Ireland championship. Victory in the competition conferred a special feather in the hurling cap of the winning county.

Reporting on the Croke Cup final, the *Independent* had this to say. 'The Wexford players were fairly outpaced by the Banner County men, whose dexterity was simply marvellous, and whose speed was sustained to the end. The victors scored goals and points with machine-like regularity.'

Jack Coughlan and his team of fellow exiles, that included two other natives of Tulla – Paddy King and John King – faced Cork with confidence; a confidence that delivered in the words of Carbery 'the epochal win of a great London Exile team of Munster hurlers . . . that carried the hurling title beyond the four seas of Éireann for the first time in GAA history.' And as we now know, the only time.

A splendidly contested game was refereed by John McCarthy of Kilkenny. The following is an excerpt from a report on the match in the *Clare Journal*. 'Cork won the toss and with the wind, pressed 'till the London captain, Jack Coughlan, drove them back with a long puck to touch. From the line puck, the Londoners came away and got a point inside a minute . . . Neutral play was the order for a considerable time but after some splendid play Cork equalised . . . the Cork forwards pressed hard until the visitors were forced to concede another point. Play was suspended when a London player received an injury but on resumption, London got possession and scored a point, thus equalising matters before half time. In the second half there were marvellous bouts of play but the strength and combination of the Londoners now told and they succeeded in scoring a goal. At the final whistle the score stood London 1:5 Cork 0:4. After the match the London captain, Jack Coughlan, was chaired and on leaving the dressing-room was again chaired and carried in this position to the hotel.'

I am grateful to Jimmy Smyth – a former Clare hurler and one of the greatest forwards the game has known – for the personal details relating to Jack Coughlan; and also to Karl Quinn, Chairman of Tulla GAA Club for his kind help.

The London team of 1901 comprised the following players, as listed on a photograph of the team.

Paddy King, John King, Jack Coughlan and J. O'Brien (Clare).
M. McMahon (Tipperary). Ned Barrett (Kerry).
Jer O'Connell, J. Fitzgerald and Tim Doody (Limerick).
Dan Horgan, Jim Lynch, C. Crowley, M. Horgan, Jim Barry, John O'Brien, Jer Kelliher, Tom Barry (Cork).

Other lineouts give P. Crowe and J. Crowley of Cork instead of John O'Brien and C. Crowley of Cork.

It is worth noting that Ned Barrett, who hailed from Ballyduff in Co. Kerry, and was, I understand, a policeman in London, added Olympic medals to his All-Ireland medal in 1908 at the Olympic Games held in London. As a member of the United Kingdom No.1 Team he won gold in the Tug of War and he also captured a bronze medal in wrestling.

Ned Hayes
TIPPERARY
1900

'You have the Irish dance as yet;
Where is the Irish hurling gone?
Of two such lessons why forget
The nobler and the manlier one?'
(Thomas Francis Meagher)

The dawn of the new century saw the birth of many positive things on the GAA front. The first steps were taken towards the establishment of the Provincial Councils. These brought a new dimension to the administration of the organisation. At the Convention in Thurles England, for GAA purposes, was declared a province of Ireland. It presented exiles with an opportunity to participate in our games at the highest level. Inter-county contests in athletics were inaugurated. For the first time since the foundation of the GAA all four provinces were represented in the hurling championship.

It was against this progressive background that Ned Hayes captained the men of Tipperary in the hurling title-race of 1900.

Ned hailed from Two-Mile-Borris and was among the most skilful hurlers of his day. As well as captaining Tipperary he also led victorious Croke Cup and Railway Shield teams.

Ned and Tipperary began their successful campaign of 1900 with a first round match against Cork (Redmonds). This was a tension-packed encounter from start to finish with hurling of a high standard. Ned Hayes's men trailed at half time by seven points to five. Great defensive work in a second half of fluctuating fortunes saw victory go to the Premier County on a scoreline of 12 points to 9.

Clare in the Munster semi-final and Kerry in the Munster final were both completely out of their depth against Ned Hayes and his men as the following scorelines show.

v Clare (6:11 to 1:6)
v Kerry (6:11 to 2:1)

A tougher and sterner contest awaited Tipperary in the All-Ireland semi-final against Kilkenny (Mooncoin) at Carrick-on-Suir on 29

213

June 1902. The game was a contest of Homeric proportions. As was the case against Cork, Tipperary were behind at half time. They were led by 1:6 to 4 points but Ned Hayes and his men had grit and staying power. They finished on a winning score of 1:11 to 1:8.

Game No. 5 for Tipperary was against Galway who had overwhelmed Antrim on a final score believed to be something like 3:44 to 1 point. Unfortunately, for those who gathered at Terenure on 21 September 1902 to watch the Home Final between Tipperary and Galway, the game turned out to be a very one-sided affair. Tipperary were superior in all departments and won easily 6:13 to 1:5.

Now came a great occasion for the GAA – the meeting for the first time in an All-Ireland final of the home champions, Tipperary, against London (Desmonds), a team of exiles. Nobody knew quite what to expect. Tipperary were perceived as being well nigh invincible. The exiles, all Munster men, knew their hurling but only about half a dozen were household names. A gathering of about 10,000 assembled at Jones's Road on 26 October 1902. The game turned out to be a contest of bewildering uncertainty. And as the hour progressed neutrals turned more and more towards the exiles who were displaying not only great skill and stamina but also remarkable resilience. At half time Ned Hayes and his men had a slight lead, 5 points to 3.

However, with three minutes to go to the final whistle, a shock result seemed imminent. London led by 6 points to 5. Then fate dealt a blow. A free to Tipperary was taken by Ned Hayes. He lobbed the sliotar into the goalmouth. The forwards rushed it through the posts for a goal. A weak puck-out saw Hayes, Gleeson and O'Keeffe thunder in on goal to carry the sliotar over the goal line again. Thus in a twinkling the game was won and lost.

Carbery had this to say about Ned Hayes and his men. 'I don't believe, since or before, that Tipperary ever sent out a combination, to equal that of Two-Mile-Borris.'

A splendidly contested final was described by *Sport* as 'the best, cleverest, and the fastest, we have ever seen in an All-Ireland final'.

It was a great occasion for Tipperary. In the curtain raiser the football team captained by John Tobin of Clonmel Shamrocks had captured the football title with a 3:7 to 2 points win over London (Hibernians).

After the games the London and Tipperary teams were entertained at the Mansion House by the Lord Mayor of Dublin. Among others in attendance were Luke O'Toole, Secretary of the GAA and Ald. James Nowlan, President of the GAA.

It had taken six games in the hurling championship of 1900 for Ned Hayes to lead his native Tipperary to their sixth All-Ireland crown.

When Ned died in 1946 he had lived to see Tipperary win their 13th title the previous year.

Denis Grimes
LIMERICK
1897

'No more upon the hurling field
Will Sunday evenings find me,
But far away from all that's gay
And the spot I've left behind me.'

(Sliabh Ruadh)

In the championship of 1897 Limerick were appearing in their fourth Munster final. Having won in 1891 against Kerry, an objection followed, and in the subsequent replay Limerick lost. In 1893 and 1895 they lost heavily to Cork and Tipperary respectively.

Kilfinane won the county title in 1897 with a 4:9 to 4:8 victory over Cappamore. Following that win a strong Kilfinane selection emerged to represent the county in the All-Ireland championship. It included a number of first class hurlers from Cappamore, Ballingarry, Caherline and Croom.

Denis Grimes – no relation of Eamon Grimes from South Liberties, that dashing hurler who captained Limerick to All-Ireland success in 1973 – proved to be an admirable captain. Under his leadership Limerick had a resounding 4:9 to 1:6 win over Cork in the Munster final and faced Kilkenny in confident mood in the All-Ireland final at Tipperary on 20 November 1898.

On the way to the final Kilkenny, with a Tullaroan selection that included players from Mooncoin and Threecastles, got a walkover from Wexford in the Leinster final. They had earlier drawn with Dublin at Carlow, 2:6 each, but won the replay easily at Jones's Road (6:13 to 1:4). At the same venue they defeated Galway in the All-Ireland semi-final on 30 October 1898 by 3:4 to 4 points. The competition in the championship had been very keen but disputes, not at all uncommon in the early years of the Association, caused the final to run in to the winter of 1898.

As Denis Grimes led his hurling men onto the pitch on that November day in 1898 one thing was certain. At the final whistle, barring a draw, a new name would appear on the All-Ireland hurling honours list, for neither county up to then had won a title.

Kilkenny had unsuccessfully contested the finals of 1893 and 1895. This was Limerick's first final. It is fascinating to record that the All-Ireland hurling final of 1897 was played as a curtain raiser to a Croke Cup football tie between Cork and Tipperary.

The referee of the hurling final was J.J. McCabe, Chairman of the Dublin County Committee. T.F. O'Sullivan recorded that 'there was a very large attendance, and the game was splendidly contested'. Kilkenny led at half time by 2:4 to 1:1. However, they failed to score in the second half. The final score was Limerick 3:4 Kilkenny 2:4.

Denis Grimes made history by being the first captain to lead Limerick to All-Ireland victory. He had some great men in his lineout. Among them was Vice Captain, Jim 'Sean Óg' Hanley who played at fullback. He has been described as 'the greatest hurler of his day'. He played with London in the All-Ireland finals of 1900 and 1903. In the mid 1950s Carbery, who had seen more than fifty hurling finals, picked 'Sean Óg' as his fullback on his 'Best Ever Team'. 'Sean Óg' died relatively young. A Celtic Cross, erected to his memory by his comrades, marks his grave in Kensal Rise Cemetery, London.

Denis Grimes led Limerick to further success in the competitions of 1897. In those days the Croke Cup competition generated tremendous enthusiasm and was no less exciting than the All-Ireland championship. The cup was a magnificent silver trophy donated in 1896 by Dr. Croke, Archbishop of Cashel and patron of the Association, as a token of his support for, and keen interest in, Gaelic games.

Disputes and disagreements caused the final to be delayed until 9 July 1899. Limerick and Kilkenny confirmed their rating as leading hurling strongholds by qualifying for the final. The game was played at Tipperary. T.F. O'Sullivan wrote as follows. 'There was a

216

very large attendance of spectators, including the most Rev. Dr. Croke, and a number of Clergymen. The Secretary of the Association (Mr. F.B. Dinneen) presented the teams before lining up to his Grace, who imparted his blessing to the kneeling players.'

Denis Grimes led his men to victory on the score 3:8 to 1:4. Limerick, therefore, became the first county to complete the double of Croke Cup and All-Ireland title in the same year of competition.

I am indebted to Maurice O'Regan of Kilfinane for the following information which he very kindly sent me on Denis Grimes and the Croke Cup competition of 1897.

Limerick played their first game in the Croke Cup against the holders Clare (Tulla) at Tipperary in October 1898 a month before they played the All-Ireland final against Kilkenny on 20 November 1898. They won by 4:6 to 2:5. In the Munster final of the Croke Cup, between Limerick and Cork, played at Mallow on 26 March 1899, the game ended all square at four points each; a score both sides disputed. The Cork followers called referee Pat McGrath of Tipperary 'A Bloody Orangeman' and he refused to handle the replay which took place at the same venue on 21 May 1899.

One journalist described the replay as 'the best since Fionn Mac Cumhaill hurled for three days at the foot of the Torc Mountains near Killarney, a game which ended when the ball got lost and was eventually located in the whiskers of a spectator'.

A fine sporting game under referee D. Woods ended with Limerick victorious by the narrowest of margins on the score 1:7 to 1:6. Cork (Blackrock) with some brilliant hurling men that included Steva Riordan and the famed Coughlan brothers, Pat, Dan, Denis and Jer, had hoped to avenge their All-Ireland championship defeat at the hands of Limerick – but in vain.

A good story attaches to this Croke Cup Munster final replay. A few over-enthusiastic Cork supporters in the huge gathering pelted sods of earth at some of the Limerick players. Denis Grimes faced up to the handful of misguided supporters and told them that the rope that hanged John Twist would not frighten his men, let alone sods of earth. It seems that John Twist was a patriot from Kildorrery parish in North Cork. A Limerick jury failed to convict him but subsequently a Cork jury did.

Denis Grimes was born on 7 August 1864 to John and Mary (née Casey). In his hurling days he played as goalkeeper on the team. He came of humble origins. Opportunities were few. He worked as a labourer. After the 1897 successes he emigrated to Wales and worked in the mines. Sadly, like many an emigrant of that era, he never came home. He died in 1920 and was buried in Wales. His son, John, attended the funeral.

The following are the men that Denis Grimes captained to All-Ireland success in 1897. The bulk of the team won the Croke Cup.

> Denis Grimes, James 'Sean Óg' Hanley, Maurice Flynn, Patrick Flynn, Mick Finn, Michael Downes, Tom Brazill, John Finn, Patrick O'Brien (Kilfinane). John Condon, John Hynes, Pat Mulcahy, Patrick Butler (Cappamore). John Reidy, Jim Cottrill (Ballingarry). Jim Flood, Dan Riordan (Caherline). Patrick Ruskin (Croom).

Mikey Maher
TIPPERARY
1895–1896 and 1898

> 'When I think of Matt the Thrasher's strength
> And Nora Leahy's grace,
> I love you Tipperary though
> I never saw your face.'
>
> (Brian O'Higgins)

Without a doubt, Mikey Maher was the first of the super captains and one of the greatest in the history of the game of hurling. He was a mighty man, standing at 6'3", built accordingly, and he lined out on the playing pitch fit at 15 stone.

Wrote Carbery – 'Of the 100 All-Ireland captains I have seen, for inspired leadership and dynamic force in a crisis, I'll give the palm to Big Mikey of Tubberadora.'

Off the field he was a man of quiet and soft disposition –'big, genial, stout-hearted, a huge man with a soft, kindly countenance, he had a quiet, easy-speaking way with him that endeared him to all who knew him' (Canon Fogarty). But on the field he had a towering presence that inspired all those around him.

He led physically fit men – hardy sons of the soil – who had stamina in abundance. It was a factor that proved to be a turning-point in the closing stages of many a game.

Mikey usually operated at centre forward or centre field. He was not a stylish player. He had a tear-away, fearless approach to the game supported by the heart and courage of a lion.

He was a born leader and was held in deep respect – even with a sense of awe – by all colleagues. He led by example – his men followed. His word was law.

Using his immense strength he could dribble the sliotar goalwards – shouldering opponents who tackled and leaving them stretched in his wake. Then he would send a mighty shot off either hand. Left or right, it was all the same to Mikey.

He lived in an era when a good captain organised his team, arranged the games, made the travel arrangements and did switches of personnel on the field. Mikey did all those things and did them exceedingly well.

Mikey was born in 1870, the second of four boys – the others being Tim, Jack and Matty, all of whom had a deep commitment to the game of hurling. Tim who started life as a national teacher was at the time of his death a chief superintendent in the Garda Síochána. Jack, the eldest, who won two All-Ireland titles and died at 50, was father of Sonny Maher who won three All-Ireland titles with Tipperary in the 1949/51 era. Matty was the youngest and hurled in the days of the great Johnny Leahy. His son Michael, who inherited many of the qualities of his Uncle Mikey, won five All-Ireland titles with Tipperary in the years 1958, '61, '62, '64 and '65.

Mikey in his time won five All-Ireland titles 1895, '96, '98, '99 and 1900. He shared those wins with Johnny Walsh and Ned Maher, father of little Jimmy Maher whose display in goal in the All-Ireland final of 1945 denied Kilkenny victory.

Mikey led Tipperary – with a Tubberadora selection – to three of those All-Ireland successes, 1895, '96 and '98. Only Christy Ring with Cork and 'Drug' Walsh with Kilkenny succeeded in matching it. Mikey Maher's men swept all before them on the hurling field in those years. They had resounding victories over all opposition. A glance at the key games confirms this.

Munster finals.
1895 v Limerick (7–8 to 0–2)
1896 v Cork (7–9 to 2–3) after a 1–3 each draw
1898 v Cork (1–13 to 1–2) after a draw 3–0 to 2–3

All-Ireland semi-finals.
1896 v Galway (7–11 to 0–4)
1898 v Galway (3–14 to 1–3)

All-Ireland finals.
1895 v Kilkenny (6–8 to 1 goal)
1896 v Dublin (8–14 to 4 points)
1898 v Kilkenny (7–13 to 3–10)

After the Munster final of 1895 a press report read as follows – 'Ably led by the strong and fearless Mikey Maher, the style of the Tipperary hurlers was fast, free and open, and their positional work perfect. In every unit there was sting and dash; in every line there was ability and method. With such a gallant combination, it looks as if Tipperary is going to make some history in the ancient pastime.'

The Episcopal Silver Jubilee of Dr. Croke, Patron of the GAA, Archbishop of Cashel, a native of Mallow, Co. Cork, was celebrated on 18 July 1895. Addresses were presented from the Central Council, the Tipperary County Committee and the Cork County Committee.

The All-Ireland finals of 1895 in hurling and football were both played at Jones's Road on 15 March 1896. It was a great day for Tipperary. They contested both finals and brought off the double. The hurlers led the way in the curtain raiser. In the second game the footballers defeated Meath in a thriller.

The story is told that in one of those All-Ireland hurling successes the men of Tubberadora walked to Thurles, got the train to Dublin, played and won the final, got the train back to Thurles, walked to Tubberadora – and milked the cows.

Tubberadora became a household name. And where is Tubberadora? To the north of the parish of Boherlahan there is a townland called Tubberadora – just a townland. Translated from the Irish, Tiobraid Ortha, it means the Well of Prayers. The Well of Prayers! Yet, the scourge of hurling opponents in the days of the great Mikey Maher.

In 1995, the Centenary year of their first All-Ireland success, a memorial plaque was constructed at Tubberadora Cross, recording the names of the Tubberadora All-Ireland winners. It was unveiled at a ceremony on Sunday 27th August by Séamus Ó Riain, a former President of the GAA.

At the age of 48 Mikey left his native place where it was said 'he carried more weight than a parish priest' and went to farm at Gleneffy, Galbally, in Co. Limerick. His friends in Boherlahan looked upon him as a king in exile. And they demonstrated it when he died.

Seamus Leahy, a great Tipperary historian, in a beautiful article in the *Tipperary Association Yearbook* of 1982 described his funeral as follows:

'When he died in 1947 many of them travelled there to help carry his giant frame to its last resting place in Tipperary's St. Michael's Cemetery. To his neighbours at Gleneffy he had been a big, soft-spoken, kindly man, who worked hard and was a well-liked neighbour. But to the men of his native place, who knew him in his prime, he was Cú Chulainn and Napoleon and Matt the Thresher. He was Big Mikey and there would never be his like again.'

Stephen Hayes
CORK
1894

'"Cut me a hurl," says the sturdy youth,
His limbs were straight and strong;
I liked his eyes of budding truth
Alight to right some wrong.

"My mates play other games," he said —
I saw his proud lip curl:
"I'll play the game my grand-dad played,
— I want to hurl."'

(Carbery)

Stephen Hayes was a Blackrock hurler. His club was officially founded in 1883 and was initially known as Cork Nationals. In 1888 the name was changed to National Hurling Club Blackrock and later in that year adjusted to read Blackrock National Hurling club. Stephen captained the club team to county honours in 1889 and 1891. He had earlier been a member of the victorious team of 1887.

In 1894 Blackrock won its fifth county hurling title. They defeated Blarney in the final by 1:5 to 1 point. That victory opened the door to the All-Ireland trail.

Only four teams took part in the All-Ireland title race. The draws took place in Thurles at the annual convention. In Munster, Tipperary beat Kerry by 2:4 to 6 points at Cork Park before losing the Munster Final to Cork (Blackrock) on the score 3:4 to 1:2 at Charleville. No team emerged from either Connaught or Ulster. In Leinster, Dublin (Rapparees) were unopposed.

The All-Ireland final of that year was played on 24 March 1895 at Clonturk Park, Dublin. Cork with a Blackrock selection, led by Stephen Hayes, now in the twilight of his hurling days, faced Dublin represented by a Rapparees seclection.

The weather was unkind. It was a day of wind, rain and hail. Cork (Blackrock) lined out on time and incredibly had to wait for two hours before their opponents turned up. However, it proved to be well worthwhile.

Dublin (Rapparees) won the toss and opted to play with the strong wind. Stephen Hayes and his men were in a defensive frame of mind in the early stages of the game as they faced the elements and studied the opposition for strengths and weaknesses. At half time they sensed victory as they led by 2:5 to 2 goals. And how right they were. Aided by the elements in the second half they ran riot and scored a further 3:15 while holding their opponents scoreless. It ended Cork (Blackrock) 5:20 Dublin (Raparrees) 2 goals. Victory brought Stephen Hayes his first and only All-Ireland medal and shortly afterwards he retired from the game. The final was refereed by J.J. Kenny of Dublin.

After such a trouncing a Dublin player is reputed to have sought consolation by stating: 'How could you beat a team like Blackrock, sure, they have been playing hurling since the time of Fionn Mac Cumhaill.'

To be a Blackrock hurler in those days conferred a special hurling status on any camán wielder. In Blackrock's *Centenary Year Publication*, the following is attributed to Carbery.

'Down by the fishing village; at the pierhead; round the Convent Road; at the quarry in Ballintemple; and Boreenmanna we practised hip to hip. To see the Blackrock hurl was a revelation. They never caught a ball after a lift, they never dallied with a ball. Their swing was long, but crisp and graceful. They drew on "lightening balls" off left and right showing a command of ash that was astonishing.

Hurling was in their blood . . . their lofty moral code and spirit was beyond all praise.'

The 1894 victory was Cork's fourth All-Ireland title. It was the second in a row won by a Blackrock selection and completed a run of three-in-a-row 17-a-side victories for Cork county.

It is interesting to take a look at the manner in which each of the other three victories was achieved. In 1890 Cork (Aghabullogue) captained by Dan Lane met Wexford (Castlebridge) in the All-Ireland final. The game was unfinished. With Wexford leading by 2:2 to 1:6 (no number of points equalled a goal in those days) the game was abandoned when the Cork team left the field alleging rough play on the part of the Wexfordmen. Following the referee's report, Cork were subsequently awarded the game by the Central Council. The voting was close, 3 to 2 in Cork's favour.

In 1892 Cork (Redmonds) captained by W. O'Callaghan faced Dublin (Flag-Davitts) in the final. The game was unfinished. The Dublin team left the pitch after fifty minutes play having disputed a Cork goal. Cork were awarded the match. At the Congress held in Thurles, on 13 January 1892, some changes were made in the rules-

- A goal was made equal to five points.
- Teams were reduced to seventeen players.
- County champions, when representing the county, were allowed to select players from other clubs in the county.

In 1893 Cork (Blackrock) captained by John Murphy had a decisive victory over Kilkenny (Confederates) on the score 6:8 to 2 points.

'Can you equal the Coughlans, the Ahernes, the Sheas,
Scannell, Cremin, Curtis, and match Stephen Hayes,
I can mention their names from the round of the clock,
The men that won credit for Cork and Blackrock.'

John Mahony
KERRY
1891

'See, o'er the springing green sward
The swift opponents dash.
And hear that echoing music
The quiv'ring hurleys' clash.'

(Rev. James B. Dollard)

In the world of Gaelic games, if the name Kerry is mentioned, the sport that immediately comes to mind is Gaelic football.

And yet, strangely enough, Kerry won a hurling title – their only one – twelve years before they came to the fore in football.

The hurling crown was won in 1891. It was the last year that the county champions had to field a team of players from within the parish. And the parish was defined as a district presided over by a parish priest.

It was also the last occasion that teams lined out with twenty-one players aside and that no number of points equalled a goal.

Ballyduff is a parish located about seven miles to the west of Listowel in North Kerry. By winning the Kerry county hurling title on 10 May 1891 Ballyduff avenged the defeat of the previous year at the hands of Kilmoyley on the score 1 goal to 2 points. Interestingly, that was also the half time score as neither team scored in the second half. Reporting on the game, the *Sentinel* had this to say – 'The Ballyduff team are therefore the champions of the county for the present year, and if they are careful to keep on practising there is little fear that they will render a good account of themselves in the All-Ireland championships.'

Ballyduff was then, and has continued to this day to be, a hurling stronghold. Down through the decades it produced many fine hurlers, among them Mike Joe Quinlan, Eamon O'Sullivan, Michael Hennessy, Brendan Hennessy, Tom Kirby, Tom McEnery, Mikey Carroll, John Carroll and John Bunyan. Captaining them in the campaign of 1891 was the indomitable John Mahony, son of Jack and Bridget (née Doran). John was born in Kilmore, Ballyduff, in 1863. He never married and made his livelihood from fishing and thatching – the former still very much to the fore in parts of Kerry – the latter an almost extinct skill.

John was a determined, fearless and outspoken individual. Instance this letter which he wrote to *The Kerry Sentinel* on 18 June 1890 and published on 21 June.

Dear Sir,

Kindly insert the following which I do not wish to escape the notice of those interested in hurling.

In the match that came off on Sunday last between the above teams, Kilmoiley had men from the Lerrig team playing with them against Ballyduff and I should think that it is no great credit to Kilmoiley to get two teams to beat one, as I am certain they will admit the fact that P. Lawlor, P. Mansell and some others from the Lerrig team played with them, which I can prove to the hilt and now in a friendly spirit, I beg to inform them that it is the intention of Ballyduff to play them again in Tralee any Sunday they suggest, so long as they leave out men from the Lerrig team and the County Board ought to give the matter their best attention.

I remain, dear sir, yours etc.

John Mahony
Captain Ballyduff Hurling Club.

Representing Kerry under the captaincy of John Mahony, Ballyduff faced Cork (Blackrock) in the first round of the Munster championship at Killarney on 21 September. Leading by 2:4 to nil at half time the Kerrymen emerged from the game with a convincing 2:7 to 0:3 victory – a game in which they demonstrated hurling skill, dexterity and physical fitness.

Because of the Parnell 'split', political matters were at boiling point in Ireland and when Parnell – one of the GAA's first patrons – died unexpectedly on 6 October 1891 it was feared that the Munster hurling final between Kerry and Limerick might not be played. Happily, however, the game did go ahead at Newcastle West on 1 November. Special trains brought supporters from Limerick and Tralee and by the time the game got underway at 3 p.m. a huge crowd had assembled. The referee was Mr. John Sheehy, Secretary of the Limerick County Board. Limerick won on the score 1:2 to 1:1.

Kerry, however, objected. There are different versions on what formed the basis of the objection, but be that as it may, the Central Council upheld the Kerry appeal. It was part of the culture of the time to settle disputes — in many of the cases — by arranging a replay. And that's what happened in this case.

On 31 January 1892 Kerry proved superior when they won the replay at Abbeyfeale under referee Michael Deering of Cork on the score 2:4 to 1 point and in so doing demonstrated their skills at overhead play and ground hurling.

They now faced Wexford (Crossabeg) in the final at Clonturk, the 'Field of the Boar' on 28 February 1892. The programme of the day was as follows:

1st game — All-Ireland football semi-final — Dublin v Cavan
2nd game — All-Ireland hurling final — Kerry v Wexford
3rd game — All-Ireland football final — Cork v Winners of 1st game.

The referee was Patrick Tobin of Dublin, then Honorory Secretary of the GAA. It was a most exciting encounter, played with great dash, vigour, fury and determination. And as one scribe wrote 'A splendid specimen of muscular hurling.' The Kerrymen played in their bare feet and everyday long pants and wore a jersey of greyish colour with a gold band.

But the encounter wasn't without some controversy. At full time the referee said the score was 1:1 each.

Wexford claimed they had won with a point from a free from the last puck of the game on the score 1:2 to 1:1. But the referee said that time was up before the sliotar crossed for a point and that he had no authority to extend the time beyond the hour.

Kerry argued that they had won by 1:1 to three points, pointing out that in the 22nd minute of the second half Wexford sent the sliotar between the points posts for a point but the sliotar rebounded off a spectator and was then sent in for a goal, and wrongly recorded as such by the referee.

John Mahony and his men were reluctant to consent to a half hour of extra time. It took the persuasion of Tom Slattery, Chairman of the Kerry County Board, and a few others to get John to eventually agree. As they lined up for extra time they received wild applause from the spectators who had witnessed a stirring contest.

They were treated to more of the same in the third half hour. The game ended Kerry 2:3 Wexford 1:5 – the first and only time extra time was played in an All-Ireland hurling final.

Writing many years afterwards on the game P.J. Devlin (Celt), the well-known GAA writer, had this to say. 'It was such a contest as has never been seen before in a native arena. It may be youthful fancy or senile myopia, but I think there was more of the spirit of the ancient Fianna that day than ever since.'

And *The Kerry Sentinel* had this to say of the men on both sides. 'Difficult indeed would it be to find two teams of twenty-one men each possessing the attributes which go to make the athlete perfect, as the representatives of Ballyduff and Crossabeg. In a word they were fast, wiry and long-winded, and strong and scientific, more even than the giants of old, of whom we read in fabled history.'

John Mahony and his victorious men were met at Lixnaw Railway station on the following Monday morning by the Ballyduff Brass Band. That night bonfires, dancing, music and song celebrated a famous occasion.

> '*Oh the days of the Kerry dances,*
> *Oh the ring of the Piper's tune.*
> *Oh for one of those hours of gladness*
> *Gone, alas, like our youth too soon.*'

I have failed to find evidence that a cup existed for the All-Ireland winners of 1891.

A Wexford bard wrote the following poem as a salute to the victorious Kerry men.

> '*We toast you men of Ballyduff*
> *You won it fair and square.*
> *Like us to Dublin you did go*
> *To venture and to dare.*
> *With Kingdom pride ranked side by side*
> *Without hindrance, let or fear*
> *You won! Well done! But you'll hear again*
> *Of the unbowed Shelmalier.*'

The year 1891 was unique in a number of ways as regards hurling. It was the only occasion that Kerry won a senior hurling title. It was the only time that extra time was played in a final. It was the only year that at least one of the 'big three' – Cork, Tipperary and Kilkenny – failed to contest the provincial final. In Munster it was Limerick v Kerry. In Leinster it was Wexford v. Laois.

It is worth while recording here that on 9 November 1891 Pat Nally, athlete and patriot from Balla, Co. Mayo, after whom the Nally Stand in Croke Park is named, died at the age of 34 in Mountjoy Prison.

The victorious Kerry team of 1891 was as follows:

John Mahony, Maurice Fitzmaurice, Maurice Kelly, John Murphy, Jack O'Sullivan, Paddy 'Carr' O'Carroll, Pat Wynne, Jim McDonnell, Michael O'Sullivan, James Crowley, Frank Crowley, Pat O'Rourke, Thade Eugene McCarthy, Thade Donal McCarthy, Michael McCarthy, Michael Riordan, Richard Kissane, Pat Quane, Jackeen Quane, Michael Kirby, Tom Dunne.

John Mahony died aged 80 after Christmas 1943 and was buried on 1st January 1944 in Rahela burial ground in Ballyduff.

Nicholas O'Shea
DUBLIN
1889

'Who shall tell their story
Who shall sing their praise
Tho' no martial glory
Round their feats may blaze?'

(Maeve Cavanagh)

The first championships under the auspices of the GAA took place in 1887. For the first and only time to date they operated on an open draw basis. Dublin were drawn against Tipperary. The Dublin champions, Metropolitan Hurlers, sought a postponement of the game from the Executive because some of their players were on holidays. The request was refused. Tipperary received a walkover. Thus ended Dublin's interest in the first hurling championship. We will never know how they might have fared.

Due to the 'U.S. Invasion' the championship of 1888 remained unfinished. Dublin, represented by the Kickham's Club, beat Kildare (Monasterevin) in the first round by 3:6 to 2 points. However, they failed to Kilkenny (Mooncoin) in the Leinster final on the score 7 points to 3 points.

That brings us to 1889. Nicholas O'Shea was captain. Despite extensive queries and research I have failed to unearth anything about Nicholas's background or his way of life, apart from confirmation that he wasn't a Dublin native. It could well be that like many of his generation he emigrated to 'far foreign fields', shortly after the triumph of 1889. At any rate it would now seem that knowledge of Nicholas has disappeared into the mists of time.

Only three counties competed in the Leinster championship. In the first round Dublin, represented by county champions Kickhams, led by their captain Nicholas O'Shea, beat Louth (Drogheda Gaelics) by 6:9 to 1 point. They then got a walkover from Laois (Rathdowney) in the Leinster final.

Clare (Tulla) emerged as champions in Munster, where all counties bar Waterford participated. The All-Ireland final took place at Inchicore, on Sunday 3 November between Dublin (Kickhams) and Clare (Tulla). The game was refereed by Patrick Tobin, Hon. Sec. Co. Dublin Committee. The attendance numbered about 1500.

Dublin were in arrears by 1:5 to 1 goal at half time – an era when no number of points equalled a goal. The second half was all Dublin. Scores, and particularly goals, came in abundance. Nicholas O'Shea and his men ran in a further 4:1. Clare could only muster 1 point. The game ended 5:1 to 1:6 in Dublin's (Kickhams) favour.

It seems that Clare for some strange reason decided to play in their bare feet. This approach was effective in the first half. However, following some rainfall at half time the surface became slippery. Sawdust was laid on portions of the ground. Bare feet on a slippery surface didn't help Clare's cause.

Even though defeat was Clare's lot, it didn't deter Jimmy Smyth of Ruan, Co. Clare from writing a ballad on the game many decades later. Here is one verse.

> 'We were nourished in the days of yore, with tales of hurling at the core –
> The noble men of Tulla who played in eighty-nine –

As barefoot then, they played the game and tried the Dublin
* boys to tame.*
A heavy downpour spoiled their fame; the sun refused to shine.
We smile at all this now I fear, but all these men we do revere,
Who came from humble holdings in the heart of Co. Clare.
They were peeping into freedom's light from out the darkness of
* the night —*
The first beginnings of a fight — the right to do and dare.'

P.P. Sutton writing on the match in *Sport* had this to say. 'The match was by long chalks the finest display of our national game I have ever witnessed, and the Kickhams covered themselves from head to foot with honours by hurling with the most extreme pluck and brilliancy. Though beaten by such a big score, the Clare men are really skilled hurlers, but their discipline and staying powers were inferior to the Dubliners.'

William J. Spain, a native of Nenagh and a fine dual player, who won an All-Ireland football final with Limerick (Commercials) in 1887, was a key figure in Dublin's hurling success. Of their tally of 5:1 he contributed three goals. He became the GAA's first dual medal winner. He later emigrated to America.

T.F. O'Sullivan in *The Story of the GAA* wrote as follows about the Kickhams Club in 1889. 'The Kickhams Club was formed on Easter Sunday 1886, and at the end of 1889 had about 180 members. At first hurling was not played, as the game was considered too dangerous. After a time, however, hurling was taken up by the members. The record of the Club in hurling and football to the end of 1889 was as follows — football matches played, 66, of which 54 were won, 9 lost and 3 drawn. Hurling, 31 matches played, of which 29 were won and 2 lost.'

The names of the teams were not published in any newspaper at the time. However, through the good offices of Frank Coghlan, a member of the victorious Dublin team, the names were supplied to T.F. O'Sullivan who published them in his book *The Story of the GAA*.

This, therefore, is the team that Nicholas O'Shea captained in 1889. Nicholas O'Shea, Frank Coghlan, Thomas Butler, John Lambe, Dan Kerwick, J.D. O'Byrne, Thomas McKenna, William J. Spain, James Harper, Charles Hackett, Thomas Maher, John Bishop, T. Belton, Patrick Ryan, J. Cahill, Ned Gilligan, Fred Palmer, 'Sil' Riordan, Patrick O'Shea, Patrick Riordan and Michael Madigan.

Jim Stapleton
TIPPERARY
1887

'Upon his native sward the hurler stands
To play the ancient pastime of the Gael,
And all the heroes famed of Innisfail
Are typified in him.'

(Rev. James B. Dollard)

Let us first look briefly at the Ireland of 1887, when the first All-Ireland championships got under way within three years of the establishment of the GAA in 1884.

Charles Stewart Parnell and Michael Davitt were the leading political figures. Both were among the first patrons of the GAA.

Home Rule and the Land Question were the burning issues of the day. The Home Rule Bill of Gladstone had been defeated in the House of Commons in 1886. The land of Ireland was in the grip of landlords – many of them absentee – and the plight of the tenants was, in many cases, woeful.

The Plan of Campaign, aimed at improving the lot of tenant farmers, was initiated in 1887. It led to the passing of coercion acts and agrarian unrest.

The GAA was making a major impact throughout the country, providing recreation and uplifting the spirits of a largely oppressed people.

Jim Stapleton was born in Thurles town in 1863. It was hurling territory and he grew up playing the game and loving it. In his hurling prime he stood 5'10" in his stockinged feet and turned the scales at 12st. 7lbs. Add to that a powerful pair of shoulders and arms, and you had what an old-timer once described him as – 'a powerful bullet of a man'. Jim had courage and stamina in abundance. All in all, he was a tower of strength to his colleagues and a formidable proposition for opposing teams. Off the field and on, he was known as a sincere and honourable man.

In 1947, Paddy Mehigan, Carbery, himself a former county hurler and outstanding sports journalist talked with Jim, just two years before he died. 'Hats off, Gaels and all you who love a grand old

231

Hurler — 84 years gone, who still reads his newspaper without glasses, and one whose mild, open, honest eyes will sparkle when recalling the great days of his youth.'

Carbery was taken by Jim's vivid recollection of the first hurling final and the sense of pride he felt in leading his team to victory.

It seems that from time to time wrong versions of the team lineout used be published. This upset Jim as he felt that those who did duty on that historic occasion should be honoured and remembered. He gave his team lineout as James Stapleton (captain), Martin McNamara, Edward Murphy, Thomas Burke, Jer. Dwyer, Matthew Maher, Thomas Maher, Andrew Maher (all of Thurles); Thomas Carroll of (Moyne); John Dunne, Pat Leahy (Ferror); Edward Bowe (Leigh); John Mockler (Newhill); Thomas Healy (Coolcroo); Thomas Stapleton (Littleton); Dan Ryan, Jerh. Ryan (Ballybeg); Jer. Dwyer (Ballyvinane); Pat Leamy, Pat Lambe, M.Carroll (Drombane).

Apart from two Christian name discrepancies, his team tallies with the team published by T.F. O'Sullivan in *The Story of the GAA,* who gave Jim Dwyer instead of Jer. Dwyer and John Leamy instead of Pat Leamy.

Fate played a role in Jim having the mantle of captain bestowed on him for the final. Because of a dispute over the railway travelling expenses, seven players including the Thurles captain Dinny Maher were left standing on the platform on the morning of the match.

The final of 1887 was played in Birr on Easter Sunday 1 April 1888 with ground and weather conditions ideal for hurling. It was a 21-a-side contest. The pitch measurements for that occasion were 200 yards by 100 yards.

Media interest in GAA affairs at the time was minimal and very often non-existent. And so it was with the final of 1887. Only in retrospect has the occasion turned out to be a historic event in the GAA calendar.

The draw for the championship that year was an open one. Not many teams participated. Galway booked their place in the final after a 2:8 to 1 goal victory over Wexford in a rather tempestuous encounter at Elm Park, Dublin.

Disputes in Limerick and Cork as to what club should represent the county led to neither county participating.

Tipperary defeated Clare 1:7 to 2 points and Kilkenny 4:7 to nil 'in a game that was refereed with much difficulty by Frank Moloney' before coming face to face with Galway in the final.

The Galway representatives – Meelick – wore green jerseys with white stripes. Tipperary, represented by Thurles, donned green jerseys with stars artistically worked in the centre. The prospect of a stirring contest, coupled with the pleasant spring weather conditions, attracted a large gathering of spectators from Galway, Tipperary and the surrounding districts of Birr. At 3 p.m. referee Pat White got the contest under way.

It proved to be Tipperary's toughest test. They were well matched by the Galwaymen in a game that was vigorously contested from start to finish. At half time Tipperary led by one point to nil. And with no number of points equalling a goal in those days the destination of the title was wide open.

However, at a crucial stage of the game in the second half, Jim Stapleton led a charge down the field. Spotting an opening he passed the sliotar to Tommy Healy of Coolcroo. He caught it and made no mistake with a low hard drive that gave Tipperary a vital goal.

The game ended on the score Tipperary 1 goal, 1 point and 1 forfeit point (the equivalent nowadays of a 70) to no score for Galway.

Tommy Healy had scored the first goal in an All-Ireland hurling final. Jim Stapleton was the first to captain a team to All-Ireland honours.

It is of interest to recall the scoring area that existed in 1887. Goals were scored within the soccer-style goal area. The crossbar was 10'6" high compared to 8' nowadays. Points were scored between the side posts which were 63' apart. For the 1896 championship the crossbar was brought down to a height of 8'.

Within six months of the All-Ireland victory a team of 50 Irish athletes and hurlers set sail from Cobh, on board the *Wisconsin*, for New York on 16 September. Jim Stapleton was among them. He took part in several hurling exhibitions at a variety of venues that included New York, Boston, Philadelphia, Brooklyn, Providence, Neward and Trenton. Exiles and native Americans were fascinated by the ancient game of the Celt.

Quite a few of the athletes remained on in America but Jim was one of those who returned to his native Thurles when the party set sail from New York on 31 October.

Jim Stapleton, first All-Ireland winning hurling captain, will always be remembered as one of the great pioneers of the early days of the GAA. He was part of a great movement.

> *'It began a revolt again degradation, leading to submission;*
> *A recall to the past so that its glories might again animate us;*
> *A tocsin for the present so that the future should find us united*
> *and strong and fit to be free men.'*
>
> (Celt)

All-Ireland Winning Camogie Captains
2002 – 1887

Jovita Delaney
TIPPERARY
2000

My early memories of this fantastic game are at home in the front lawn where I spent many hours at a young age practising and perfecting the skills of the game. I was frequently put between the two apple trees in the front lawn while the boys battled it out between them.

However, it was not until I attended secondary school (Scoil Mhuire, Cashel) that I received my first taste of competitive camogie under the direction of a man I greatly admire – Martin Quirke. With his leadership we were steered to both junior and senior Munster titles in '89 and '90. Unfortunately, however, an All-Ireland title eluded us due to the magnificent run of St. Raphael's, Loughrea, who won eight Senior Schools titles from '85 to '92 under the direction of none other than the famous Cyril Farrell. We were defeated by St. Raphael's in '89 at both junior and senior level in the All-Ireland semi-final and in the All-Ireland senior final in 1990. Nevertheless, we eventually managed to overcome St. Raphael's in an All-Ireland schools seven-a-side competition in '90 by a mere point. This proved to be a memorable day for myself as I scored the winning point in the dying minutes of the game.

By attending school in Cashel I got involved with Cashel camogie club under the watchful eye of Kirsty McClousky – an individual who devoted much of her time to coaching the juveniles of the club and whom I later had the pleasure of playing with at both club and county level. With Kirsty's guidance, Cashel won numerous county titles at under-age level.

The club also had a fantastic run of success at senior level from '86 to '91 (the latter three of which I myself played in the forward line), and again from '98 to 2001 each of which I played in the fullback line.

However, in spite of contesting previous Munster club finals it was not until 2001 that we achieved Munster glory by defeating the great Granagh/Ballingarry team who had won numerous All-Ireland titles prior to this. We also contested the All-Ireland club final in 2001 but were bitterly disappointed to lose out by a single point to Pearses of Galway.

After the All-Ireland county senior successes of 1999 and 2000, it came as no surprise to many that we returned in 2001 with the aim of retaining our title and achieving the three in a row.

A semi-final clash with Cork proved to be a tremendous game. Cork were edging ahead in the final minutes of the game only to be halted by Deirdre Hughes' levelling point. The final result – a draw. Tipperary 2:8 Cork 0:14. Two weeks later the replay was a similar affair. With two minutes of normal time remaining only a point separated the teams. It was clear that if a goal was to come that it would surely be the key score. My heart sank when Una O'Donoghue from Cork lashed the ball past me. Cork had taken the lead. However, this was followed by an unforgettable rally from Tipperary, beginning with magnificent scores from Noelle Kennedy and Philly Fogarty, followed by a delightful goal from Claire Grogan. Deirdre Hughes also pointed and Emer McDonnell hammered home another goal, resulting in a one-point deficit, just a few minutes earlier, being turned into a seven-point victory margin. This sent us one vital step further in search of that three-in-a-row achievement.

All-Ireland final day arrived and a sea of blue and gold could be seen in Croke Park. It was a very special day for Tipperary as we were contesting both the junior and senior finals. The atmosphere was electric and expectations high – we did not disappoint. The Tipperary junior team gave a fine display defeating Offaly by 4:16 to 1:7. We, the senior team, proved much too strong for Kilkenny on this occasion, defeating them by a margin of 16 points to take our third successive All-Ireland senior title. The final score was Tipperary 4:13 Kilkenny 1:6.

As my playing days draw to a close I look back and realise how fortunate I am. Apart from the many hours of enjoyment I have received, I have made numerous friends who undoubtedly will remain, long after my playing days are over.

> 'For here today, in contest fleet,
> Tipperary's best and Cork will meet.'

Jovita Delaney grew up surrounded by an atmosphere of hurling activity. 'Our house was a big GAA house and my Dad was actively involved with the juveniles of Boherlahan. In his younger years he hurled with Boherlahan and won a mid-Tipp. title with the club. My two older brothers, Pio and Dave, were members of the winning Boherlahan team of 1996.'

On her mother's side – also named Jovita – there is a link with a great Tipperary hurler of the past. Arthur O'Donnell, a cousin, won All-Ireland medals with Tipperary in 1916 and '25. 'He toured America with the Tipperary team in 1925. His pucks of the ball were of such length that they called him the Babe Ruth of hurling over there, after their baseball hero.'

As a youngster Jovita's late father Dick used take her 'to watch Tipperary and other matches'. Inevitably there were heroes – past and present; 'Nicky English was unreal; Michael Cleary was a fine player; Declan Ryan was a powerhouse and Brendan Cummins was magical to watch.'

And she had of course words of admiration too for camogie players – among them Angela Downey 'in a league of her own'; Fiona O'Driscoll 'a fabulous player, an unbelievable motivator who does trojan work on and off the field'; fellow county colleague Deirdre Hughes 'a class act, delightful to watch'.

Jovita's first taste of success in the camogie world came at the age of 16 in 1990 when Tipperary defeated Kilkenny in the All-Ireland minor final – the county's first camogie title in any grade. 'The final score was 2:11 to 3:6. Playing at centre forward I scored 7 points in what was my last game at minor grade. I had been playing since I was 12.'

A future senior colleague on that team was Sinead Nealon. More honours came in 1992 when her native Tipperary won the county's first junior title at the expense of Galway. Seven of that team would form the nucleus of a historical senior breakthrough in 1999 – Claire Madden, Meadhbh Stokes, Sinead Nealon, Noelle Kennedy, Deirdre Hughes, Helen Kiely and Jovita. The build-up to greater things continued in 1997 when Tipperary won the intermediate title with a great victory over Clare – 'an unforgettable day for Noelle Kennedy who scored 1:19 of Tipp's total of 2:19'.

Glory and honour and undreamed-of success was around the corner at senior level. And yet, such success must have seemed impossible when a rampant Cork team trounced Tipperary in the league final of 1999 on the score 9:19 to 2:7.

That defeat, humiliating on the day, bred a grim resolve. 'After the league final something had to be done in preparation for the championship. Colm Bonner became a mentor. He decided to ask Michael Cleary to be there when he wasn't available. Michael hesitated. It would be new territory for him. However, after some thought he agreed to give it a go. After the first training session he was hooked. He saw our potential and was impressed by our commitment. We really wanted to prove we were better than the league final form. That league game was played in Thurles before the Tipp. v Kerry Munster championship senior hurling game. It was a big occasion for us and the first time before a big crowd.

'In the training programme there was emphasis on fitness under Sean Hennessy. Michael and Colm concentrated on a lot of ball work. They upped the pace and at the same time looked for quality.'

Jovita had watched the disastrous league final from the bench — suffering from an ankle injury. In her camogie career to date she had played in a variety of positions — centre forward, fullback, wing forward. Back in training she was asked to 'stand in goal there — give it a go — only a step back from fullback'. She did. And that's where she was for the All-Ireland title race of 1999. Victories over Clare and Down brought them face to face in the final with Kilkenny who had beaten Cork in the semi-final.

'To be in the All-Ireland final of 1999 was a major breakthrough for us. We felt we had a 50/50 chance against Kilkenny. Psychologically it was good not to be playing Cork. We gave it everything.' Well, give it everything they certainly did. From the throw-in they tore into the game with zeal and zest. They played with abandon and élan — spread the ball wide, hustled and harried, blocked and hooked — and they ran and ran and ran. At the final whistle the scoreboard read Tipperary 0:12 Kilkenny 1:8. It was a famous victory in a nail-biting contest that was anyone's game right up to the final whistle.

It was unbelievable — our first time in a senior All-Ireland final and victorious — last final of the century. We had a bit of luck on the day.

An absorbing and spectacular match that produced a high standard of play was witnessed by a crowd of 15,084, that included President Mary McAleese and Taoiseach Bertie Ahern.

For the championship of 2000 Jovita was voted captain by her club Cashel. Down, Clare and Galway fell to them. Now came the acid test. Their opponents in the final were Cork.

> Without a shadow of a doubt this was my most memorable game – beating Cork in the All-Ireland final of 2000 – even more memorable than beating Kilkenny in 1999 because we had to prove ourselves worthy. We got two goals in the first 15 minutes – you can't beat a bit of luck on the day. It was a fabulous match, very fast – 15-a-side has done great things for camogie. The 1999 win gave us the confidence to keep going and dig deep.

In goal, Jovita was coolness personified and an inspiration to her team mates outfield. In the closing stages Cork redoubled their efforts and piled on the pressure. They whipped in a few vicious shots at Jovita but she dealt with them all, as she had throughout the hour, with the confidence and aplomb of a Tony Reddan. One stole past her with seconds to go. But it mattered not. The final whistle saw Tipperary triumph with five points to spare. A team's pride and honour was restored.

Jovita's brilliance in goal in the 2000 championship was well rewarded.

- She was the *Daily Star*'s Player of the Year
- She was RTÉ's Player of the Match in the final
- She was Sportstar of the Week in the *Irish Independent*
- All-Star honour
- Cidona Award in Tipperary
- Canon Hayes Recreation Centre County Award
- Honoured by Manchester Tipperary Association and Tipperary Men's Association, Kilkenny.

In 2001 the Tipperary senior camogie team made it three in a row, with a resounding and comprehensive win over Kilkenny. They were now playing with the confidence and assurance of champions. They had developed into a cohesive unit with a wonderful range of skills – sweet ground striking, precision movements, first touch control. They scored textbook goals that were the products of their sublime skills.

So let's name the heroines of those three finals: Jovita Delaney, Suzanne Kelly, Una O'Dwyer, Claire Madden, Meadhbh Stokes, Ciara Gaynor, Sinead Nealon, Emily Hayden, Angela McDermott, Noelle Kennedy, Therese Brophy, Helen Kiely, Emer McDonnell, Deirdre Hughes, Niamh Harkin, Paula Bulfin, Joanne Ryan, Claire Grogan, Philomena Fogarty, Caitriona Hennessy.

Len Gaynor, father of Ciara; Donie Nealon, father of Sinead and John Grogan, father of Claire, all starred with the Tipperary senior hurling team in bygone days.

The county now joined the elite of the game – Antrim, Cork, Dublin and Kilkenny – who in their time had won three or more successive titles. In the spring of 1999 the idea of three in a row would, for Tipperary, have been just a dream. And yet, what followed was the stuff of dreams.

Elsie Cody
WEXFORD (LEINSTER)
1988, 1991

It would be impossible to write about Brian Cody in this book without referring to his wife Elsie (née Walsh). For she too had a most illustrious career with the camán – spanning a period of over twenty years.

With her native Wexford she progressed from county junior in 1969 to the senior team the following year. She played in four All-Ireland finals – losing in three (1971 to Cork, 1977 and 1990 to Kilkenny). In 1975 she won a coveted All-Ireland medal with a 4:3 to 1:2 victory over the Leesiders. Her skills on the camogie field were recognised by the inter-provincial selectors and she played many times for Leinster in the Gael-Linn sponsored competition. She captained her province to victory in 1988 and 1991 and was also a member of the winning teams of 1971, '72, '81 and '83.

Some of her greatest days were with her club Buffers Alley. In a remarkable and record-breaking run the club contested seven All-Ireland club finals in a row with the following results: 2 defeats, 5 wins.

Tommy Quaid, a great Limerick custodian.

Jimmy O'Brien captained
Wexford in 1967.

Billy Rackard (*left*), Wexford captain in 1962.

Noel Lane, (*second from right*), captained Connaught to victory, in the Railway Cup in 1986.

Niall Patterson, outstanding goalkeeper with his club, Loughgiel, his county, Antrim, and his province, Ulster.

Tom Dempsey, captain of the 1993 Wexford team defeated in the Leinster final by Kilkenny.

Jackie Power (Limerick) in
1991 when he received his
All-time All-star award.

Jackie Power (*second from left*) with the National
League Cup in 1947 and team-mates (*left to right*)
Sean Herbert, Thomas O'Brien, Mick Herbert.

Jackie Power

Cork v Wexford – National League final 1993
(*Courtesy of Ibar Carty, Enniscorthy.*)

All-Ireland final 1996 – Wexford v Limerick.
(*Courtesy of Ibar Carty, Enniscorthy*)

Frank Lohan from Clare in action against Kilkenny captain Andy Comerford, in
the 2002 All-Ireland Hurling Final. (© Damien Eagers/SPORTSFILE)

1968 All-Ireland final, Tipperary v Wexford. Tipperary threaten the Wexford goal.

Action shot from the 1956 All-Ireland final, Wexford v Cork. Wexford attack the Cork goal.

Historic All-Ireland final of 1954, Cork v Wexford – the old-style throw-in with forwards and midfielders all lined up at midfield.

1956 All-Ireland final, Cork v Wexford. Cork goal under siege.

Martin White (*right*), the oldest living All-Ireland medal holder, now 93 years old. Won his first All-Ireland medal in 1932 with Kilkenny. (*Courtesy Michael Brophy.*)

Tony Doran, Wexford hurling star in full flight for his club, Buffers Alley, in the All-Ireland club final against O'Donovan Rossa in 1989.

Mick Mackey and Christy Ring – captains of Ahane and Glen Rovers, 1946.

Fergal Hartley (Waterford) with the Munster Cup 2002 rejoicing with supporters.

1978 v Ballyagran (Limerick) 1:3 to 0:1 (lost)
1979 v Athenry (Galway) 2:6 to 1:2
1980 v Killeagh (Cork) 4:2 to 1:7 (lost)
1981 v Killeagh (Cork) 2:6 to 1:4
1982 v Athenry (Galway) 3:2 to 0:2
1983 v St.Mary's (Galway) 3:7 to 0:6
1984 v Killeagh (Cork) 2:4 to 1:4

Those five titles leave the club in second place on the roll of honour at the present time – behind St. Paul's of Kilkenny with eight titles to their credit and followed by Glen Rovers of Cork who won on four occasions.

> At the time the significance of what we were achieving passed us by. We were very young. It's only when I look back now that I can take in and appreciate what we did. We had a reunion recently. Those All-Ireland finals were played with a total of only 22 or 23 players over the seven-year period.

Halcyon days! Days of wine and roses!

Angela Downey
KILKENNY
1977, 1988, 1991

> Angela Downey is a matchlessly talented individual, performing her wonders independently of the quality and circumstances of the game going on around her.
> (Kevin Cashman)

Camogie has always been central to the lifestyle of Angela Downey and her twin sister Ann. They have played the game since they were nine years old. 'A neighbour named Mr. Lawlor made my first hurley for me. Daddy varnished it for me with linseed oil. I was proud of it. Ann and myself used play 'three goals in' out in the backyard against the slaughterhouse shed. On Sundays we played on the road.'

243

Daddy of course was none other than Shem Downey who played for his native Kilkenny for almost a decade. He took part in the classic final of 1947 when a last-minute point from Terry Leahy gave Kilkenny a one-point win over Cork. And in 1950 in the National League Home Final against Tipperary he played the game of his life with an individual display that matched anything ever seen in Croke Park. Determination and never-say-die spirit accompanied the genes inherited by Angela and Ann.

In due course they joined St. Paul's camogie club – one of the most successful in the country until it disbanded in 1990.

Angela played her first All-Ireland final at the age of 15 against Cork in 1972 and lost by four points. She was captain in 1995 when she played in her last All-Ireland final – again against Cork – and again they lost by four points despite Angela's personal contribution of 2:4 out of a total of 2:10. But in between, during which time Angela won twelve All-Ireland titles, they never lost to Cork. In fact they beat them on six occasions – twice after replays. On the occasion of the 1995 All-Ireland final, Angela's daughter, Katie, aged 2, was the team mascot. Before the game the team were doing various stretches and loosening up on the pitch. Katie joined in all the exercises much to the amusement of the spectators.

Angela's father, Shem, was a team mentor with St. Paul's and later with the county team. He lived the games on the sideline and played every stroke. 'You'd hear him roaring on the sideline – telling us what to do. And if anyone hit us he'd be in like a ton of bricks. He reacted one day in Naas and got suspended for a while. One Sunday morning in a game against Buffers Alley, whatever happened on the pitch, himself and a father of a Buffers Alley player became involved in a roaring and shouting match.' However in the famous words of Sonia O'Sullivan's father 'no one died'.

Angela looks back on a career that lasted a quarter of a century with tremendous satisfaction. It is strewn with trophies and triumphs – above all great memories.

She recalls that in the league campaign of 1988 Cork inflicted a heavy defeat on the team. Both teams met in the All-Ireland final. 'The same result was expected. But we won to make it four in a row. I thought it was as far as we could go but we went on to record seven in a row.' In all Angela played in fourteen All-Ireland finals. She won twelve to leave her one behind Una O'Connor and two behind Kathleen Mills, both of Dublin. Her twin sister Ann, of course, shared in all those successes and was captain on two occasions. Ann has now taken to training the county team.

In Angela's last game with Lisdowney, in an All-Ireland club semi-final, she recalls that 'it was a ding dong match. Granagh were winning and a supporter in the stand shouted – Where's Angela Downey now. Then I got a goal. One of our fellows in the stand shouted – "Now you know where she is".'

Angela looks upon the All-Ireland club final of 1994 between Lisdowney (Kilkenny) and Glen Rovers (Cork), played at Ballyraggett, as one of her best games. 'We robbed Glen Rovers that day. They had great players including Linda Mellerick and Sandy Fitzgibbon. Sandy had a great side step, there was no catching her when she got the ball. She was marking me that day and having a great game. With ten minutes to go we were down ten points. Then Ann got a free – that was the start of the comeback. I went on a scoring spree and got four goals. We won by six points. Katie was the team's mascot.'

Being captain in 1991 evokes special memories. It was Angela's third time being so honoured. President Mary Robinson made her first official visit to an All-Ireland camogie final. 'Meeting the President was a huge thrill. I had led my team behind the Artane Boys Band and walked up the steps to collect the cup. We felt we were being treated like the hurlers. My mind went back to when I was captain in 1977 – only 20 years old – marching behind the Artane Boys Band – and then going back to college with an All-Ireland medal.'

And then there was the unforgettable moment in an All-Ireland final against Cork. There was Angela bearing down menacingly on the Cork goal. Liz O'Neill's tackle left Angela skirtless. Onward she went undaunted. Marian McCarthy advanced from goal and whipped the hurley from Angela's grasp. Unfazed, Angela continued and palmed the sliotar to the net.

A very special treat was when Angela and Ann travelled as guests to Toronto with the All-Stars – richly deserved it was.

At Maynooth University, Angela played camogie and won a Dúthracht shield. During one of the summer breaks she went to the U.S. and played camogie in Chicago with St. Bridget's who reached the final of the competition. Angela came home to start her diploma on Monday and returned to Chicago the following weekend to play in the final and take victory with St. Bridget's.

Where Angela was concerned camogie was a magnetic attraction – in the back yard, with club, county, college, province and in far foreign fields – a career spread over a quarter of a century. No wonder she admits to missing it.

The honours were legion. Chief among them were:

22 county titles (20 with St. Paul's)
12 All-Ireland medals
10 inter-provincial titles
8 National Leagues
6 All-Ireland club titles
Camogie Player of the Year 1994
Texaco Award 1986
B&I Award 1977, '86 and '89
Tailte Skills Award 1984, '85 and '86

Her training schedule was rigid and disciplined. 'At the height of it Ann and I would go to Hotel Kilkenny gym and do a workout. We would be in and out in about one and a quarter hours. We would arrive at the hotel at 7 a.m. From there we would go home for breakfast or sometimes take breakfast to school and have it before class time. In the evening for four nights a week we would do county training mostly. On Sunday morning we would have a match or a training session. In latter years we did stretching, cool downs and warm ups. My father used to laugh and tell us there was no such thing as hamstrings in his day, adding that he would leave the slaughterhouse, travel by bicycle, play the match, cycle home and back to the slaughterhouse.'

Angela selected a team as nonplaying captain. It combines a lovely blend of the stars of the past and outstanding players of the present day. This is it – a twelve-a-side, as in Angela's day.

Marie Fitzpatrick
(Kilkenny)

Biddy O'Sullivan
(Kilkenny)

Elsie Cody
(Wexford)

Liz Neary
(Kilkenny)

Una O'Dwyer
(Tipperary)

Linda Mellerick
(Cork)

Sandy Fitzgibbon
(Cork)

Therese Maher
(Galway)

Emer McDonnell
(Tipperary)

Breda Holmes
(Kilkenny

Pat Moloney
(Cork)

Deirdre Hughes
(Tipperary)

Brigid Doyle
WEXFORD
1969

'And hand in hand, by the edge of the sand,
They danced by the light of the moon,
The moon,
The moon.
They danced by the light of the moon.'

(Edward Lear)

I come from a very large family of nine girls and eight boys. When we were old enough to walk we were all given a hurley stick. When the farm work was finished in the evening all of us would take our hurleys to the field at the back of the house and hurl until dark. We picked a mixed team each night of boys and girls and made two goals at either side of the field. We tried our hearts out to see who would win on the night. It was here our love of the game began and probably also here that we were 'toughened up' by our brothers.

Shortly after I married I came to live in Adamstown (having married an Adamstown man), and Fr. Aidan Redmond C.C. formed a camogie club. He asked me to play and it was that man who really got me going. I rambled over to that field every evening and soon the county team spotted my talents. That time we wore big black tights and a heavy uniform and we had to change in the ditch – and nobody minded!! I imagine now if I was young and fit and had all the gyms and jacuzzis they have nowadays that I would be a superhuman person.

I thoroughly enjoyed my playing days with my club and county and made many good friends over the years. I probably won more than most, winning six county championship medals, Leinster medals, three All-Ireland medals, Powers Awards, Gael-Linn trophy and a B&I Award.

My greatest thrill in life was lifting the All-Ireland cup in Croke Park in September '69 with all my family around me and my two-year-old son holding the cup with me.

In the sixties Wexford reaped a fine harvest in the hurling arena. The decade opened with the senior hurlers producing one of the games greatest shocks with a resounding 2:15 to 0:11 victory over a star-studded and highly fancied Tipperary team in the All-Ireland final. They repeated that success over the same opposition in 1968.

Other All-Ireland triumphs were as follows:

Minor 1963, '66, '68
under-21 1965
Intermediate 1961, '64
St. Peter's College 1962, '67, '68

A camogie All-Ireland title in 1968 made it a unique quartet of successes for the Model County in that year. The decade ended with a flourish when Wexford's camogie stars made it two in a row for the senior team.

Brigid Doyle, daughter of Edward and Johanna Kehoe of Clonleigh, Palace East, Co. Wexford was one of a family of seventeen children, consisting of nine girls and eight boys.

The two eldest girls, Mary and Liz, played club camogie with Ballywilliam and won county titles in the 1950s.

All the others represented Wexford at county level and wore the purple and gold with pride. All-Ireland medals eluded Bernie and Eileen. However, Eileen gained inter-provincial honours with Leinster in 1988 and '89 and won two Gael-Linn medals.

Kit won two All-Ireland titles with Dublin in 1965 and '66 in the distinguished company of Eithne Leech, Órla Ní Shíocháin, Una O'Connor, Kay Ryder, Ally Hussey and Kay Lyons. She was with her native Wexford in 1975 and added a third All-Ireland medal to her collection.

Josie (1968), Annie (1969) and Gretta (Captain 1975) all tasted All-Ireland senior success in the purple and gold.

Brigid together with camogie colleague Margaret O'Leary Lacey are the only camogie players to have won three All-Ireland medals with Wexford (1968, '69 and '75) — indeed the only All-Ireland camogie crowns won by Wexford to date.

Brigid was captain in 1969. And a wonderful and inspiring leader she proved to be. 'I loved training and practising. I couldn't wait to get to the field in the evening and tog out and start hurling.' Wexford under her leadership were in search of two in a row, having defeated Cork in 1968 by 4:2 to 2:5 to take their first ever title under the captaincy of Mary Walsh.

Wexford emerged from Leinster with victories over Kilkenny and Dublin. They then faced Tipperary in the All-Ireland semi-final at Wexford Park. It turned out to be a rather tempestuous affair. Grim resolve, fierce determination and passionate play led to a brief outburst that displeased the referee. A Tipperary player and Josie Kehoe, sister of Brigid, found themselves watching the rest of the game from the sideline. It cost Josie a team place on All-Ireland final day.

Victory brought Wexford face to face with Antrim on Sunday 21 September. Antrim, champions in 1967; Wexford, champions in 1968. A titanic contest was in prospect between two teams that possessed some brilliant exponents of camogie.

The game exceeded expectations. It turned out to be a wonderful advertisement for camogie. It was a fantastic final — one of the great camogie contests. The standard of performance reached new heights in a free flowing game that produced a classic contest. And what a finish. It was nerve-racking, nail-biting and heart-stopping. Just picture it. Wexford, playing against the wind, a point behind as the game entered the fiftieth minute. (It was a fifty-minute game in those

249

days). Then a goal, entering injury time, to put the Model County two points up; then three minutes of injury time: three minutes of torture as Antrim twice almost pulled the game out of the fire; then the final whistle; relief and glory to the Wexford team and supporters. Full-time score – Wexford 4:4 Antrim 4:2.

Brigid had given an outstanding display at centre-back. She was able to draw on all the experience gained playing in those family contests in the field at the back of the house and in the farmyard where they broke more windows than she could remember. Add to that her temperament. 'I never had any nerves. I never saw the crowd on the sideline or in the stand. All that was ever in my mind was to go out and follow the ball and get that ball. I never gave a second thought as to whether a knock from an opponent was accidental or not – just get that ball.'

On Saturday 27 Septemer the *New Ross Standard* wrote as follows: 'Captain Brigid Doyle also had an inspiring game at centre-back . . . she was the "rock" on which many of the Antrim attacks perished, and she was the central figure of the defence in every way. She imposed a steadying influence on her colleagues and was capable and efficient in everything she did. This was a superlative performance in any circumstances and even more so when Brigid was carrying an injury for most of the game.'

The Echo of 27 September had this to say:

> Though possessing a different style to Margaret (O'Leary), team captain Brigid Doyle was just as brilliant. Her injury in the last half only partly curbed her efficiency, but it was in the last five minutes that she heroically repulsed Antrim's final desperate onslaughts. Gifted with a really fine sense of position and unlimited amounts of courage, the store of knowledge she had accumulated in only two years of playing the game makes her one of the greatest players on view today. The Adamstown girl showed that she was a natural leader, and like Margaret O'Leary, is an integral, indispensable part of the team. How anyone can simply ignore her, under any circumstances, when selecting the best in the Province is truly amazing.

The reference to selection for the province relates to the fact that a rule at that time barred a married lady from being selected for the provincial team. As a result it wasn't until Brigid's final years, when the rule was lifted, that Brigid played for her province.

The honour of leading her team as they marched behind the Artane Boys Band, and the joy of liting aloft the O'Duffy Cup in triumph in 1969 were only matched, 32 years later in 2001, as she proudly watched her son Philip – playing in the same position she herself adorned – win a county senior hurling medal at centre halfback with Faythe Harriers.

Brigid played her last game in the purple and gold in the All-Ireland final of 1977 when Wexford lost to neighbours Kilkenny, powered by such greats as Liz Neary, Bridie Martin, Ann and Angela Downey on the score 3:4 to 1:3.

Brigid left the camogie scene – a little prematurely she would now admit – bearing many honours, among them:

3 All-Ireland medals
B & I Camogie Player of the Year 1975
Sports Star of the Week – *Irish Press* – after 1968 All-Ireland win
6 county titles
2 Powers Sports Star Awards as a player
1 Powers Sports Star Award as a player of the past.

In an Academic Presentation, Jean Quigley, niece of Brigid and daughter of Gretta, captain of the 1975 winning team who married Ray Quigley the Saturday before the final, quotes her mother as saying – 'My sister Brigid inspired me the most. She had skill and determination. She was an excellent all-round player. At the time, standing on the sideline watching Brigid play, you could hear many of the men shouting – "She should be on the men's team." She was that good, and better than many of the men and Wexford would have won more hurling All-Irelands if they had to have her!!' (Laughs)

Brigid selected two teams – a Wexford team and an All-Ireland team. After some deliberation she decided to omit her sisters, all of whom have been honoured in this article. After all, if she did pick them, there would be very few positions left to fill.

Her Wexford team:

Teresa Sheils

Mary Sinnott   Joan Murphy   Dorothy Walsh

Brigid O'Connor   Brigid Doyle (Capt)   Margaret O'Leary

Bernie Murphy   Elsie Walshe

Mairead D'Arcy   Maggie Hearne   Bridie Jacob

Eileen O'Gorman   Mary Shannon   Mary Doyle

Her All-Ireland team:

Jo Golden
(Kilkenny)

Maeve Gilroy   Alice Hussey   Bridie Martin
(Antrim)   *(Dublin)*   *(Kilkenny)*

Mary Fennelly   Brigid Doyle (Capt)   Sue Cashman
(Kilkenny)   *(Wexford)*   *(Antrim)*

Mairead McAtamney   Orla Ní Shíocháin
(Antrim)   *(Dublin)*

Ann Downey   Margaret O'Leary   Maggie Hearne
(Kilkenny)   *(Wexford)*   *(Wexford)*

Judy Doyle   Una O'Connor   Angela Downey
(Dublin)   *(Dublin)*   *(Kilkenny)*

Una O'Connor
DUBLIN
1963 & 1964

'I know a maid with sparkling eye,
She looks so sweet, she seems so shy –
But she smiled at me as she passed by,
Going down to Mass last Sunday.'

(Carbery)

Meet one of the all-time greats of the camogie world. I am referring
to Una O'Connor – a modest superstar, a forward supreme, a prolific

scorer who loved to practise and who saw beauty in the art of ground strokes. She was endowed with natural athletic talent but confessed that she had no idea from where in her ancestry she inherited her athleticism.

Playing camogie, whether with her club Celtic or her county Dublin, made Una feel good. For this was something she could do better than most. The game enriched her life and brought her fame – a fame that rested lightly on the shoulders of a kind and gentle personality.

At an early age Una learned discipline and when we met she spoke of its merits. She remembers their trainer, Nell McCarthy, blowing the whistle, calling them all to the mid-field position, telling them they weren't doing their best and sending them home. And home they went without a protest.

She was in awe of Kevin Heffernan. They lived in the same parish. He would offer counsel and guidance before a game and give Una a goal-scoring target. If she failed to deliver she would be fearful of meeting him.

Una was the youngest of a family of eight and at eighteen years of age experienced the pain and sadness of loss when her mother died. Her father who hailed from Co. Kildare went to all the games she played and this sporting bond meant a lot to Una.

In 1967 she received the Caltex Award for the best player of the year – the first camogie player to be so honoured. Una's big regret was that her father wasn't there to share in the glory. 'He died the year before. Jack Lynch presented the trophy. He would have got such a thrill out of that.'

In 1953 at the age of 15 Una won her first of thirteen All-Ireland medals and in so doing demonstrated her scoring potential by netting three goals. Dublin defeated Tipperary by 8:4 to 1:3. After that honours just flowed and flowed at provincial, inter-provincial and All-Ireland level as Una combined speed and skill with craft and cunning in her many magical displays.

In 1963 and '64 she had the signal honour of captaining her county to All-Ireland success. She was well equipped for the task. Her vast experience, infectious enthusiasm, dedication to training and shining example on the field of play were leadership qualities designed to make her ideally suited to take on the richly deserved mantle of captain.

In each of those years the camogie players of Antrim were defeated.

| 1963 | 7:3 to 2:5 |
| 1964 | 7:4 to 3:1 |

Those victories recalled for Una the final of 1957 between the same counties. Inexplicably, she was out of favour. With ten minutes to go and defeat facing Dublin, Una was sprung from the bench. Her genius paved the way for the goal that shattered Antrim hopes and elated Dublin fans with a final 3:3 to 3:1 score line. Thus began a run of successes that by 1966 saw Una take ten All-Ireland victories in a row – an achievement unique to Una and one unlikely to be ever equalled.

The following year, 1967, saw the ladies from the 'Glens' exact sweet revenge for the defeats of 1957, '63 and '64 in which Una had played a major role. After a 4:2 apiece draw, Antrim won the replay by 3:9 to 4:2.

In 1975 Una was persuaded to come out of retirement to play a Leinster championship game against Wexford. She lined out at fullback and this former forward showed her true versatility by turning in a sterling performance.

In the record books Una, with thirteen All-Ireland medals, stands second to her fellow county camogie colleague Kathleen Mills who heads the honours list with fifteen titles.

Fad agus a bheidh caint agus trácht ar chamogaíocht, beidh ainm Una i mbéal na ndaoine go deo deo. Imreoir den chead scoth a bhí innti; scil thar bharr aici; í ábalta imirt ins na cúil nó ins na tosaithe. Banlaoch ab ea í ar pháirc an imeartha agus i dteannta cúpla imreoir eile beidh sé an-deacair a leithéid nó a sárú a fháil arís.

Kathleen Mills
DUBLIN
1958

'Had I the gold of England's King,
The wealth of France or Spain,
Or all the jewels that the big ships bring
From o'er the Spanish main;

I'd leave them all, the great and small
For a verdant Irish lawn,
My comrades all, the flying ball
And a stout grained ash camán.'

(Sliabh Ruadh)

I first met Kathleen in March 1994 following which she featured in my book *Hurling Giants*. She was then in her 71st year – warm and welcoming, hospitable and informal, vivacious and lighthearted. May I call you Kathleen, I enquired. 'Do, it will make me feel young,' she replied.

Kathleen was born in 1923 of a Dublin mother and Cork father. Sadly, when she was eighteen months old her mother died. She was then reared by her maternal grandmother. 'When I was five years old I first held a hurley and from that day to 1961 I never left it out of my hand.' As Kathleen grew up she took a keen interest in a wide range of sports and games – gymnastics, table tennis, running and soccer. She was a natural athlete. She used go to Dalymount and remembers a special occasion when she went to see Jackie Carey play.

Camogie, however, was her first love. It was her sporting passion. The game absorbed her energies and at the same time generated vibrancy within her. She was brilliant at the game and became its first superstar. In her playing days she became a legend and will remain one as long as Gaelic games are talked about. Kathleen was to camogie what Mick Mackey and Christy Ring and Nicky Rackard and Lory Meagher were to hurling. She could inspire a team like Mick Mackey and Dublin's supremacy in the camogie world was built to a large degree on Kathleen's brilliance. She had the dedication and range of skills of Christy Ring and her career lasted almost as long. In defeat she could be as philosophical and sporting as Nicky Rackard. She had the magic of Lory Meagher.

Kathleen made her camogie début with her club GSR – later to become known as CIE – in 1938. In 1941, at the age of 18, she found favour with the county selectors and played her first All-Ireland final against a great Cork team seeking a three-in-a-row run of successes. The Rebel County ladies proved too good and won well on the score 7:5 to 1:2. For Kathleen it was a case of *bíonn gach tosnú lag*. However, great harvests lay ahead.

In 1942 as Europe struggled with the horrors of World War Two, the train taking the Dublin camogie team to Cork to play the All-Ireland final, chugged and huffed and puffed its way for about eleven hours as poor quality fuel kept the engine functioning at under-capacity. The game was a draw but victory came in the replay at Croke Park. Kathleen collected her first All-Ireland medal.

When the same counties met in 1943, for the third final in a row, much excitement was generated and a crowd of 10,000 turned up at Croke Park. Dublin, with Kathleen Mills in devastating form, swept to victory on the score 8 goals to 1:1. The following year, 1944, brought a third All-Ireland medal.

Disputes in the camogie organisation in 1945 and 1946 kept Dublin out of the All-Ireland race despite winning in Leinster.

Kathleen married George Hill in 1947. She won a fourth All-Ireland medal in 1948 and didn't participate in the championship of 1949. The next eleven years – 1950 to 1961 inclusive – brought an avalanche of successes. Kathleen collected eleven All-Ireland medals in a row. There were, of course, lots of other successes and awards. Kathleen was the first camogie player to be honoured as Sports Star of the Week in the *Irish Independent*.

The honour of captaincy was bestowed on Kathleen in 1958. Led by her, Dublin defeated Tipperary in the final by 5:4 to 1:1. She proudly accepted the O'Duffy Cup and raised it aloft. A replica of the O'Duffy Cup is among her many trophies. It was presented to her in 1961 by the Camogie Board. That was the year Kathleen won her last All-Ireland medal. The occasion had a special appeal. It was her birthday. She called it a day. She was 38 and yet 'I was playing as good as ever.'

On the camogie team, which lined out twelve-a-side in her day, she played at left wing. In that position she was devastating – a natural lefthander, hurley held righthand under. And she could strike left and right with equal ease and take frees in similar fashion. She had a great turn of speed, many deft touches, and was known to send sideline cuts over the bar – Josie Gallagher of Galway, style.

On the pitch her sweeping play, lengthy striking, accurate distribution, uncanny accuracy, fleetness of foot, superb wrist-work and ball control made her stand apart. In her own words 'I could fly along and rise the ball and strike in the one motion.' Yes indeed, she could fly along all right and as she did this remarkable performer cut a tall, blonde, lithe, athletic figure – an athlete fit for a story from Na Fianna.

At the launch of *Hurling Giants* at Croke Park on 17 November 1994 Kathleen was present. It was good to see her there. She was, after all, the most decorated player of the GAA world with fifteen All-Ireland medals to her credit. Among her playing colleagues present were Sophie Brack, who captained Dublin on six occasions and won a total of eight All-Ireland medals; also Una O'Connor who stands second to Kathleen with thirteen All-Ireland successes.

In August 1996 Kathleen Mills died. She was 73. *Solas na bhFlaitheas ort, a Kathleen, is i seilbh ghrámhar Dé go raibh tú go deo.*

Other Outstanding
Hurling Captains
2002 – 1887

Fergal Hartley
WATERFORD
2002

'Twas a new feeling – something more
Than we had dar'd to own before'

The sound of the final whistle in the Munster hurling final at Páirc Uí Chaoimh on Sunday 30 June heralded the release of joy unconfined from supporters and players of the Waterford team. A famous victory had been achieved after a lapse of 39 years.

Fergal Hartley, now aged 30 and winner of an under-21 All-Ireland title in 1992 at left halfback, gave a regal display – sure hands, endless courage, hugely inspirational. He was rock-solid and defiant at centreback. Time and again he held the centre and repeatedly repulsed Tipperary attacks.

He captained great men who gave a gripping, pulsating and breathtaking display of energy-sapping hurling. And oh, how Carbery, if he were alive, would have loved it – hurling in all 'its stern naked grandeur'.

We saw 'all that delirium of the brave' at the final whistle – scenes of wild delight. The Waterford players remained on the pitch for a half hour after the game – heroes all, acknowledging the acclaim and congratulations of their wildly enthusiastic supporters. There they were, players and supporters, now gripped in a unison of celebration.

It was Waterford's sixth Munster title. Let's now look back briefly at the county's earlier wins. The hurling championships were in their 52nd year when Waterford under the captaincy of Mick Hickey of Portlaw defeated Clare by 3:5 to 2:5 in the Munster final of 1938. Great men on that team included Charlie Ware, John Keane, Christy Moylan and Willie Barron.

Ten years would elapse before their next success in 1948 – this time at the expense of Cork (4:7 to 3:9). The late Micheál O'Hehir captured the excitement of that occasion for me. At one stage in the second half Waterford led by eight points. Gradually, Cork chipped away at that lead until only one point separated the sides. With seconds remaining the attendance held its breadth as Christy Ring gained possession about forty yards out. To the relief of Waterford followers his shot shaved the upright on the outside. Legendary names from that victory – which was later converted to All-Ireland success – include Jim Ware who captained the team, Andy Fleming, Vin Baston, Mick Hayes, John Keane, Christy Moylan and Johnny O'Connor.

Nine years later in 1957, the Suirsiders, led by Phil Grimes, again got the better of the men from the Lee on the scoreline of 1:11 to 1:6.

That victory was the harbinger of a great Waterford era. In 1959, led by Frankie Walsh, they defeated Cork at Thurles 3:9 to 2:9 with a wonderful display in a great game of hurling. They went on to take their second All-Ireland title by defeating Kilkenny in a replay, after an epic drawn contest.

Waterford were back again in 1963. Joe Condon led them to victory over Tipperary in the Munster final, 0:11 to 0:8.

Apart from the captains, the other great players of that era included Austin Flynn, John Barron, Seamus Power, Tom Cheasty, Martin Óg Morrissey, Larry Guinan, Johnny Kiely, Mick Flannelly and Tom Cunningham.

Let's now return to 2002. Waterford booked their place in the Munster final with a one-point win over Cork in a game where they displayed grit, tenacity and never-say-die spirit.

Having won the toss in the Munster final Waterford decided to play against the wind in the first half. After a tentative start they gradually came to grips with the task on hand. At half time the omens looked good – only a point behind on the score (1:10 to 1:9).

Slowly but surely Waterford began to assert themselves in all positions in the second half. About midway through that half the scores were level for the sixth time, 1:16 to 3:10 for Tipperary. From then to the end Waterford hurled with a fury and intensity to which Tipperary had no answer. In the last twelve minutes the Tipperary posts were under constant siege. If all the shots had found the target the victory would have been closer to fourteen points instead of the 2:23 to 3:12, eight-point win. It was fairytale stuff. Jim Sullivan, writing in the *Irish Examiner* the following day, summed it up well – 'it was one of those days when you had to see it happen to believe that it was true'.

In an after-game comment Fergal Hartley said – 'Unbelievable. This is the day we always dreamed of and, thank God, it has finally arrived.'

Vincent Hogan of the *Irish Independent* observed Fergal Hartley as he departed with the Cup.

Meaty hands slap their approval across Fergal Hartley's back as he brings the Cup down the tunnel. What a story.

Fergal's been hurling nine years for the county, hurling and hurting. Losing time, wrestling with the banalities of grief.

Yet, here he comes, his complexion florid, his irises now wide as hubcaps. This moment ought to be embalmed. A good man vaguely nonplussed by his good fortune. Fergal looks like there's a stranger roaming about inside his head. Waterford. Champions. Say it again, Sam.

Waterford hurling lovers will savour this victory for many a day. What a memorable occasion. What a great captain – modest and gracious in victory. The supporters will watch the video over and over again; they will relish the moment; they will inhale the glory; 1:6 from the hurley of Paul Flynn – the goal, a defiant effort from a 21 yards free as he picked his spot and lashed the sliotar past five Tipperary men who lined the goal; seven points from the elegant Ken McGrath who served up a majestic performance; a great display, especially in the second half from midfielder Tony Browne, who followed through on a mighty long free from goalkeeper Stephen Brennan, to send a well-timed ground stroke past the advancing Brendan Cummins to the Tipperary net that sent Waterford into a one goal lead in the 52nd minute and on their way to Munster glory. From heroes all, it was vintage hurling – a spectacle of sport that beggars description. Truly a game for the gods.

The homecoming, the welcome and the celebrations have rarely been surpassed. The Munster Cup rests with Fergal Hartley, proud captain of the Déise hurling men. *Níor chaill fir an mhisnigh riamh.*

Tom Dempsey
WEXFORD
1993

'Is fearr déanach ná ró-dhéanach.'

My greatest memories revolve around the Buffers Alley GAA grounds in the mid seventies. It's a bright summer's evening and the ball is flying. Passions run high as a group of ten to fourteen year olds contest their 'All-Ireland final' under the expert supervision of my father, Ger, Billy Lee, John Doyle, the late Joe Kinsella and Fr. Jim Butler.

Every ball is life and death as the Whelans, Donohoes, Gahans, Har Lee, Fintan O'Leary, Mattie Foley, Marney Burke, Eamon Sinnott and myself amongst others play out our dream.

This was indeed the most wonderful time of my life.

The pride I felt fourteen years later when these same boys (now men) backboned Buffers Alley in winning the All-Ireland club title was incredible. The best club team in Ireland, 'a dream realised'.

Much of my youth was spent banging a sliotar against the wall at the front of my house in Kilmuckridge village. Every so often a badly directed shot made short work of my mother's roses and, no matter how hard I tried, I couldn't get across to her that the shot just taken was the winning goal for Wexford in an All-Ireland final.

Again I was lucky enough to realise the aforementioned dream and score that vital goal in 1996. The deaths of my mother's roses were not in vain.

It was a great privilege to serve with thirty wonderful men in 1996 and also of course to have hurled with many wonderful Wexford men over fifteen years in the purple and gold jersey.

It saddens me to think of the unlucky players who served Wexford so well but did not win a 'Celtic Cross', as they were all as entitled to the honour as the '96 players.

So as I look back now I feel lucky and honoured to have achieved the two main goals in my GAA life. I appreciate the fact that I played with and against many great men (better than me) that weren't so lucky.

Finally, thanks to my family and to Sinead for the patience.

At county level the final whistle, more often than not, heralded disappointment rather than rejoicing for Tom Dempsey in a career that stretched from 1984 to 2000. However, defeat, while always a burden, never diminished his ardour for the game.

Tom hails from the same territory as Mick Butler and the great Tony Doran – 'the Happy Warrior'. He was three years old when

Tony was doing *gaiscí* for Wexford in the All-Ireland final of 1968. In due course Tom would play beside his childhood hero in the Buffers Alley colours and win an All-Ireland club title.

Tom's potential as an athlete was in evidence from an early age. For three years in a row he played minor hurling and minor football with his native Wexford. He remembers well the 1983 Leinster minor hurling final against Dublin. Wexford lost by 5:14 to 4:12. Chief architect of Wexford's defeat was corner forward Niall Quinn, destined for international soccer renown, who scored 3:5.

At St. Peter's College, Tom captained the senior hurling team that won the Leinster title in 1982. He experienced the first of many major disappointments on the playing field when losing the All-Ireland colleges final to St. Flannan's of Ennis by five points after a replay. 'It still affects me to think we lost. Colleges hurling is the most personal game you'll ever play – it's like a family affair. We should have won the first day. Ned Power, one of our teachers, was a great influence on hurling in St. Peter's and in Wexford – one of the most knowledgeable of hurling men.'

Tom played at midfield for St. Peter's. It was his favourite position – 'Midfield or halfback, my best position. I was centre-back for the under-21 team that lost the 1986 final to Galway. It was one of my regrets that I found myself being placed in the forwards throughout my hurling days. I would have loved a career at midfield.' That comment of Tom's reminded me of a letter I received from Larry Rice of Belfast in July '93. Here is an excerpt:

> To me the greatest and most thrilling final ever played in my time was the 1935 game between Limerick and Kilkenny, and the next best to follow that was Wexford v Cork 1956 . . . Mick Mackey was the greatest ever to play hurling and two others deserving of national acclaim but never received it, Mattie Power and Paddy Phelan of the great 1935 Kilkenny team . . . I hope Wexford take the Leinster title crown this Sunday. Had Tom Dempsey been in at centre field on the first playing of the National League they would have taken the trophy, not Cork.

That's an interesting comment from my Antrim correspondent. Tom would regard the 1993 Wexford team as the best he played on. And with good reason too. Victory over a fine Limerick team in the National League semi-final brought Wexford, under Tom Dempsey's captaincy, face to face with Cork in the final. Lost opportunities saw Wexford lose – after three games – a league title that was there to be won, especially in the first game that ended 2:11 each and also in the second game that ended level at Wexford 3:9 Cork 0:18, after extra time.

But even greater heartbreak lay in store for Wexford and Tom Dempsey in the championship of 1993. They met Kilkenny in the Leinster final. A wonderful display of power-packed hurling saw Wexford dominate the first half – a superiority not reflected on the scoreboard. With the final seconds of the game ticking away Wexford held a one-point lead and looked winners – winners that is until Kilkenny from the very depths of defence executed a movement that produced a remarkable equaliser. 'We were like a team that hadn't won before. We should have gone forward. Even though I got nine or ten points I was very disappointed. We should have been putting Kilkenny away.' Defeat in the replay was Wexford's lot. 1993 was a year when Wexford undoubtedly had the ability and potential to have brought off a league and All-Ireland double. The Fates ordained otherwise. It will always be Tom's year of greatest regret.

Fortunately, at parish level there were many moments of rejoicing. A central figure in the Buffers Alley club was Tom's father Ger – 'a fanatic about the game, he hurled himself in the early fifties. My mothers helps neutralise things.' Victory in eight county finals led to three Leinster club successes and one of those paved the way to an All-Ireland club victory. That was in 1989.

Rathnure were defeated after a replay in the county final of 1988. Then the following games ensued:

v Ballyhale Shamrocks (1:12 to 1:9) at Carlow
v Four Roads (Roscommon) (2:19 to 0:9) at Wexford
v O'Donovan Rossa (2:12 to 0:12) at Croke Park.

'The atmosphere in the dressing-room was indescribable. In every corner you saw a friend. The club had achieved a lifelong ambition. My father predicted after the All-Ireland final defeat by Kilruane McDonaghs in 1986 that we would soon win a club title – that we'll have the best club team.' That victory celebrated the 'honour of the little village' – an honour that stirs all hearts.

The years were passing. Tom was in the autumn of his career. He had seen many a promising harvest blighted. Then came 1996 and

Liam Griffin. Injury kept Tom out of the first-round game against Kilkenny until the second half was well under way. From then until the end of the championship he hurled with the passion and flair of a player rejuvenated. 'You're prepared to shed 500 beads of sweat to win an All-Ireland,' said Liam Griffin to me at a training session. 'I am,' I said, as I walked away. 'Tom,' he shouted. 'Make that 1000 beads.'

Tom became Wexford's most consistent forward. In the remaining games he was the county's leading scorer; 1:5 against Offaly in the Leinster final – 3 beauties (points) in the closing stages on a day when Wexford's hurling graph peaked in a thrilling and absorbing contest; 0:6 against Galway in a dour, mental and physically sapping, semi-final encounter; 1:3 against Limerick in the All-Ireland final. It was the only goal of the game and a vital one it proved to be. It came from a ground stroke at a crucial time for Wexford, twenty minutes into the first half. It proved to be a winning score in Wexford's two-point win – 1:13 to 0:14.

Victory brought Tom a cherished All-Ireland medal and his outstanding hurling throughout 1996 brought him an All-Star Award. Oh, and by the way, that goal he scored against Limerick subsequently attracted an added value element. In appreciation of the role the goal played in Wexford's victory, the Management of Murphy Flood's Hotel in Enniscorthy told Tom that for the rest of his life a free cup of coffee would be available to him at all times.

Tom encountered and observed many great hurling men during his career. The selection hereunder, excluding Wexford men, is just some of many.

Joe Quaid
(Limerick)

Brian Corcoran   Brian Lohan   Martin Hanamy
(Cork)   (Clare)   (Offaly)

Seannie McMahon   Ger Henderson   John Taylor
(Clare)   (Kilkenny)   (Laois)

Brian Whelehan   John Fenton
(Offaly)   (Cork)

Nicky English   Joe Cooney   Ciaran Carey
(Tipperary)   (Galway)   (Limerick)

Liam Fennelly   D.J. Carey   Pat Fox
(Kilkenny)   (Kilkenny)   (Tipperary)

Tommy Quaid
FEOHANAGH (LIMERICK)
1990

'From seventy six to ninety three, he
played a starring role
Leading by example as he guarded
Limerick's goal.
'Tis hard to understand it all as in
cold clay he's laid,
Why did he have to die so young,
Feohanagh's Tommy Quaid'

(Garry McMahon)

The adjectives that describe the personality of Tommy Quaid are kind, sincere, humble, warm, endearing, shy and soft-spoken.

As a hurling goalkeeper, he ranks with the elite in that position. Lynx-eyed, agile and with cat-like reflexes he produced many magnificent saves. Good-humouredly he used to say that it was the ones he let in that were remembered. No doubt all custodians can identify with that. Tommy's innings of eighteen years – 1976 to1993 – between the posts at senior level for his native Limerick is a record for the county. As a youngster, his hero was Ollie Walsh of Kilkenny fame. Where longevity between the posts is concerned Tommy stands in the noble company of Damien Martin of Offaly, Ger Cunningham of Cork, Jim Ware of Waterford, Pat Nolan (Oilgate) of Wexford and Dr. Tommy Daly of Clare and Dublin.

On the pitch Tommy was a sportsman supreme, whether in goal for his county or outfield for his club where his scoring feats were quite phenomenal. Intimidation, retaliation and ugly play were alien to his make-up.

Tommy Quaid at the age of 41 died tragically in 1998 in a freak accident following a 14 ft. fall from scaffolding. Ironically on the day he died, Saturday 10 October, the Limerick intermediate team that he had coached, defeated Kilkenny in the All-Ireland final at Semple Stadium in Thurles.

In latter years Tommy had thrown in his lot with Effin where he had come to reside. His presence was largely instrumental in the club winning three South Limerick titles. A week before his death he played in the county quarter-final victory against Fedamore and scored 1:5.

> 'We remember you in Páirc Uí Chaoimh
> For many a wonder save
> Whether, on your feet, or on your knees
> No-one was so brave.
> We remember you in Thurles town
> For many a game so fine
> Eagle-eyed between the posts
> With the courage of a lion.'
>
> (Seamus Benson)

Tommy was the son of Bridie (née Collins) and Jack Quaid who won an All-Ireland junior title with Limerick in 1954 and a Munster senior medal the following year when 'Mackey's Greyhounds' sensationally defeated Clare in the Munster final at Limerick Gaelic Grounds.

Tommy Quaid made his début in the green and white of his native Limerick at minor level in 1974. He was still a minor in 1975 and after that graduated to the No. 1 jersey at under-21 level from whence he moved to senior in 1976.

He won many awards at club level and one of his proudest moments came in 1990 when he captained his native Feohanagh to a West Limerick senior hurling title. The honour of the little village stirs all hearts.

Unfortunately, Feohanagh never won a county senior title. As a consequence the opportunity to captain his county never arose for Tommy.

Among his many awards one finds a long overdue All-Star in 1992; All-Ireland Poc Fada over the Cooley Mountains; Munster senior medals in 1980 and 1981; National League medals 1984, '85 and '92; Railway Cup honours; an All-Ireland inter-firm with Golden Vale; football successes with his club that include a county junior title – for Tommy was no mean footballer either.

Many times he dreamt of an All-Ireland senior medal but the great honour proved elusive. Galway foiled Limerick's efforts in the final of 1980. The following year, after a replay, Galway again shattered Tommy's hopes at the All-Ireland semi-final stage.

He was once described as 'the ultimate GAA man'. His commitment to Gaelic games and the development of the youth was enormous. He had a temperament that oozed equanimity which enabled him to cope with success and failure with philosophical grace. He was a man of ideals and values.

Where the youth were concerned, Tommy was a visionary. He was an instigator of a five-year plan. He knew that the foundations of future success were built on caring for, nurturing and encouraging the youth. *Mol an óige agus tiocfaidh sí*, would have been his motto. His counsel, guidance and game plan strategy were all delivered in soft, measured tones. And as those in his charge took the field he would always place emphasis on 'playing the ball'. As a non-smoker and non-drinker he set a fine example too.

In years to come hurling lovers look forward to seeing Tommy Quaid's sportsmanship and hurling skills replicated in his three sons Tommy, Nickie and Sean – now ardently coached by their Kilkenny-born mother Breda.

> *'For he gave the young men dreams to dream,*
> *The old ones tales to tell*
> *To the youth he gave the five year plan*
> *Their skills to nurture well*
> *That is the sporting picture*
> *The other side brings tears,*
> *The great one now is gone from us*
> *All in his prime of years.'*

(John Carrig)

Noel Lane
CONNAUGHT (GALWAY)
1986

> *'But hark! a voice like thunder spake*
> *The West's awake! the West's awake!'*

My earliest recollection of gripping a hurley is in the field beside our house at home in Lavally Connor. Playing with my

270

three brothers and some neighbours we used 'stones' for goalposts and generally a sponge ball. The pace of the ball was nothing like the present sliotar which probably helped all hurlers at that time. I notice now that my kids will not play with a sponge ball because of its pace and speed – a pity really as it's great for the eye.

My first hurley was made by Pat Monaghan (R.I.P.) and I was very proud of it and treated it like a precious jewel – linseed oil, hanging up each night and running repairs by my late father.

My brothers were the first to influence me locally and my father, but it was probably Micheál O'Hehir on radio that developed my passion and spirit for the game. Playing for Ballyglass N.S. under Tom O'Doherty and Sean Devlin at Our Lady's College, Gort, also had a tremendous influence on me. Of course my club Ballinderreen – playing with Joe McDonagh, Michael Coen and many others – were also a huge influence.

Playing with Galway was a dream come true. I made my début in Tulla in 1977 v Clare in N.H.L. Togging out with John Connolly, Sean Silke, Iggy Clarke, P.J. Molloy, Frank Burke and all the others who had made the great breakthrough in 1975, was a great honour and one I'll never forget.

My wife Carmel was probably my greatest supporter and biggest influence of all.

Funny enough my childhood heroes were the Galway football three-in-a-row team (1964–1966).

However, Babs Keating, John Connolly, Mick Roche and Kieran Purcell all impressed me. I thought Babs was God the day he took off his boots and socks.

My own club senior players – Eamon Fahy, John Coen, John Faul, Mick McTigue and Paddy Shiels – to name a few were 'giants' when I was young. Letting Paddy Shiels take the black insulated tape off my hurley at half time on a very warm day to put on his big hurley as a grip, was my claim to fame for a long time.

I had many special moments, good and bad:

- Captain of Ballyglass N.S. and winning a South final v Labane N.S. was special. We met a delivery truck while cycling home from the game – they stopped and filled our cup with orange – it was fantastic, we felt so proud. Tom Doherty brought us on a tour around the area and the parents had a big bonfire and all the goodies to celebrate.

- Playing in a Colleges final v St. Peter's of Wexford – a draw the first day – they beat us well in the replay. I scored a few points.
- Seeing my name in the *Irish Press* – in my bedroom in digs in Aughrim, Wicklow – selected on the Galway team to play Clare in Tulla in the 1977 N.H.L. – that's how I found out – no mobile phones those days.
- Playing with my club in the 1978 county final, draw, replay and extra time – very special.
- Winning a junior 'B' county final in 1996 – my only county medal – scoring two line balls to win the final.
- Winning the 1980 All-Ireland final, the homecoming and having the MacCarthy Cup in my home, local pub and club – very special.
- Scoring a 'Goal of the Year' in the 1979 final v Kilkenny.
- All my goals but particularly the goal v Tipp. in the 1988 All-Ireland final.
- Finding out about my 'All-Star' selections in '83 and '84.
- On Galway 'Team of the Century'.
- Watching my kids play for Ballindereen.

1986 was a very mixed year. I heard that the Management were going to name me as captain on the way down from Dublin after the defeat in the 1985 final. Personally, I was happy but was unsure if I was ready for such a role – I had a lot of commitments at home with a young family and at work in the Forestry.

Connaught won the Railway Cup and receiving the Cup as captain was special – my first – little did I know it was also my last. We were beaten in the Oireachtas, National League and All-Ireland finals. It was a huge disappointment.

Winning the All-Ireland semi-final v Kilkenny in Thurles was a great day. The thought afterwards of leading my county on All-Ireland final day was made of dreams. I had a recurring back injury at the time and it acted up the week before the actual final. It was a huge worry and in hindsight affected my performance – mentally in particular – on the day. Playing two inside forwards – a repeat of the semi-final – backfired badly and Cork beat us well in the end. I also failed to score.

The subsequent days and weeks were the worst ever in my life – such a disappointment for myself and my family but also for Galway. However, it was a great honour and experience. We were a young team and went on to win the next two finals.

I played in eight All-Ireland finals, winning three, and I'm happy enough with my lot as a player. I would love to have won a county senior final with my club.

I love hurling and did since I was four or five. I still puck around with my kids – it's my favourite way to unwind after a day's work.

In 1527, following a Royal Edict, the Statute of Galway ordered loyal subjects 'at no time to use the hurling of the little ball with hockey sticks or staves'. It would, however, take more than Royal Command to suppress the ancient pastime of the Gael. The game of hurling lived on in Galway.

The 1980s was a wonderful decade for Galway hurling and Noel Lane figured prominently in the county's many successes.

Noel hails from the rural parish of Ballindereen in South Galway – a parish that also produced such hurling heroes as Mick Gill, Joe McDonagh and Tom Helebert.

So rich in hurling talent was Galway in the 1980s that there were occasions when Noel found himself in the role of super-sub. So let's recall two in particular.

In the All-Ireland final of 1987 against Kilkenny, Galway having played with a strong wind in the first half led by only five points to four at the break in a game of tense, tough, torrid exchanges. Five minutes into the second half, Noel Lane emerged from the subs bench to replace Michael Naughton. It was to prove to be a vital move. With eight minutes to go it was still anyone's game. Two points separated the sides. It was then that goal-poacher Noel Lane pounced. He finished a build-up, involving Steve Mahon, Éanna Ryan and Joe Cooney, to the Kilkenny net with a hard angled shot. With that goal – the only goal of the game – the match was won and lost. A further point followed from Tony Keady. The game ended Galway 1:12 Kilkenny 0:9. Victory heralded a treble of successes for Galway and Noel Lane in 1987 – Railway Cup, National League and All-Ireland honours.

The following year, 1988, Noel was again to the fore in a similar role. This time their opponents were Tipperary – appearing in their first All-Ireland final since 1971. Galway played with a strong wind in the opening half and led by ten points to six at half time. Noel, who had played in the earlier games of the championship, replaced Anthony Cunningham in the second half. In the closing stages of the game with Galway under fierce pressure and clinging to a two-point lead Noel went into action. He rounded Tipperary fullback Conor O'Donovan and his well placed ground shot found the net. It clinched victory for the Tribesmen. As in the previous year it was the only goal of the game. Noel had demonstrated once again that he possessed the flair, temperament and opportunism to produce a winning score in tight pressure situations. The final of 1988 ended on the score Galway 1:15 Tipperary 0:14.

It is significant to note that in both of those finals, seven Galway men scored in 1987 and ten scored in 1988, while John Commins in goal brought off some superb and crucial saves.

In 1980 Noel was at left full forward for Galway in the All-Ireland final against Limerick. He was one of Galway's many stars on that historic occasion when the men of the West, after a lapse of 57 years, captured their second All-Ireland crown. Noel with three points to his credit was among Galway's leading scorers. Peadar O'Brien writing in the *Irish Press* on Monday 8 September had this to say – 'At the other end of the field the much vaunted and respected Limerick fullback line was torn to pieces by cornermen Bernie Forde and Noel Lane . . . ' and their ability 'to pick off long range points must have broken every Limerick heart in Croke Park'.

Throughout the eighties Noel won major honours on a regular basis. The list is impressive.

All-Ireland Titles 1980, '87, '88
Railway Cups 1980, '82 '83 '86 and '87
National Leagues 1987 and '89
All-Star Awards 1983 and '84.

In the spring of 1980 Noel was playing at right full forward when Galway hurlers made the breakthrough that opened the gates to greatness in the 1980s. On 17 February at Ballinasloe, Galway, representing Connaught, defeated Leinster by 1:13 to 1:10 after extra time in the

Railway Cup semi-final. On St. Patrick's Day at Croke Park they beat Munster in the final by a point – 1:5 to 0:7. It was their second victory in a competition that was inaugurated in 1927 and their first since 1947 when they defeated the might of Munster by 2:5 to 1:1.

Six years later in 1986 Noel had the honour of leading the western province, represented by Galway, to Railway Cup honours. In the semi-final at Galway on 16 February they beat Leinster by 1:10 to 1:9. On St. Patrick's Day at Ballinasloe they had a convincing win over Munster on the score 3:11 to 0:11. Noel took the Railway Cup to the West for the fifth time. He then proceeded from being winning Railway Cup captain in 1986 to being super-sub extraordinary in the All-Ireland finals of 1987 and '88.

Noel played in eight All-Ireland finals. We have referred to the three that were won. So let's briefly look at the five that were lost, some of which on any other day might well have been won.

1979 v Kilkenny (2:12 to 1:8)

Galway were favourites. Noel got the only Galway goal early in the second half to put his county into the lead. With less than ten minutes to go and Galway just two points in arrears a John Connolly penalty was superbly saved by Noel Skehan.

Kilkenny's goals, both of the fortuitous variety, came at critical stages of the game – the first with less than five minutes to go to half time came from a seventy that deceived defence and goalkeeper, the second three minutes from time travelled all the way to the net from about fifty yards out.

1981 v Offaly (2:12 to 0:15)

It's a title Galway will feel they let slip. For much of the game they looked the superior outfit but failed to reflect that on the scoreboard. With about ten minutes remaining and Galway still three points to the good, Noel Lane broke through the Offaly defence. His shot was heading to the top of the net at Damien Martin's right in the Offaly goal, only to be blocked by a superb reflex save from the Offaly man. It was one of the game's turning points and kept Offaly's hopes alive.

1985 v Offaly (2:11 to 1:12)

This was another local derby between the Shannon River neighbours. The scoring was almost a carbon copy of 1981. Galway were left to rue their scoring efforts that registered nineteen wides.

1986 v Cork (4:13 to 2:15)

Galway entered the game firm favourites and deservedly so after crushing Kilkenny in the semi-final at Thurles. Two early goals to Cork, playing against the wind, rattled Galway who had an uphill battle thereafter.

1990 v Cork (5:15 to 2:21)

Cork as in 1986 were underdogs. Galway will always wonder how they lost this magnificent game. The fates certainly conspired against them. It was Noel's last All-Ireland final. He was 36. Retirement beckoned.

However, his fame will live on in hurling circles and his scoring deeds will always be remembered in the folklore of Galway hurling.

Niall Patterson
LOUGHGIEL (ANTRIM)
1983

'The Blue Hills of Antrim I see in my dreams,
The high hills of Antrim, the glens and the streams;
In sunlight and shadow, in weal and in woe,
The sweet vision haunts me wherever I go.'

Niall Patterson was born on 2 January 1962 and was the second eldest of a family of seven consisting of four boys and three girls – Anthony, Niall, Aidan, Jarlath, twins Maggie and Anne, and Katrina.

He lives in a small village in North Antrim called Cloughmills. It is in the parish of Dunloy but, like his father Neil before him, he played his club hurling with Loughgiel Shamrocks.

Niall's earliest memories of hurling centre around 'the great Loughgiel team of the late sixties who won five county titles in the space of six years between 1966 and '71, losing the final of 1969 by one point after having three goals and one point disallowed, and pucking a ball about before and at half time on the Sunday of the games'.

He started playing when he was nine years old at fullback. 'I went further back to goalkeeper for the under 12s and that's where it all began in 1971. I was coached by Johnny Coyle, the goalkeeper on the senior team, a legend in his own right.

I started playing senior for Antrim straight out of minor. I replaced Jim Corr, a great keeper, and made my début against Kilkenny in Nowlan Park in the National League in 1979. I played until 1992 against Down in the National League in December.

Niall is very proud of his club, his county and his province. He has represented them all at the highest level on the hurling field and captained Ulster in the Railway Cup against Leinster in 1983. His club has a very proud tradition and boasts 15 county titles, four Ulster titles and one All-Ireland title.

Memories abound.

I met some great people. One of my mates, and now a life-long friend, Ger Rogan, was playing with me in a Leinster minor final against Kilkenny in 1979. The night before the match we got our new jerseys. Rogie, as he was affectionately known, was so proud of his jersey that he slept with it on all night. That was the first Antrim jersey we got to keep.

Noel Skehan was probably the best goalkeeper I have seen. John Commins of Galway was a fine goalkeeper too. Then there was Joe Cooney, midfielder, half forward, full forward – play him nearly anywhere. Brian Whelehan has to be one of the most complete hurlers of this modern era. Also D.J. Carey, Nicky English, Eugene Cloonan – where do you stop?

The fifteen Niall would like to have captained reads as follows:

Niall Patterson
(Antrim)

Sylvie Linnane	Brian Lohan	John Horgan
(Galway)	*(Clare)*	*(Cork)*
Brian Whelehan	Ger Henderson	Denis Coughlan
(Offaly)	*(Kilkenny)*	*(Cork)*

Frank Cummins   John Fenton
(Kilkenny)   *(Cork)*

Martin Storey	Joe Cooney	D.J. Carey
(Wexford)	*(Galway)*	*(Kilkenny)*
Pat Fox	Joe McKenna	Nicky English
(Tipperary)	*(Limerick)*	*(Tipperary)*

Offaly's magnanimous gesture in 1989 will always be remembered by Niall.

> I have never come across anything like what Offaly did, lining up a Guard of Honour for us after us beating them in the All-Ireland semi-final of 1989. To be knocked out of a game like that and still have the presence of mind to realise what the occasion meant to the people from Antrim is something I will never forget and I have, and will have until the day I die, the greatest respect for Offaly hurling.
>
> One of my biggest lows on a personal level on the field was the day I punched Pat Fox in the National League quarterfinal. Pat was marking Declan McKillop, a young lad from my club in his first year at county level. The experienced Pat was using his craft on and off the ball and I got involved telling Declan to give it back. One thing led to another verbally, and the ball went wide into the side netting and I went to pick the ball up. Pat stepped in behind me and hit me on the hand. I just turned around – and whack. I should have been sent off. Instead I got booked and the ref. gave a penalty which I didn't understand because the ball had already gone wide. But I wasn't going to argue as long as I wasn't sent off. For the remainder of the match I was booed every time I touched the ball. That was the worst feeling I have had on a pitch. I was so embarrassed I didn't even hang around to apologise to Pat. It was a lesson well learned.

Niall was chosen as B&I 'GAA Personality of the Month' for April 1983. 'This was a dream come true to win such an award. This was regarded at the time as being second to an All-Star award. I was honoured to learn I was the first hurler from Ulster to win the award and it was the first and only time it was given to a player for a club game. So with Kilkenny just having won the hurling league and Down the football league and me just the third goalkeeper joining Noel Skehan and Seamus Durack, I was actually a little embarrassed but proud.'

Other honours that came Niall's way include:

• Two All-Ireland B medals in 1981 and 1982
• O'Neill Sports Star Award for Antrim in 1983

- Two All-Star nominations 1983 and 1991
- Ulster GAA Writer's Award 1990
- RTÉ Save of the Year 1990
- Two county titles – 1982 and 1989
- Ulster Club champions – 1982 and 1989
- Four Ulster titles with Antrim

On the occasion of the Silver Jubilee of the All-Ireland club championship, 25 years after its inception in 1971, a team was chosen. Niall was honoured. The team read:

Niall Patterson
(Loughgiel)

Tony Maher	Conor Hayes	John Horgan
(St. Finbarr's)	*(Kiltormer)*	*(Blackrock)*

Joe Hennessy	Frank Cummins	Denis Coughlan
(James Stephens)	*(Blackrock)*	*(Glen Rovers)*

Gerald McCarthy   Joe Cooney
(St. Finbarr's)   *(Sarsfields)*

Francis Loughnane	Ray Cummins	Ger Fennelly
(Roscrea)	*(Blackrock)*	*(Ballyhale Shamrocks)*

Charlie McCarthy	Tony Doran	Liam Fennelly
(St. Finbarr's)	*(Buffers Alley)*	*(Ballyhale Shamrocks)*

In 1983 Loughgiel won the All-Ireland senior hurling club title. It must surely rank as Ulster's greatest hurling success. Here is how Niall Patterson recalls the campaign that led to glory.

> I'd say it was one of the best prepared teams to come out of Loughgiel with lots of passion, ability and will to win. The path to the club championships:

Semi-final, Antrim – Loughgiel 3:7 Cushendall 1:11

> Cushendall were champions and we were a young side – nine under-21s in the side – given no hope of dethroning the

champions. From what I remember it was a windy day in Dunloy. We won the toss of the coin and elected to play with the breeze. We rattled in three goals in the first half and had a commanding lead. In the second half it was backs to the wall. Our defence fought tooth and nail as it did all the year and we held on.

It was only after that game that we realised we had a chance to win the championship. We decided to put in a lot of work over the next four weeks in preparation for the final against a great Ballycastle side who were the team of the eighties in Antrim – winning six or seven titles in that decade.

Final, Antrim – Loughgiel 5:9 Ballycastle 3:8

My first memory of the game was that we were going in as under-dogs again – our first final in eleven years. I remember winning the toss and being so nervous played against the breeze by mistake in the first half. We had a team meeting before going out on the pitch and decided to play with the advantage of the breeze. Although it was an honour for me to captain this great team, I felt I only had to win the toss because we had leaders in every line of our team. So it made things easier for me as a goal-keeper to be captain. During the match we got off to a great start. After seven minutes Brendan Laverty goaled from thirty yards to leave us leading 1:2 to 0:1. We got goals on either side of half time – just on the stroke of half time and straight after half time.

Those goals by Martin Coyle and Dominic McKinley made it 3:4 to 0:4 immediately after the break. Seamus McNaughton got a further goal and Brendan Laverty with another thirty yarder left the score with ten minutes remaining, 5:7 to 1:5.

Ulster semi-final – Loughgiel (Antrim) 3:15 Clontibret (Monaghan) 0:6

A game where we didn't play very well. We seemed to struggle all over the pitch that day. With some very heavy tackles coming in, it was hard to play to our potential. Although the going was tough we ran out easy winners.

Ulster final – Loughgiel (Antrim) 1:9 Ballygalget (Down) 0:9

Proved to be one of our toughest games that year. Aidan McNaughton pointed a free in the third minute to open the scoring, followed by a sixth minute goal by Aidan (Beaver) McCarry, followed by points by Dominic (Woody) McKinley and Aidan McNaughton to leave us six points clear after ten minutes. Gradually Ballygalget roared on by a large home crowd started to get going and pegged back our lead. If Paddy McIlhatton excelled at centre halfback in the county final he had an even greater performance that day. Paddy played on the great team of the early seventies. That day our defence was outstanding – Martin and Sean Carey, P.J. Mullen, Aidan McNaughton and Eamon Connolly all stood firm. Our midfield, half forward line and full forward line fought tooth and nail for every ball and blocked and hooked like a fullback line when we hadn't got the ball. That was the secret of our success – hard work and a will to win. We were playing for the pride of our club, families, ourselves and our parish.

All-Ireland semi-final 13 February 1983 – Loughgiel (Antrim) 2:7 Moycarkey-Borris (Tipperary) 1:6

We were facing a very fancied Moycarkey-Borris team – favourites to win the club championship. Moycarkey came to Loughgiel, kingpins of Munster and Tipperary, to play us off the park and have an easy passage to the final, which all the papers had written about all week. This was a great incentive for us. All the players had worked hard pre season. The game was just about one minute old when I picked the ball out of my net. I thought, maybe the papers are right. But thank God the players outfield had other ideas. We clawed our way back into the game by playing the Tipperary team at their own brand of hurling – making the ball do all the work. Our defence cleared their lines and halfbacks and midfield kept the ball moving to our forwards who picked the ball up and took their scores. It was a fine game of hurling by both sides and goals by Brendan Laverty and Aidan McCarry left us winning the match by four points. Moycarkey were gracious in defeat and helped us as much as they could in preparing for the final – their team mentors actually came into the dressing-room in Croke Park before the St. Rynagh's game and gave the team a talk and gave us a belief, which we already had from our own mentors, that we could win the All-Ireland club title.

All-Ireland club final Croke Park 17 April 1983 – Loughgiel (Antrim) 1:8 St. Rynagh's (Offaly) 2:5

Having travelled down to Dublin and stayed overnight with the team, it was nice to be in the Clarence Hotel with all your clubmates and family. It was something special. It seemed to bond us all together. Most of us headed to the pictures and played snooker that night. In the morning we had a workout in Phoenix Park. Mick O'Connell was an injury doubt. We were worried because Mick was a stalwart on the team. But he was passed fit and played the game of his life that day. I remember arriving at Croke Park and no one gave us tickets to get in. We had to queue with the spectators while the St. Rynagh's players stepped off the bus and got straight in. We thought 'these boys are superstars – they don't need tickets'. We were just the boys – down to make up the numbers. How wrong could I have been, because they turned out to be a very fine bunch of lads who have remained good friends with us over the years.

On to the match. I remember looking down into the stand when we came out onto the pitch and I thought, I hope who ever was last out of Loughgiel remembered to turn the lights out. Every family in the parish must have been there.

Our Bishop of Down and Conor was Dr. Cathal B. Daly, a native of Loughgiel. He had just been moved to our diocese from Ardagh and Clonmacnoise which is the diocese St. Rynagh's belong to. (A coincidence or what!)

The game started with a great point out on the right hand wing by Martin Coyle. That sticks out in my mind along with a great Brendan Laverty goal. There were points by Aidan McNaughton (0:3), Mick O'Connell (0:2), Aidan McCarry (0:1) and Paddy Carey (0:1). Two other things that stand out in my mind were two clearances, which were blocked wide, which the umpire gave St. Rynagh's seventies for – they scored points from both.

282

I remember saying to the umpire (not in English I fear) I hope you haven't cost us a club title. But just like the Beefeaters outside Buckingham Palace I got no reply. Two other things that stand out were the St. Rynagh's goals either side of half time. I deflected the shots onto the woodwork only to see the ball bounce directly to a St. Rynagh's player to score goals.

Otherwise we were in command of the game, but like in any game St. Rynagh's had the luck for the two goals. We had the luck when Padraig Horan missed a 40 yards free to win the match. I had asked the umpire how long was to go. He said one and a half minutes. I said give me a ball for a quick puck out because I was expecting Padraig to get a point. When he missed the ref. blew for full time. I remember going into the dressing-room and thinking we'd missed the boat. You only get one chance at this level down here, and the Southern teams seem to learn more than the Northern teams do for a replay. But we got back to training and on Tuesday recollected our thoughts and got down to business as usual.

Replay at Casement Park, Belfast – 24 April – Loughgiel (Antrim) 2:12 St. Rynagh's (Offaly) 1:12

My first memories from that day are introducing the players to Bishop Daly before the match and then being led around the field by the band. Now this was really like an All-Ireland final – beautiful sunshine, perfect pitch – the scene was set for what was to be a memorable game and a great day in the life of every player and member in the squad.

The match itself was exceptional, as a good game of hurling, with great scores coming from everywhere on the pitch. The second half was score for score – real good end to end stuff. Our goals came from Brendan Laverty and Aidan McCarry. We led by six points with minutes to go when St. Rynagh's got a penalty and scored to leave injury time seem very long and nervous for our defence. I think we had fifteen defenders in the last couple of minutes.

Again, every player on the team and subs played their part. In the winning of this title we had a large panel which was important for training, for team morale and for challenge games.

283

The team selectors need great praise for the work they did. Dominic Casey, Liam McGarry and Neil Patterson, now deceased. A great deal of thanks goes to our trainer Danny McMullan who made this probably the best prepared team to come out of our club – a special word of thanks to Dunloy physio Tommy Quinn, who made sure all our injuries were looked after.

All the team of 1983 have represented Antrim at senior level. The team was:

Niall Patterson

Martin Carey	P.J. Mullen	Sean Carey
Eamon Connolly	Paddy McIlhatton	Aidan McNaughton
Mick O'Connell	Gerald McKinley	
Aidan McCarry	Brendan Laverty	Dominic McKinley
Paddy Carey Snr.	Paddy Carey Jnr.	Seamus McNaughton

Martin Coyle and Brendan McGarry played in the drawn game.
Paddy Carey Snr. and Paddy Carey Jnr. are cousins.
Gerald and Dominic McKinley are brothers.
Martin, Sean, Harry (sub) and Paddy Carey Jnr. are all brothers.

Niall's father was a great motivator. He held a very special place in his son's heart.

My father Neil (deceased) played for Antrim for a long time. His claim to fame was holding Christy Ring scoreless from play. The match took place in Corrigan Park, Belfast in the mid fifties – I think 1956 or '57. Christy Ring scored a point from a sideline cut.

My father became Vice President of the County Board in 1991. He was Manager of the Antrim team in 1970 that won the county's first Intermediate title. In 1978 Antrim won their first Senior 'B' hurling title. He was a selector in 1981 when we won a second Senior 'B' title in London by three points. He was a selector on the 1983 Loughgiel team which won the All-Ireland club championship and was made an Honorary Life Member of Loughgiel in November 1991.

Hurling was his life. He died on 22 February 1993. I buried my stick in his coffin and never played again. He was a great man and was my main motivator. I played just to please him and when he died a big part of me died with him.

Sean Stack
CLARE
1978

If this great game holds bad memories for me, it is that the disappointing days keep haunting. The pains that we felt after our Munster final defeats are still tangible. Those Mondays will never leave my memory and still to this day hurt greatly. There were days when any kind of company was avoided – especially those keen on talking about the 'game'. 1978 keeps on coming back – excuses that Cork had a marvellous team, their great forwards were held goalless etc. etc. are just not erasing the pain. This was to be the pinnacle of all our careers. Croke Park beckoned, but damn it, we did everything in our power. Two miserable points separated us from glory. Five years of growing up together working up and down that field of Tulla. This was to be our dream. The fact that Cork subsequently 'sailed' away with the All-Ireland made it even worse.

But this great game of ours is not easily left aside. I love everything about the game of hurling. Watch any player on the pitch over an hour and then you know what kind of character he is. Now, I had my great days too. The Clare championships won with Sixmilebridge are special. 1983 in a replay was one of those 'moments in time'. Coming back to the village in late December 1984 with the provincial trophy was memorable. We sang everything that night from 'Singing in the Rain' to 'Jingle Bells'. I took as much joy in winning the county championship in 1993 (at the age of 40) as any of the others.

Great players I recall:
Ray Cummins was a genius. He made players around him look good. He could catch, run and finish like no other full forward

I ever saw. Iggy Clarke (Galway) has everything. His artistry at frees, lineballs was out of the top drawer. He was so durable and strong and his discipline and dedication to detail was exemplary. I was so lucky to have played at College level with him. I definitely would not have two Fitzgibbon Cup medals but for Iggy.

There were many others like John Horgan, Sean Silke, Brian Whelehan, Colm Honan but if ever hurlers entered the transfer market who would be the No. 1 target of today? It would have to be Tommy Dunne. He is poetry in motion. He has to be the best striker of a ball on the run that I have seen.

Hurling – a beautiful game. It's a crime that the 'authorities' in this organisation are killing it and being allowed to do so. Where will the hurlers of the future come from? If this question is not addressed soon, then our great game is going to wane away.

Why do so many clubs in this country play so little amount of games of any significance during the playing period?

Why in the name of heaven did hurling need a 'back-door' system at inter-county level to further complicate a fixtures programme? An example of what is prevalent throughout the country is my experience from the year 2001. Toomevara (current Tipp. champions) played no game for a ten-week period during June, July and August.

Are clubs just producing players now to lose them to county teams?

Every hurler dreams of success – with club, county and province. A glance at the past can produce a fair indicator of prospects, so when Sean Stack of Sixmilebridge donned the blue and gold jersey of his native Clare at senior level for the first time in October 1973, in a National League game against Galway, he would have looked into a past that produced many wonderful individual hurlers – Pa 'Fowler' McInerney, Tom McInerney, Dan McInerney, Tull Considine, Brendan Considine, Amby Power, Tommy Daly, John Joe Doyle, Larry Blake, Jim Mullane, Matt Nugent, P.J. Quane, Jimmy Smyth, Mick Hayes, Jim Carney, Pat Cronin and Jimmy Cullinane – just some of a litany of greats. Successful teams? Sadly, very few. Munster titles were secured in 1889, 1914 and 1932. The All-Ireland final was contested in each of those years – only 1914 brought glory. A league title was won in 1946; an Oireachtas was won in 1954 following a thrilling replay against the then glamorous and emerging Wexford. Apart from that the only other success of note was a junior All-Ireland title in 1914.

Sean Stack was born in 1953 in Listowel where he spent the first year of his life, followed by a three-year spell in Glin, Co. Limerick. His father Stephen, 'a great friend of Gus Cremin's of Kerry football fame in the forties', was a Kerryman while his mother Bridget (née McNamara) – affectionately known as Pydge – was a native of Glin. In 1957 Stephen purchased a farm of 97 acres in East Clare together with 25 cows and a range of machinery for £7500. And so fate ordained that Sean would star in the colours of Clare rather than those of either Kerry or Limerick.

His hurling days were many; the glory days were relatively few. However, in a most illustrious career, which ended following a National League game against Wexford in 1987, he did have his moments of success, interspersed with quite a few near misses particularly in Munster finals. The late Raymond Smith referred to Sean as 'a hurler of cultured grace'. A most apt description indeed, for Sean was a sportsman to his fingertips. And he was versatile too – a forward in his juvenile days, a midfielder in his college days, cornerback in his first Munster final in 1974, later moved to wing-back and finally to centre-back where he played many magnificent matches.

Sean first gripped the camán with the juveniles of Sixmilebridge. And from that very moment a hurling fervour gripped him. In 1993 at the age of 40 he won his seventh Co. Clare senior hurling title and played in the Munster club final against Toomevara (a team he was then coaching). He lost to the team he had coached.

The following year his American-born wife Pat asked him to promise her he would give up playing hurling. She didn't mind him giving as much time as he wished to coaching and training but she feared for his safety as a player. 'Some day someone will get you.' Pat explained she had given up a lot for him – left her job in America in order to come to live in Ireland and was now asking him to make his promise.

'I said I couldn't. Hurling was my way of life. I couldn't give it up. Anyway I thought about it and after a while I went back and promised.'

A few years later Pat went off to America on summer holidays. Sean was on the sideline watching Sixmilebridge playing an intermediate match. 'Things were going badly for the team. I went on with about fifteen minutes to go. I just couldn't stop myself. I got a lash of a hurley – sustained a broken arm in two places, spent four days in hospital in Limerick – and during that time Pat was trying to contact me without success.'

It was the year they had moved into their new house and Sean had undertaken to put down a patio and paths around the house during the summer holidays. On discharge from hospital he set about this work and didn't take good care of the broken arm. When he returned to the hospital he was told the plaster would have to stay on for six months.

Pat was due home in August. Two days before she was due to return Sean pleaded with the doctor to remove the plaster – but no, no way. He then went home and removed it himself.

For about a week he succeeded in hiding the injured arm. But Pat noticed he was holding it quite badly. The cat was out of the bag. Sean had to confess it had been broken playing hurling – broken, following a broken promise!

Sean captained the Clare minor hurling team in 1971 but suffered a heavy defeat at the hands of Cork in the Munster final at Killarney. In 1972 and 1974 Sean came tantalisingly close to Munster titles at under-21 level. Again the Fates frowned on The Banner. Victory went to Tipperary and Waterford by three points and five points respectively.

In 1981 Sean received a well-deserved personal honour when he was named at centre back on the All-Star team. Fellow countymen on that team were Seamus Durack in goal and Johnny Callinan at right half forward. Sean was centre-back on the victorious Munster Railway Cup teams of 1984 and '85.

He played in three successive league finals – all against Kilkenny – in 1976, '77 and '78. The first encounter ended in a draw at Thurles (Clare 2:10 Kilkenny 0:16). Unfortunately for Clare, the Kilkenny forwards went on a goal-scoring spree in the replay and the game ended Kilkenny 6:14 Clare 1:14. That defeat was avenged on the double the following two years. In 1977 it was Clare 2:8 Kilkenny 0:9. Eventually 30 April 1978 was a very proud day for Sean Stack and

Clare. He led his county in their third National League success with a great win over the Noresiders on a final score-line of 3:10 to 1:10.

Around this time Clare hurling was reaching new heights. An All-Ireland title seemed a possibility. Sadly, a dream it remained as hopes were dashed in stories of so near and yet so far.

Let's look at them.

Sean played in five Munster finals without success.

1974 v Limerick (6:14 to 3:9)
1977 v Cork (4:15 to 4:10)
1978 v Cork (0:13 to 0:11)
1981 v Limerick (3:12 to 2:9)
1986 v Cork (2:18 to 3:12)

Apart from 1974, when everything went wrong for Clare early on, the other four finals all carried the label of might-have-been. I asked Sean which, on reflection now, left him with the greatest sense of loss. Was it 1977 when Clare saw their fine fullback Jim Power sidelined, rather harshly, in the first half, or 1978 when Clare were firm favourites playing before a huge crowd of 55,000 – one of the largest ever for a Munster final – and facing the second half only a point behind and the wind in their favour, or 1981 as they watched Joe McKenna at full forward for Limerick find the net three times and match it with points – 'John Flanagan, the farmer from Feohanagh, gave me a terrible time that day' – or 1986 when Sean trained like a Trojan in the U.S. – flew home for the defeats of Limerick and Tipperary and flew home again to face Cork?

> It was 1986. I knew that day it was going to be my last chance to win a Munster medal. In the other defeats I knew there would be other days. We gave away two soft goals that day. My chance was gone – that made it sad for me.

Disappointments there may have been but Sean's hurling fervour lives on, active and healthy, as reflected in his successful coaching of Toomevara and his deep concern for the future of our ancient game.

Jimmy O'Brien
WEXFORD
1967

The most memorable game and the best match that I ever played in was the 1962 All-Ireland final when we were beaten by Tipp. A number of incidents occurred which had a profound impact on the result.

I remember vividly the puck around before the game. Normally, at a time like this I would be very nervous and certainly would not notice or be interested in anything but the upcoming game. We had been pucking about for a considerable time when I noticed the late Nick O'Donnell coming out on his own. He was as white as a ghost but it was after the match I was told of what had happened. Nicko was bringing out his son to sit in the dugout with the subs when a GAA official stopped him. He refused to let the boy out whereupon Nicko made a swing at him and then went back to the dressing-room and refused to come out. Anyone who knew Nicko would know that he was a very focussed person who would not change his mind very easily. After some very considerable persuasion he relented and what I saw was a very enraged Nicko.

However, the game started and in a flash Tipp. had scored two goals. Tipp. were awarded a sideline cut and the late Martin Lyng swore to me that it was a Wexford ball. The sideline cut was taken and we conceded a soft goal. In a rage Nicko grabbed the ball to puck out and missed his stroke. The ball trickled to a Tipp. player who had the easiest of tasks to tap it in.

Nicko, a Kilkenny man, was in my opinion the greatest player to put on the Wexford jersey. He was an absolutely brilliant ball player and to miss the ball out of his hand would be physically impossible but for his state of mind. Two goals down against a great Tipp. team left us with a mountain to climb.

From then on the game exploded into life and the atmosphere was electric. Bit by bit we edged forward and with about ten minutes to go we were leading by two points. Before half time Billy Rackard got a very badly broken thumb and wanted to come off. Billy was told there was nothing wrong with him and to play on. About ten minutes into the second half the Wexford selectors decided to switch Billy with Tom Neville. Tom had an absolutely brilliant first half but with the pattern of the play he was being redundant in the corner and Billy was in serious trouble at centre half. Unfortunately for us the decision was never conveyed to the players involved.

Midway through the second half Jimmy Doyle (Tipp.) was forced to retire with a shoulder injury. Up to then the main focus of attack was through Jimmy but when he went off the Tipp. half forward line started to run at us and we were immediately in trouble. Soon afterwards they scored the goal to give them the lead which they never lost. We got some chances which unfortunately for us did not come off.

One in particular was when Tim Flood, who in my opinion was the best Wexford forward of all time, strode through the Tipp. defence leaving the defence in his wake. Out of nowhere came Donie Nealon, the Tipp. wing forward, who must have covered back almost eighty yards, hooked Tim and the ball was cleared. The foregoing incidents are not in any way meant to diminish Tipp.'s great victory. I know it's very much open to speculation whether we could have won had not these events occurred, but they did, and they did have an adverse effect on us.

The excitement of the crowd, which must have touched every player on the field, was truly electric and could not be forgotten and I am personally very grateful to have been involved. To any of the Tipp. team who may read this article I want to send my warmest regards.

I have been very privileged to have been a part of Wexford hurling from 1957 to 1968. I have great memories of people I was associated with, both team mates and opposition, on and off the field. And for this I am truly grateful.

By 1957 the Model County had left an indelible imprint on the hurling scene with their displays since the Leinster final of 1950 which they lost to Kilkenny at Nowlan Park by 3:11 to 2:11. The purple and gold jersey spelt glamour: the hurling men of Wexford personified all that was admirable in sportsmanship; the fans flocked in record-breaking attendances to see them in action. Their successes included four Leinster titles, two All-Ireland crowns, a National League and four Oireachtas triumphs.

It was against the foregoing background that Jimmy O'Brien joined the Wexford senior panel for the National League of 1957. He played his first game against Dublin in January of that year at Enniscorthy. From then until he retired after the All-Ireland final of 1968 he was one of the leading right half forwards in the country and was a regular on Leinster Railway Cup selections throughout the sixties.

Jimmy's style of play, which was always incisive, reflected spirit, tenacity, grit, urgency and verve. He was courageous and fearless and had a grand turn of speed. He made life difficult for many a fine defender including the stout-hearted John Doyle of Tipperary. 'Going on to the field I never thought about winning. I always went out to do my best – play as well as I could – never give up.'

In 1966 Geraldine O'Hanrahans of New Ross defeated Shamrocks (Enniscorthy) in the county hurling final. That victory paved the way for Jimmy to captain his native county in 1967. They reached the Leinster final. 'A freak goal set Kilkenny on the road to victory.' Earlier that year Jimmy led Wexford to their third National League title with a 3:10 to 1:9 win over their Noreside neighbours. 'I didn't play well at all that day. I was suffering from the effects of 'flu. Going up to collect the Cup I said to a colleague that mine must have been the worst display ever by a winning captain.' But Jimmy, I interjected, they didn't take you off. 'No, I was never taken off.'

Jimmy believes that Christy Ring was the greatest he ever saw. 'He had everything. He stood apart – away out on his own. I remember well a league game in Cork in November '59 when he scored 6:4 against us. Ned Fenlon, Jim English and Billy Rackard all had turns on him. It didn't matter – the man ran riot.' I decided to check the final score. It read Cork 7:9 Wexford 5:4. Christy had scored enough on his own to beat Wexford – and he in his fortieth year. 'After Ring I would put Eddie Keher.'

Jimmy is in no doubt as regards who masterminded the rise of Wexford in the fifties.

Nicky Rackard was the man that inspired Wexford. He was a leader. Without him Wexford wouldn't have made the breakthrough. It was his leadership and the arrival of his brothers Bobby and Billy and also Nick O'Donnell, Ned Wheeler, Jim Morrissey and Padge (Kehoe) that made the team.

Jimmy played in some of hurling's most memorable contests. The opening paragraph has dealt with his recollections of the 1962 All-Ireland final against Tipperary – one of the truly great hurling contests. Let's now look at the three other encounters.

He had the honour of coming on as a sub for Harry O'Connor in the league final of 1958 against Limerick – a super contest to watch – greater still to play in. This was a game of delightful hurling – an epic of changing, lurching fortunes that left journalists searching for superlatives to describe it. It ended 5:7 to 4:8 in Wexford's favour. 'Nick O'Donnell and Billy Rackard won it for us.' It was a dream beginning to Jimmy's hurling career.

He played in his first of four All-Ireland finals in 1960. Wexford's opponents were red hot favourites Tipperary. Right from the throw-in Wexford tore into the game. They took a grip on proceedings and terrier-like refused to loosen that grip. There was power and majesty in their hurling – glorious stuff to behold. A stunned Tipperary team and equally stunned supporters left GAA headquarters in disbelief. Gaeldom had witnessed one of the biggest upsets in the history of the game. It was Tipperary's first All-Ireland defeat since 1922 and only their fifth in 22 appearances. It was also their biggest defeat – 10 points. The scoreboard read 2:15 to 0:11. Jimmy played at right half forward and was marking John Doyle.

Before the All-Ireland final of 1968 between Wexford and Tipperary Jimmy had to get a pain-killing injection in his knee. He lined out at right full forward. Tipperary were firm favourites. The half time score confirmed that rating, 1:11 to 1:3, but it didn't at all reflect their superiority. Wexford's performance could only be described as vapid and dull. Nothing in their first half display presaged what would unfold in the second half. Wexford made switches and hurled with a fury and fluency that bewildered Tipperary. It was resurrection stuff. Entering the 28th minute of the second half Wexford led by the incredible scoreline of 5:8 to 1:12. In the couple of minutes remaining Tipperary got two goals. But it mattered not. The Liam MacCarthy Cup was on the way to the Slaneyside for the fifth time. Wexford had shredded the formbook.

It was Jimmy's last championship game. He was thirty years of age. The injured knee could take no more. His career ended as it had begun – in a blaze of hurling glory.

Jimmy's team for the 20-year period 1950–1970 reads as follows:

Ollie Walsh
(Kilkenny)

Tom Neville   Nick O'Donnell   Jim Treacy
(Wexford)   *(Wexford)*   *(Kilkenny)*

Phil Grimes   Billy Rackard   Martin Coogan
(Waterford)   *(Wexford)*   *(Kilkenny)*

Ned Wheeler   Mick Roche
(Wexford)   *(Tipperary)*

Jimmy Doyle   Tom Cheasty   Eddie Keher
(Tipperary)   *(Waterford)*   *(Kilkenny)*

Christy Ring   Nicky Rackard   Tim Flood
(Cork)   *(Wexford)*   *(Wexford)*

Billy Rackard
WEXFORD
1962

'And maybe, God, a singer or two
To lilt a ballad for me and You.
Then all I'll wish is to spend each day,
Watching all the great hurlers play;
With Ring and Mackey and Rackard too
And Tom Semple and Lory, to name a few.
To see Scanlon and Daly mind the net
"You'll promise too – that it won't be wet."'

(J. Ryan)

Billy Rackard often recalled for me how raw he felt as a hurler when he played at corner back in his early days at county level. He didn't particularly like the fullback line. It was too congested in there for him. His style demanded more space – more freedom. When he moved to centre halfback – in the absence through illness of his brother, Bobby – against Clare in the Oireachtas final of 1953 he said to himself 'this is it; this is where I feel comfortable; this is where I feel confident and in command on the hurling field'.

Billy was introduced to the county senior scene in league games against Laois at corner forward and Dublin at corner back in 1949. In the championship of 1950 after victories over Offaly and Laois, Billy lined out at right fullback for the Model County against Kilkenny at Nowlan Park in the Leinster final before a capacity attendance.

While he wasn't playing badly, his display was causing concern to the Wexford mentors. So at half time, County Chairman Sean Browne told him to lie down injured at the first opportunity in the second half. Those were the days when a player could only be replaced if he was injured. What ensued is a story Billy enjoys telling.

'When the ball was thrown in for the second half I began thinking about getting injured. The next thing was the ball came in between Liam Reidy and myself. I pulled first time and cleared upfield. I was thinking of lying down when the ball came back again. I reached up and grabbed it, side stepped my opponent and made a long clearance. No time to lie down as the ball came back again and I made another clearance. This time play remained outfield, so with the referee not looking I lay down and began holding my ankle as if in agony. The next thing I saw was Sean Browne rushing in, gesticulating and telling me to get up, saying 'You're alright, you're alright.' From that moment onwards Billy was a fixture on the Wexford team until he retired in 1964, at the age of 33, after defeat by Kilkenny in the Leinster championship.

Billy played in six All-Ireland finals and it is interesting to recall the details of those games.

1951 – left halfback v Tipperary – lost (7:7 to 3:9) Attendance 68,515
1954 – left fullback v Cork – lost (1:9 to 1:6) Attendance 84,856
1955 – centre halfback v Galway – won (3:13 to 2:8) Attendance 72,854
1956 – centre halfback v Cork – won (2:14 to 2:8) Attendance 83,096

1960 – centre halfback v Tipperary – won (2:15 to 0:11) Attendance 67,154 (This was Tipperary's first defeat in a final since 1922.)
1962 – centre halfback v Tipperary – lost (3:10 to 2:11) Attendance 75,039

During his career Billy played in eight Railway Cup finals, beginning in 1953 when he came on as a sub and finishing in 1964 with a 3:7 to 2:9 victory over Munster, to give him his third Railway Cup medal.

Following Rathnure's senior hurling success in 1961 Billy was chosen for the first time to captain the men in purple and gold in the All-Ireland championship of 1962.

He experienced the elation and ecstasy associated with walking up the steps of the Hogan Stand, in triumph, to collect the Bob O'Keeffe Cup after victory over Kilkenny (3:9 to 2:10) in the Leinster final. He looked forward with hope to All-Ireland final day.

I watched the 1962 All-Ireland final from the Hogan Stand. My heart and hopes were with Billy Rackard that day. Over the years his displays had given me immense enjoyment. In my time I had seen no greater exponent of centre halfback play in action. In that position, Billy stood supreme and hurled with an art that concealed art. His reading and positional sense were uncanny. He had a great pair of hands. And he had strength too. It was a hidden strength. I say that, because it wasn't always apparent. His sportsmanship was of the highest order. He never drew a foul stroke. It wasn't in his nature. And yet, it was a foolish man who might think that Billy couldn't fight his corner – if pushed.

Billy had always been a great horseman. That sport called for patience, discipline, control and forbearance. All these qualities were reflected in his displays and demeanour on the hurling field.

Before the 1962 All-Ireland final was five minutes old, the Wexford men had suffered three body blows that would have necessitated a mandatory count of eight in a boxing contest. Within 90 seconds of the throw-in by referee John Dowling of Offaly, Tipperary had the ball in the Wexford net twice, via Tom Moloughney and Sean McLoughlin. Minutes later, following a melée, Billy tumbled to the ground and suffered a multiple fragment fracture of the hand, as a result of a flying hurley connecting with the base of his thumb. That injury was in plaster of Paris for eight months and took a year to fully heal.

296

At half time Billy, though not aware of the extent of his injury, asked to be replaced but his request wasn't heeded – not even by the medical team. Apart from the discomfort of his injury, he didn't feel in peak hurling condition at all that day. Like his brother Bobby he always had reservations about collective training. He preferred to follow his own programme and reach match fitness in that way. However, being captain in 1962, he felt obliged to attend all the special training sessions at Enniscorthy. As Billy paraded in front of his team around Croke Park he knew that the preparation routine he had been through had left him inadequately equipped both mentally and physically for the challenges of an All-Ireland occasion.

He always blames himself for Wexford's failure in the final of '62. He believes if he had been taken off that Wexford would have won.

From my seat in the Hogan Stand, I watched enthralled as one of the really great All-Ireland finals unfolded. It was spell-binding stuff; a wonderful exhibition of our ancient game; played at hectic pace and replete with all the skills that produce an epic contest. Right from the start, the excitement generated on the pitch produced a supercharged atmosphere that had the attendance of over 75,000 in a state of suspense until the final whistle brought a halt to a classic encounter. And despite Billy's discomfiture, of which, of course, I was unaware at the time, I could find no flaw in his display.

Entering the final quarter, Wexford's fighting qualities saw them take a one-point lead and victory began to look a distinct possibility. Unfortunately, however, the hectic pace was beginning to tell on Wexford. Quite a few of the players were at the veteran stage, men

'of heroic hearts,
Made weak by time and fate'

In the twentieth minute of the second half, Tom Ryan of Killenaule found a gap in the Wexford defence and engineered a third Tipperary goal that gave them a one-point lead. With seven minutes left to play Padge Kehoe levelled for Wexford but Tipperary finished with points from Donie Nealon and Sean McLoughlin.

As Tom Ryan careered through for his all-important goal, Billy Rackard was tempted to throw his hurley after him – concede a free – possibly save the game. The temptation was great – very great. But Billy resisted. To act in such a manner would be going against the grain. It would be alien to his nature. The discipline of the horseman, the discipline of the sportsman prevailed.

Billy didn't have the honour of walking up the steps of the Hogan Stand to collect the MacCarthy Cup but he is not remembered for that. Rather does his name conjure up an outstanding hurler and wonderful sportsman whose presence on the hurling field adorned the great game for a span of fifteen years.

Jackie Power
LIMERICK
1947

'Time like an ever rolling stream bears all its sons away . . .'

Jackie Power was, without a doubt, one of the greatest hurlers not only of his era but of the century. He was fast, strong, skilled, durable and dexterous. He was a hurling artist who played with grace and elegance – an opportunist and a predator – a master of his craft. He was immensely versatile – could play in any position – and no matter where he played he starred. It made him a hurling colossus and his remarkable versatility added lustre to his greatness. He rarely had an off day.

For nine successive years from 1940 to 1948 inclusive he was chosen on the Munster Railway Cup team. It was an era when it was a supreme honour to be chosen for your province, 'the proudest feather in any hurler's cap' according to Carbery. Competition for places was intense. Jackie was victorious on seven occasions – losing only twice; to Leinster in 1941 by 2:5 to 2:4 when a family bereavement deprived Munster of the Mackeys, John and Mick; to Connaught in 1947 by 2:5 to 1:1.

Jackie's positional selection in those years is an indication of his utility value and versatility.

1940 left halfback
1941 right halfback
1942 left full forward
1943 '47 and '48 centre forward
1944 and '45 centre back
1946 centre field

298

Little wonder then that he would be switched from time to time and assigned the task of curbing the brilliance of the likes of John Keane, Jimmy Langton, Terry Leahy, Tommy Doyle and Christy Ring. And if Limerick needed to strengthen their defence, enhance their midfield or add punch and scoring power to the attack, Jackie Power was their man. According to Jim O'Sullivan of the *Irish Examiner*, Ring once said when speaking of Jackie Power, 'He would be the first man I would pick on my team.'

Jackie was born in Annacotty, Co. Limerick, on 30 May 1916 to David and Ellen (née Fitzgerald). He was introduced to the game of hurling in his national school days under the tutelage of his teacher John Kelly who in Jackie's words was 'a hurling fanatic'. As a teenager Jackie showed tremendous promise as an athlete but his potential in this field was sacrificed in the cause of hurling and football. As a footballer he was quite talented. He played at junior and senior level for his native Limerick and won five successive county senior titles with Ahane from 1935 to 1939 inclusive. It is no surprise therefore to find that his son Ger excelled as a footballer and gave brilliant displays with Kerry in their all-conquering era of 1975 to 1986 inclusive – winning eight All-Ireland medals, five All-Stars and three Railway Cups.

In his leisure hours Jackie enjoyed nothing more than fishing in the Mulcair River near his native home.

Jackie won his first of fifteen senior county medals with Ahane in 1933 when Croom were defeated 1:7 to 1:1. It was the first of seven in a row. Ahane's onward march was halted by Croom in 1940 and '41 but a further seven in a row followed from 1942 to 1948 inclusive. He won his last county title in 1955.

Jackie made his début on the Limerick senior hurling team in 1935. The following year he established himself permanently on the team. He was in the company of stars – men like Paddy Scanlan, Paddy and Dave Clohossy, Mick and John Mackey, Timmy and Mick Ryan, Mickey Cross, Garrett Howard, Jim Roche, Paddy McMahon, Paddy Carroll, Tom McCarthy and Mick Kennedy.

When Jackie was appointed captain of the Limerick team for the National League campaign of 1947 he was a vastly experienced and much revered hurler who had won every honour in the game and was now in search of his fourth league medal.

Victories over Galway (8:7 to 3:2) and Clare, the reigning champions (8:1 to 1:4) brought Limerick face to face with Kilkenny in the National League final on 15 November 1947 at Croke Park. Kilkenny were favourites. They were the reigning All-Ireland champions, having defeated Cork by one point in a thrilling and classic final the previous September. Apart from Ramie Dowling in goal instead of Jim Donegan and one change outfield, Kilkenny fielded their All-Ireland winning team. Croke Park was like a home ground to them.

Limerick were new to Croke Park. Most of the players had never played there. Jackie Power, Dick Stokes and John Mackey were there in 1940 when Limerick beat Kilkenny in the All-Ireland final of that year. This trio, together with a few others, would have played Railway Cup games in Croke Park but that was it. While Limerick had been somewhat unlucky to lose the Munster final of 1947 to Cork by 2:6 to 2:3, it was felt that Kilkenny's experience and familiarity with Croke Park would tilt the game in their favour.

However, Jackie Power and the men he captained had other ideas. The game turned out to be a thriller. It matched the All-Ireland final for excitement and brilliant hurling. One journalist wrote that the only difference was that instead of the red jerseys of Cork it was the green jerseys of Limerick. In the All-Ireland final against Cork Terry Leahy got the winning point for Kilkenny with the last puck of the game. Against Limerick it ended all square – Limerick 4:5 Kilkenny 2:11.

The replay took place on 7 March 1948 with Croke Park again the venue. According to a press report 'it was a magnificent game that really thrilled a splendid crowd . . . reminiscent of a Munster final . . . traditional hard hitting . . . shoulder to shoulder encounters'. Fans had witnessed a hurling epic, fiery, yet classical. And when it was all over, so enthralled had the spectators been that they chanted 'Give us sixty minutes more.'

Jackie Power was at centreback in a defence that was heroic. Paddy Collopy in goal brought off two incredible saves from close range that proved to be the difference between the teams at the final whistle. Sean Herbert, at right halfback, played the game of his life. Dick Stokes at centre forward gave an exhibition. John Mackey wasn't going to travel at all. Luckily he did and when he came on as a sub he injected new life into the Limerick attack. Over the hour every player on the team gave a lion-hearted performance.

The game ended with a famous victory for Jackie Power and Limerick on the score 3:8 to 1:7. The team lined out as follows:

Paddy Collopy

Jim Sadlier   Mick Herbert   Tom Cregan

Sean Herbert   Jackie Power   Tommy O'Brien

Mick Ryan   Paddy Fitzgerald.

John Mulcahy   Dick Stokes   Mick Dooley

Paddy Fitzgerald   Denis Flanagan   John Barry

John Mackey replaced Mick Dooley and Jim O'Donoghue replaced Denis Flanagan.

Jackie Power's career at county level was now drawing to a close. In the Munster final of 1949, against Tipperary, Jackie tore through the Tipperary defence in the closing stages to score as great a goal as he ever engineered in his long career. A controversial decision, that deprived Limerick of a draw, saw the goal disallowed. It was Jackie's last game in the green and white.

However, the future still held moments of glory and recognition.

In 1969 he received the Cú Chulainn Award for the outstanding hurler of the past.

In 1971 he coached the Limerick team that won the league title – defeating Tipperary in the final.

In 1973 he coached the Limerick team that won the All-Ireland title – defeating Kilkenny 1:21 to 1:14.

A wonderful honour awaited Jackie in 1991. At the All-Star Banquet in the Burlington Hotel he was presented with the All-Time All-Star Award. I had the pleasure of talking with Jackie that night for I had known him in Tralee when I was stationed there. As always he was genial and modest and enjoyed nothing more than reminiscing about hurling days and hurling men and 'battles long ago'.

Dick Stokes was a colleague of Jackie's on Limerick and Munster teams right through the forties. In *The Life and Times of Jackie Power* by Sean Murphy, Dick described Jackie as follows:

'What were the attributes that made Jackie Power a great hurler? Very well built, good feet and hands, balance, unusual strength and courage that could be applied as required; great hurling skill; stamina; speed of action and accuracy; a good hurling brain with an uncanny sense of position. He had the ability to read the game and avail of any opportunities that presented, to the best advantage.'

Jackie died on 23 February 1994. Gaeldom mourned.

> 'The harvest moon shines bright to-night upon the sweet Mulcair,
> As it tumbles in a silver foam o'er Annacotty's weir;
> 'Twas on its banks how oft you fished as the mighty salmon ran,
> With rod and line you were sublime a hurling fisherman.
> No more you'll roam the lovely roads from Mountshannon to Rich Hill,
> Or cycle out to Daly's Cross and home by Garden Hill.
> Nor meet old friends at journey's end and at Lisnagry alight;
> And meet the lads who played with you in Limerick's green and white.'
>
> Jack Ryan (July '94)

Jimmy Walsh
KILKENNY
1932 & 1939

> 'Then suddenly a thunder clap stirs your soul,
> And thousands clamour "A goal, A goal!"
> The green flag waves in a moment more
> And proclaims to all 'tis indeed a score.'
>
> (Sliabh Ruadh)

Jimmy Walsh, the farmer from Carrickshock, was one of the youngest captains from Kilkenny to lift the MacCarthy Cup in triumph.

And what is more, he belonged to a special elite band that had the privilege of receiving the cup on more than one occasion on behalf of his county.

When he led the men in black and amber round Croke Park on 4 September 1932 it was his first year in championship hurling. Kilkenny's opponents, Clare, were captained by John Joe 'Goggles' Doyle.

There was a great hunger on both teams in 1932. Kilkenny hadn't won an All-Ireland title since 1922, when a great closing rally snatched an unexpected victory from Tipperary. In between those years they were beaten by Cork in 1926, and in 1931 they fell to the same opposition after a marathon three games.

Clare, whose only All-Ireland success had been in 1914, came to Croke Park with excellent credentials. They had been threatening to break through in Munster since 1928. They did it in style in 1932 with a Munster final defeat of star-studded reigning All-Ireland champions Cork on the score 5:2 to 4:1 at Thurles.

They then accounted for Galway in remarkable fashion in the All-Ireland semi-final at Limerick. Outplayed, and down 13 points at the break, they fell further in arrears when Galway added points early in the second half. With the game in the final quarter, spectators from both sides began leaving the grounds. Suddenly Clare went on a scoring spree via Tull Considine and went on to win an incredible victory by 9:4 to 4:14. Those who left early, and later heard the result rejected it in utter disbelief. Then it was rumoured that a few Galway players had over celebrated at half time.

Kilkenny too arrived in Croke Park with first class credentials. They had won a total of eight All-Ireland titles. But more importantly, the vast bulk of the battle-hardened 1931 panel were in the lineout.

Their road to Croke Park was as follows:

v Meath at Navan (4:6 to 0:2)
v Laois at Portlaoise (4:12 to 2:5)
v Dublin at Portlaoise (4:6 to 3:5)

This is how Kilkenny GAA historian, the late Tom Ryall, in his wonderful book *Kilkenny, the GAA Story 1884–1984* described the Leinster final.

> It was back to Portlaoise for the Leinster final against Dublin. It was one of the great provincial deciders with strength pitted against strength, skill against skill, and alternating changes of fortune . . . Dublin went 1:1 up before Tommy Leahy had Kilkenny's first score, a point. Two goals by Mattie Power and Dan Dunne gave the Noresiders the lead for the first time. Another goal by Fitzpatrick put Kilkenny into a half time lead of 3:1 to 2:3.

With fifteen minutes to go, Dublin were back in front with a two-point lead. The crucial stage came when Jimmy Walsh goaled and Kilkenny held out to win by 4:6 to 3:5.

Despite a world depression that had impacted adversely on Ireland and driven its economy into dire straits, a record attendance of 34,372 turned up for the game. The Kells Pipers Band led the teams in the pre-match parade. Dr. Collier, Bishop of Ossory, threw in the sliotar and Sean Robbins of Offaly got the game under way.

Clare were the heavier team and Kilkenny had to draw on all their craft and experience to win this one. Down three points to two at the break they faced the second half defending the canal goal. They proceeded to deliver three early hammer-blows – a goal from Mattie Power followed by two more from Martin White. The score then stood 3:2 to 3 points.

Undaunted, Clare hit back with two goals from Tull Considine. Croke Park was now agog. With time running out Tull gained possession again. 'Tull's got it!' exclaimed the Clare crowd excitedly, sensing a score and victory, as he bore down menacingly on the Kilkenny goal. However, solid defender Padge Byrne was equal to the challenge. He cleared for Mattie Power to add the last point of the day. Final score was Kilkenny 3:3 Clare 2:3.

A proud young Jimmy Walsh, playing in his first All-Ireland final at right half forward, collected the Liam MacCarthy cup and prepared for a triumphant journey home to the Noreside.

His next day as captain was in 1939. All kinds of drama surrounded the All-Ireland hurling final day of that year, when Jimmy Walsh led Kilkenny to victory for the second time. To begin with World War Two was declared – a war that would engulf the world, and Europe in particular, in horror for almost six years.

Kilkenny arrived in Croke Park on final day via the following route:

v Laois at Nowlan Park (6:9 to 1:5) – the first round
v Dublin at Portlaoise (2:12 to 4:3) – Leinster final

This was a great Leinster final. Dublin were All-Ireland and National League champions and entered the game as favourites. But it proved to be Kilkenny's day. Jimmy Walsh led by example and had a fine hour on one of hurling's greats, Harry Gray – a Laois man playing with his adopted Dublin.

v Galway at Roscrea (1:16 to 3:1) – All-Ireland semi-final

Cork reached the All-Ireland final with a resounding 7:4 to 4:3 victory over reigning Munster champions, Waterford, at Fermoy before a crowd of 22,000, followed by a dramatic 4:3 to 3:4 win over Limerick in an epic Munster final contest at Thurles described by one newspaper report as 'Hurling in Excelsis'. With no team from Ulster participating, Cork were now in the All-Ireland final. It would be the first All-Ireland final meeting of Cork and Kilkenny since 1931.

At half time, thanks to two fine goals by corner forward Jimmy Phelan, Kilkenny led Cork by 2:4 to 1:1 in the All-Ireland final of 1939, despite having played against the breeze. Cork had won the toss and opted for wind advantage in the first half.

Each side added points early in the second half. Then the elements took over – lightning, thunder and torrential rain; the gods in seeming wicked mood. The final has gone down in hurling lore as 'the thunder and lightning final' – and one of the great ones too it was.

One report on the game carried the following passage. 'While peels of thunder seemed almost to shake the giant stands, and rain swept in sheets across the pitch, thirty hurlers, deaf to thunder and heedless of the deluge, battled in Croke Park yesterday in a last ten minutes that will long be talked of. No enthusiast could wish for better; and there were forty thousand of them, whose cheers almost challenged the thunder.'

Despite the elements, the game continued and the attendance of 39,302 was treated to a thrilling contest, brimming with excitement, Herculean effort, and almost unbearable suspense as both sides battled with Fianna fury for supremacy.

The epic contest was now testing more than physical endurance. It challenged the metal of the spirit as well. At midfield, Jimmy Walsh and his partner Jimmy Kelly were immersed in a battle royal with their Cork counterparts, Connie Buckley and Jack Barrett.

Now only two minutes remain. Jimmy Walsh is back helping his defence. Cork win a free at midfield. Willie Campbell, Cork's right halfback and a superb exponent of the ancient craft, stands over the sliotar, the dye now running freely from his red jersey to his togs. His stroke is straight and true. Through backs and forwards and goalkeeper it travels and rests in the back of the net. The teams are level. Surely a draw now. Both sets of supporters are drained from the tension of excitement.

Kilkenny win a seventy. The immaculate Paddy Phelan takes it. It is said that with the line markings almost washed away the sliotar was placed on the wrong seventy line. The puck falls short – twenty-five yards or so. A weak clearance reaches Jimmy Kelly of Carrickshock and the great midfielder gathers and slots the sliotar between the posts for the lead. The puck out brings the final whistle. The drama of a saga has ended.

> *'Fear no more the lightning-flash*
> *Nor the all-dreaded thunder-stone'*

Jimmy Walsh, playing at midfield, now a hurling veteran, holder of seven Leinster medals and four All-Ireland crowns becomes the second Kilkenny man to have the signal honour of leading his county on the field to more than one All-Ireland hurling victory.

After the game Jimmy Walsh said 'I am immensely proud of my team, who have brought the title back to Kilkenny. It was a game of which any Gael might be proud. We never faltered once we got to the front, and I think, although our victory was a narrow one, it was well deserved.'

Jimmy Walsh was to taste success again – this time in 1947 as a selector – when Kilkenny had a stunning one point win over arch-rivals Cork in one of the all-time great finals.

This is the team Jimmy captained in 1932:

Jim Dermody

Paddy Larkin   Peter O'Reilly   John Carroll

Paddy Phelan   Padge Byrne   Eddie Doyle

Eddie Byrne   Lory Meagher

Jimmy Walsh   Martin Power   Tommy Leahy

Dan Dunne   Martin White   Mattie Power